338.9001 Olson, Mancur.
OLS
     The rise and
     decline of
     nations

DATE			

The Rise and Decline of Nations

THE RISE AND DECLINE OF NATIONS

Economic Growth,
Stagflation,
and Social Rigidities

Mancur Olson

Yale University Press
New Haven and London

Designed by James J. Johnson
and set in Times Roman type by
The Composing Room of Michigan, Inc.
Printed in the United States of America by
Murray Printing Company, Westford, Mass.

Library of Congress Cataloging in Publication Data

Olson, Mancur.
  The rise and decline of nations.

  Includes bibliographical references and index.
    1. Economic development.   2. Unemployment—Effect of
inflation on.   3. Caste–India.   4. Economics.
I. Title.
HD82.0565   1982   338.9′001   82–40163
ISBN 0–300–02307–3   AACR2
        0–300–03079–7 (pbk.)

10   9   8   7   6   5   4   3   2

For Ellika, Mancur Severin, and Sander

Contents

Preface

It may seem strange, at a time when so many find fault with economics, that an economist should claim to extend existing economic theory in a way that not only explains the "stagflation" and declining growth rates that have given rise to the recent complaints, but also provides a partial explanation of a variety of problems usually reserved for other fields— the "ungovernability" of some modern societies, the British class structure and the Indian caste system, the exceptionally unequal distribution of power and income in many developing countries, and even the rise of Western Europe from relative backwardness in the early Middle Ages to dominance of the whole world by the late nineteenth century. Yet the successful extension or improvement of something we have found unsatisfactory is commonplace: the technology that was impractical or full of bugs may after further development become economical and reliable. So also economics, even when it has encountered increasing skepticism, may with the aid of a new idea help to explain matters it could not explain before.

If we step back to gain perspective, we see not only the embarrassments of many economists in the last decade, but also more than two centuries of cumulative intellectual advance. I am fond of quoting Newton's assertion that, if he had seen farther than others, it was because he stood on the shoulders of giants. If Newton could say that in the seventeenth century, surely the trained economist today, however limited in stature, can claim at least as high a perch. The economist is the heir of several thinkers of recognized genius, such as Smith, Ricardo, Mill, Marx, Walras, Wicksell, Marshall, and Keynes, as well as of the yeoman labor of many hundreds of intelligent men and women. Indeed, since the giants of economics usually stood in turn on the shoulders of their predecessors, it is as though the economist today were standing atop a great pyramid of talent. Why, then, have so many economists failed to anticipate the emergence of new economic realities in the 1970s and 1980s? Perhaps it is because, wearing professional blinders, they have looked only straight ahead at phenomena economists have habitually examined. This book attempts to show that if we take the trouble to look to the side, at the domains of other disciplines, we shall gain a different conception of the entire landscape.

In part because this study encompasses several disciplinary domains, and even more because it aspires to reach policy-makers and students, I have worked hard to write this book in a language different from the one I use for articles in technical economic journals. This book is accordingly longer than it would need to be for the fellow economists who are my first concern, but I believe it is (with the exception of some notes and parenthetical expressions) also accessible to intelligent men and women in any profession. Luckily, most of the ideas I have come upon here turn out, once they are properly understood and explained, to be astonishingly simple.

I am indebted not only to the economists of the past, but also to an unusually large number of generous critics who have commented on drafts of this book and the papers out of which it has grown. These kind critics are so numerous and scattered that I have added a special acknowledgments section at the end of the book in an effort to do justice to them. The foundations and other organizations that have supported my research are less numerous, so I can mention them here. The most important source of support for my research has been the economics, social science, and policy research programs of the National Science Foundation—the Innovation Processes Research Program, the Economics Program, and the Measurement Methods and Data Resources Program. Despite their slender means and the manifold demands upon them, these programs have provided invaluable support for the research that underlies this and my other professional writings. I am also grateful to Resources for the Future, not only for support and stimulating hospitality, but also for patiently agreeing to wait when I delayed a book on their concerns to finish this book. The Environmental Protection Agency and the Sloan Foundation have also been helpful, and the Lehrman Institute, the Hoover Institution of Stanford University, and the Woodrow Wilson International Center for Scholars have also put me in their debt with fellowships that provided some months of freedom for my writing.

My thanks to the foregoing institutions are surpassed only by my gratitude to my family. A book such as this requires intense concentration over many years, and my wife and children have, above all else, given me the peace of mind that made such concentration possible. Since *The Logic of Collective Action* was dedicated to my wife, Alison, it is fitting that this book, a descendant of that one, is dedicated to our three children.

The Questions, and the Standards a Satisfactory Answer Must Meet

Many have been puzzled by the mysterious decline or collapse of great empires or civilizations and by the remarkable rise to wealth, power, or cultural achievement of previously peripheral or obscure peoples. The collapse of the Roman Empire in the West and its defeat by scattered tribes that would otherwise have been of no account is only one of many puzzling examples. On repeated occasions the imposing empires of China have decayed to the point where they could fall prey to far less numerous or sophisticated peoples like the Mongols or to uprisings by poor peasants in remote provinces. The Middle East provides several examples of such collapsed empires, and so do the Indian civilizations of MesoAmerica; even before the Aztec empire was destroyed by a small contingent of Spaniards there had been a succession of empires or cultures, each of which seems to have been supplanted by a previously obscure tribe, its grand pyramids or cities abandoned to the wilderness. The pattern was not greatly different in the Andes, or at Angkor Wat, or in still other places. It was evident among the Greek city-states at the time of Herodotus, who said that "the cities that were formerly great, have most of them become insignificant; and such as are at present powerful, were weak in olden time. I shall therefore discourse equally of both, convinced that human happiness never continues long in one stay."[1]

There are many examples of insignificant tribes and peripheral peoples rising to greatness. It was not in the awesome Egyptian empire that the Mediterranean achievement attained its fullest expression, but among the previously inconsequential peoples of the Ionian Peninsula. The empires of the great city-states of Greece were of course eventually supplanted by the Romans, who before their amazing conquests had been a people of little note. The civilization of Western Christendom that had by the end of the nineteenth century come to dominate the entire world sprang from the backward and chaotic societies of Western Europe in the Middle Ages, which were usually unable even to defend themselves against the advances of the Moslems, the Magyars, and the Vikings. The parts of Western Europe that paced the advance of the West were often areas that had previously been peripheral or unimpressive; the center of growth in the seventeenth century was in the northern provinces of the Netherlands, which had never been important or wealthy before and had only lately escaped subjugation by Spain. In the eighteenth and early nineteenth centuries it was England, rather than the far larger and more imposing France, that gave us the Industrial Revolution. In the second half of the nineteenth century it was long-quiescent Germany and distant ex-colonies in North America, rather than the British Empire at its apogee, that carried that revolution farthest.

There will be no attempt here to account for the rise and fall of the ancient empires or civilizations in the manner of universalist historians like Spengler or Toynbee. If their disappointing experience is any guide, it is perhaps not even very fruitful to identify allegedly common patterns in the rise and decline of ancient civilizations or jurisdictions for which we have only scanty records. There will accordingly be no attempt here to draw universal inductive lessons from the historical experience of ancient societies.

By contrast, the suggestion here is that the hurried historical references indicate how little is understood of the rise and fall of nations and peoples. If the causes of the collapse of various ancient empires had been straightforwardly explained, the way we explain the conquest of a small and weak country in terms of an attack by a larger and stronger one, there would be no "mysterious" decay to attract continued speculation. Broad historical pageants of the kind painted by universal historians are, then, a better source of motivation for further inquiry than for immediate conclusions. But if other evidence, such as recent experience on which there is unprecedented quantitative evidence, or presumptions from oft-confirmed theory, should resonate with the familiar historical tales of the rise and decline of civilizations, then there would be a case for examining the universal histories in a systematic way, with precise questions and orderly procedures for weighing evidence. It is upon the other evidence that I shall rely here and it is to this that we now turn.

II

The economic history of the last century, and especially of the years since World War II, has its own examples of rise and decline. They are not so melodramatic as some accounts of ancient civilizations, but they are no less mysterious, and the rises and declines are probably more rapid. At the end of the Second World War the economies of Germany and Japan were devastated and observers of diverse persuasions and national origins wondered whether these abjectly defeated societies would be able to provide themselves with even the rudiments of survival. As everyone knows, the economies of West Germany and Japan have enjoyed "economic miracles" and are now among the most prosperous in the world. The German and Japanese economies not only grew substantially when these countries were rebuilding their factories and recovering to their prewar level of income, but also (and even more rapidly) after they had recovered and exceeded their previous levels of income. The problem of what we awkwardly but meaningfully call *stagflation,* or inflation combined with unusual levels of unemployment, has on the whole also been less serious in Germany and Japan than in most developed economies.

The last century also offers remarkable evidence of relative decline. The most notable case is that of Great Britain. Since World War II it has had one of the slowest growth rates of the developed democracies. Its growth rate has indeed lagged behind that of most developed countries since the last two decades of the nineteenth century. By now the per capita income in Great Britain is decidedly lower than in most of Western Europe. In the past decade, at least, Britain has also suffered relatively greater increases in both inflation and unemployment than comparable countries like Germany and Japan. The slow growth and other difficulties of the British economy have driven many people in Britain as well as in other countries to speak of the "British disease."

Within the United States there are dramatic examples of decline and at the same time notable instances of growth. The states of the Northeast and the older Middle West, and especially the great cities in these regions, have declined substantially in relation to the rest of the nation and the world. The near bankruptcies of New York and Cleveland are only extreme manifestations of a general loss in relative per capita income and outmigration in the industrial states of the Northeast and the Middle West. Most states in the West and the South, by contrast, have grown rapidly in the last few decades. These reversals of fortune have not been satisfactorily explained.

It might be thought that the examples of growth and decline that have been mentioned have been explained in the literature on the "sources" of economic growth. This literature is certainly impressive; Edward Denison's estimates of the relative contributions to growth of capital accumulation, of technical advance, and so on, have been altogether constructive, while Dale Jorgenson and many other economists have made herculean efforts to provide ever more sophisticated estimates. Yet estimates of the sources of growth, however meticulous, subtle, and useful, do not tell us about the ultimate causes of growth. They do not tell us what incentives made the saving and investment occur, or what explained the innovations, or why there was more innovation and capital accumulation in one society or period than in another. They do not trace the sources of growth to their fundamental causes; they trace the water in the river to the streams and lakes from which it comes, but they do not explain the rain. Neither do they explain the silting up of the channels of economic progress—that is, what I shall call here the "retardants" of growth.

The literature on the sources of growth helps to delineate another example of puzzlingly rapid growth. We know from this literature that capital accumulation, though considerably less important than the "advance of knowledge," is still a major source of economic growth. Since new technologies are often embodied in new capital equipment, some of the "residual" increase in productivity usually attributed to the advance of knowledge would not have occurred without investment in physical capital. Any uncertainty about economic policy, and especially political or military instability so great that it creates skepticism about whether any investment in durable capital goods will be protected, will tend to reduce productive investment. Of course, businessmen have a political incentive to exaggerate their need for stable and predictable public policies, but there can be no doubt that their insecurities can have some effect on both the level and the type of investment in new capital goods. Virtually all economists agree that events, or even expectations, that discourage investment or destroy productive capital will lower the level of income. Thus societies that are politically unstable or often subjected to foreign invasion are likely to have less productive investment and lower rates of growth than they would otherwise have had. There will be more flights of capital and fewer investments in plant or equipment that can pay off only in the long run. Savings are more likely to be hoarded in easily portable but socially unproductive assets such as gold.

In view of this, the rapid growth of the French economy in the postwar years is remarkable. It is not only that France was defeated and occupied in World War II: in less than two centuries that country has experienced some of the most profound and protracted revolutions in human history, has gone through constitutions almost as though they were periodical literature, and has suffered partial or total occupation four times. Even in the postwar period near-revolutions and fears of popular front government brought some capital flight. Given this extraordinary succession of political upheavals and foreign incursions, why did France in 1970 (the year for which we have the best adjustments for national differences in cost of living and thus the best real income comparisons)[2] have a per capita income decidedly above that of Great Britain, about the same as that of Germany, and only a fourth lower than the United States?

III

France and West Germany, with Italy and the three Benelux countries, founded the Common Market in 1957. It is remarkable how rapidly all six initial members of the European Economic Community have grown. A glance at table 1.1 reveals that in general they have grown more rapidly than Australia, New Zealand, the United Kingdom, and the United States, all of which had been spared the invasion and upheaval that "the Six" suffered. In some of these initial Common Market countries growth was more rapid in the 1960s, when the Common Market took effect, than in the 1950s, even though by then recovery from the war had been completed and they had already caught up with some of the more secure societies. One of the questions this book will attempt to answer is why the Six enjoyed such rapid growth.

In the nineteenth century there were also remarkable examples of economic growth and national advance that have never been satisfactorily explained. In little more than a century, between the adoption of the Constitution and the outbreak of World War I, the United States became the world's largest economy with the highest per capita income. In the first part of the nineteenth century the German-speaking areas that were destined to become a united Germany were relatively poor, but after the creation of the Zollverein and the German Reich Germany

Table 1.1. Average Annual Rates of Growth of Per Capita Gross
Domestic Product at Constant Prices (in percent)

Country	1950–1960	1960–1970	1970–1978
Australia	2.0[a]	3.7[b]	2.4[c]
Austria	5.7	3.9	3.8
Belgium	2.0[d]	4.1	3.1
Canada	1.2	3.7	3.1
Denmark	2.5	3.9	2.2
Finland	3.3	4.2	2.5
France	3.5	4.6	3.0
Germany, Fed. Rep. of	6.6	3.5	2.4
Ireland	1.8	3.8	2.3[e]
Italy	4.9[f]	4.6	2.1[g]
Japan	6.8[h]	9.4	3.8
Netherlands	3.3	4.1	2.3
New Zealand	1.7[i]	2.2[j]	—[k]
Norway	2.7	4.0	3.9
Sweden	2.9	3.6	1.2
Switzerland	2.9	2.8	−0.1
United Kingdom	2.3	2.3	2.0
United States	1.2	3.0	2.0

NOTE: Data are from *Yearbook(s) of National Account Statistics* for 1969 and 1978,
Statistical Office of the United Nations, New York, published in 1970 and 1979,
respectively.
a. 1952–1960;   b. 1963–1970;   c. 1970–1976;   d. 1953–1960;
e. 1970–1977;   f. 1951–1960;   g. 1970–1977;   h. 1952–1960;
i. 1954–1960;   j. 1960–1968;   k. The statistics for New Zealand in this
period are not separated from those for "Oceania."

grew so rapidly that by 1914 it was overtaking Britain. In the mid-
nineteenth century the Japanese were desperately poor and could be
almost effortlessly humiliated by the warships of Western countries, but
within little more than a half-century after the Meiji Restoration in
1867–68, Japan had become the only industrialized country outside the
West and one of the world's significant powers. Another of my questions is, Why did these three countries figure so prominently in nineteenth-century economic growth?

There was a commercial revolution and considerable aggregate (if not per capita) growth in parts of Western Europe in the sixteenth and seventeenth centuries, followed by the Industrial Revolution that began in Britain in the second half of the eighteenth century. Some of this growth occurred in the northern provinces of the Netherlands just after they succeeded in gaining their independence from Spain. Much of it occurred in Britain and (to a lesser extent) in France after centralizing monarchs seized effective power from the baronies, manors, and towns that had enjoyed considerable autonomy in medieval times, and then began to eliminate local tolls and restrictions that stood in the way of nationwide markets. In the aggregate these episodes of economic growth transformed the Western Europe that had been relatively primitive in the "dark ages" into a civilization that by the nineteenth century dominated almost the entire world.

The rise of the West no doubt was due to a number of different factors, many of which are explained in the history textbooks, and it would be foolish to seek any monocausal explanation. The standard accounts do not, however, provide anything resembling a complete or compelling explanation for the rise of the West, much less of the specific advances of Holland, Britain, and France during the commercial revolution or of Britain during the Industrial Revolution. Something important must have been left out. Accordingly, one of my questions is, What has been left out or overlooked in the conventional accounts? Or more precisely, What has been left out that is so crucial that we cannot get a convincing and satisying account without it?

IV

There are several further questions that may seem unrelated to the foregoing questions about anomalous examples of economic growth or decline, but these further questions turn out to be answered by the same logic that explains the notable instances of growth and decline. The first of these questions is, Why does involuntary unemployment occur, and sometimes (as in the Great Depression of the 1930s) strike a large proportion of the work force? Those who are not economists naturally may suppose that this question had been adequately answered long ago; most leading economists today agree that it has not been. In the 1930s John Maynard Keynes offered a dazzling and influential account of unemployment and depression, but now leading Keynesian and anti-Keynesian economists agree that Keynes's contribution, however brilliant and important it might be, assumes certain types of behavior that are not reasonable or fully consistent with the interests of those individuals or firms that are assumed to engage in it. In other words, Keynesian *macro*economic theory (a theory of the economy in the aggregate) does not have an adequate basis in *micro*economic theory (a theory of the behavior of individual decision-makers in the particular markets or contexts in which each operates). The non-Keynesian theories of the "monetarist" and "rational-expectations equilibrium" economists do assume rational individual behavior, but these theories do not explain involuntary unemployment—indeed, one of the reasons many economists do not accept these theories is that they implausibly imply that all unemployment is voluntary. This book shows for the first time how involuntary unemployment, and also deep depressions, can occur even when each decision-maker in the economy acts in accordance with his or her best interests. As soon as we understand how involuntary unemployment can result from rational and well-informed individual behavior, it also becomes obvious how inflation and unemployment— which we once thought could not occur simultaneously—can be combined, as they have been in the recent stagflation.

At about the same time that the ugly word *stagflation* was introduced among economists, many political scientists began to describe certain modern societies as "ungovernable." The term *ungovernability* was used by various writers in Great Britain when the Heath government fell as it attempted to assert the authority of the government at the time of a miners' strike. The term was used in the United States to describe the politics that led to the virtual bankruptcy of New York City. It has also been invoked by observers of the failures of several administrations to obtain the legislation or authority to implement most of their programs, even when, as in the Carter administration, the president's party had a large majority in both houses of Congress. The concern about ungovernability in the United States often takes the form of complaints about "single-issue" politics and the limited influence and discipline of American political parties. Thus our next question is, Why are some modern societies to some degree ungovernable? That is, Why has it seemed that governments in some countries did not govern or control their societies as well as they had in the past?

There are also a couple of questions that it will not be possible to state even roughly until much of our analysis is complete, so I will make only an oblique reference to them here. One concerns what I have chosen to call the "top-heavy" societies, because of the unusual influence of the top firms and families in the largest cities. Such societies are most likely to arise where there is political instability and an underdeveloped economy, and lead to a great degree of inequality in the distribution of income.

The last major question is a bit different. It also requires the use of a controversy-laden and ill-defined concept, so this question cannot be stated as precisely as might be wished without tedious length. In a casual sense, though, the question is straightforward: What makes the class structure more rigid or exclusive in one country or period than in another? There may be some ambiguity partly because the word *class* is sometimes used to refer simply to differences in income or status, almost as a synonym for income brackets or educational levels; but here the concern will be with any exclusivity and barriers to entry in a social structure that at least to some degree limit opportunities and countervail meritocratic tendencies. The word *class* is used in approximately this sense fairly often in Great Britain, and the model offered in this book has striking implications about one important aspect of the evolution of class structure in that country. Those who believe that class rigidities in the sense described could not occur, or would never have much quantitative significance, will change their view the moment they think of the Indian caste system, an extreme form of class rigidity, which has limited untold millions of people to particular occupations. The same theory that generates testable answers to our other questions also happens, quite by accident, to generate an explanation of the Indian caste system as well as of class or group barriers.

V

Answers of sorts have been offered to many of the questions I have posed, and sometimes these answers are even established in the folklore. This is particularly true for the anomalous growth rates since World War II. The remarkably rapid economic growth in postwar Japan and West Germany, for example, is often ascribed to the wartime destruction of plant and equipment, which induced these countries to rebuild with the latest technology. It is similarly attributed to the exceptional industriousness of their peoples, while in the same spirit the slow growth of Great Britain is ascribed to the allegedly exceptional British taste for leisure.

Perhaps because Britain has had an anomalous growth rate for a longer time, its economic performance has been the object of an unusual number of such ad hoc explanations. Britain's slow growth is often laid to the strength or narrow-mindedness of British unions, to the resistance to change or the uncooperativeness of British workers, or to socialistic economic policies. Others emphasize a lack of entrepreneurial drive and willingness to innovate on the part of British managers; establishmentarian, anticommercial attitudes that keep the ablest and best-educated people away from business pursuits; and an addiction among the British ruling classes for Concorde-type purchases of national prestige. A common denominator of most of these explanations is that they emphasize some allegedly distinctive trait of one social class or another or the rigidities in the British class system.

The above folk wisdom is not set out as a straw man easily knocked down. On the contrary, I will argue that some of the folk wisdom is partly true, and I will endeavor to provide an intellectual foundation for some of the popular suppositions. The point is rather to make it clear that the foregoing arguments, like many others, are only ad hoc explanations, and ad hoc explanations cannot be sufficient.

One reason that ad hoc arguments are insufficient is that they are usually not testable against a broad enough array of data or experience to enable us to tell whether they are correct. Each country, region, historical period, and indeed each human being is unique in many ways. Thus the fact that a country with an unusually high growth rate has this or that distinctive trait provides no justification for the inference that there is a causal connection. Only the British have Big Ben and only the Germans eat a lot of sauerkraut, but it would of course be absurd to suggest that one is responsible for the slow British growth and the other for the fast German growth. No causal explanation can claim any more credence than the Big Ben/sauerkraut argument unless it identifies an attribute that explains a number of cases or phenomena or is logically derived from a theory that has wide explanatory power. Often explanations based on a unique attribute of a country provide in statistical terms a sample of the size of one; they are equivalent to concluding, from a single toss of a pair of dice that resulted in two ones, that tossing a pair of dice will always result in "snake eyes." In some other cases where a unique attribute of a country is considered, this analogy is unfair; the unique trait may be present in different parts of the country in different degrees, or there may be enough variability or richness of other kinds to make an argument persuasive. This is what accounts for the appeal of the conclusions drawn in the better historical monographs. Nonetheless, only when a wide range of diverse phenomena is explained concisely can there be a compelling basis for belief.

Another reason we should be cautious about ad hoc explanations is that, when outcomes are already known, it is almost always possible to work out an irrefutable "explanation" if one can use any amount or type of information in constructing the explanation. Even if there should be no unique attribute to which appeal can be made, reality is normally so complex and variegated that any cases with different results are almost certain to differ in other ways as well. Any two countries, periods, or significant historical events differ in so many ways that if there is no limit to the amount or type of information that may be used, then it will almost always be possible to construct an explanation of any differences in outcome by appealing to one or more of the other ways in which the pair differ. Unless the differences that are invoked also apply to other cases, we are again back to making inferences from a sample of one. It is because it is so easy to rely on the unique attributes or distinctive sets of attributes that are likely to characterize any human or social phenomena that we must insist that any explanation fits some data or observations beyond those from which it was derived.

The seriousness of the shortcomings of ad hoc explanations is aptly illustrated by a set of photographs in a magazine I read as a child. The magazine article pointed out that some of those portrayed were convicted criminals and others were highly respected citizens, and the reader was invited to judge which was which before turning to the page with the answers. Neither my friends nor I did well in picking out the criminals—the most villainous-looking of the lot, I seem to remember, turned out to be a distinguished author. Yet it was remarkable how often, *after* looking up the answers, we would "discover" the sneaky eyes or suspicious chin that was, or should have been, a dead giveaway.

Now suppose that, after looking up the answers, we also received descriptions of the childhood and ancestry of each of the individuals. Would it not then also have seemed easy to explain why the criminals had turned to crime? This one fell on evil ways as a reaction against his severe and distant father, that one because he had no father, the next because he had too much of mother; yes, the successful businessman also had a severe and distant father, but he did not repress his hatred. Admittedly, the successful artist had no father and a doting mother, but this was the catalyst for his creativity. Whenever there is some astonishing behavior, be it a crime or a great achievement or whatever, there is someone ready to offer a confident psychological explanation based on one or the other of the special features of the astonishing person's history. Sometimes there are several different explanations by different experts. But few, if any, select those who will be so aberrant beforehand. One should be as suspicious of some of the historical and psychological explanations we hear as of the discoveries of evil features in the faces of men who have already been identified as criminal.

The limitations of ad hoc arguments also help to explain why the histories of each country and period are rewritten periodically and a different story told each time. Part of the explanation is that new sources are found, new interests emerge, and better analyses are developed; but partly, when there is no limit to the length of an explanation and no rules about which of the infinite number of outcomes is selected for explanation, an enormous—if not infinite—number of plausible stories can be told, and it is mainly a matter of taste which of these explanations is preferred. Scholar after scholar can then write plausible book after plausible book, but none need be definitive and there is no accumulation of knowledge of causes and effects.

We can begin to have confidence in an explanation when a large number of phenomena are explained—that is, when the explanation has "power"—and explained "parsimoniously." Since it is costly to acquire and remember information, parsimonious or concise and simple explanations must, other things equal, be preferred; the principle of Ockham's razor—that any inessential premises or complexities ought to be cut out of an argument—has been useful to philosophers, mathematicians, and scientists since the Middle Ages. But when the parsimony of an explanation is taken into account along with its power, it bears also on the likelihood that it is true. For one thing, if the explanation has both power and parsimony it is hard to see how its author could have resorted to unique or distinctive features to explain the outcomes. For another, when a simple explanation explains a great deal—when the ratio of power to parsimony is high—it is improbable that mere chance could explain its success. As Charles Darwin put it in the sixth edition of *The Origin of Species:*

> It can hardly be supposed that a false theory could explain, in so satisfactory a manner as does the theory of natural selection, the several large classes of facts above specified. It has recently been

objected that this is an unsafe way of arguing; but it is a method used in judging of the common events of life, and has often been used by the greatest natural philosophers.[3]

The persuasiveness of a theory depends not only on how many facts are explained, but also on how diverse are the kinds of facts explained. Darwin's theory offers insights into the origin and evolution of creatures as diverse as whales and bacteria, and this makes it more convincing than if it could explain only mosquitoes, however many millions of mosquitoes might be satisfactorily explained. If a theory explains facts of quite diverse kinds it has what William Whewell, a nineteenth-century writer on scientific method, called "consilience." Whewell argued that "no example can be pointed out, in the whole history of science, so far as I am aware, in which this con-silience . . . has given testimony in favor of an hypothesis later discovered to be false."[4]

There is also a need to ensure that an explanation is not consistent with the evidence presented in support of it merely because those cases that happened to fit the theory were the only ones examined; there could, of course, be other cases to which the theory is supposed to apply that contradict it. Since it is usually impossible in practice to consider all relevant cases, the best approach is often to consider all the cases in one pre-established category or another; this rules out selection bias at least in this category. Possibly different principles apply to the category considered than to other categories, and this suggests examining other cases outside the test category as well. If the facts are not selected because they fit a theory, and they are also numerous and in very different classes, then it is most improbable that a false theory could explain them and at the same time remain parsimonious.

VI

The reader should accordingly not accept the argument in this book simply because he or she finds it plausible and consistent with known facts. Many plausible stories have been told before and often also wide-ly believed, yet they failed to stand up. The reader should not place even a small degree of confidence in the argument here unless he or she finds that it explains a large number of facts in different categories and with such a limited set of "causes" or postulates that it is clear I could not consciously or unconsciously have been adding as many as were needed to cover every outcome I could have been aware of at the time I worked out the theory. (In fact, I did not know some of the facts this book explains when I developed the argument, but unless the reader knows me well, he or she, as a matter of scientific principle, ought not take this claim into account in deciding whether my explanation is right, for those who do not know me have no way, even indirectly, to test the truth of my assertion.) Finally, the reader should also be wary about whether the cases I have set out to explain are simply those that happen to fit the theory.

Lest the reader think I have been excessively sporting in emphasizing the need for high standards in judging the evidence in support of my theory, I should point out that it has occurred to me that intelligent people will judge all alternative explanations by the same high standards. And almost all of the competing explanations are separate and ad hoc explanations of each of the many phenomena at issue, and often explanations that focus on some unique alleged cultural or racial characteristic of each country, region, and historical period. In the aggregate these ad hoc explanations are anything but parsimonious, and even when they are partly right they do not take us far, or explain how the key causal attribute originated, or provide much guidance on public policies that might improve matters.

VII

Although we should not be satisfied with any theory that fails to explain a lot with a little, we need not of course expect any one theory to explain everything, or even the most important thing. Absolutely nothing in all of epistemology suggests that valid explanations should be monocausal. An explanation may be entirely valid, yet explain only a part (and even a small part) of the variation at issue. I am reminded by the pilot's announcement on the aircraft on which I am writing this paragraph that the groundspeed of the plane depends on the direction and the speed of the wind, and of course accurate navigation requires that they be taken into account, yet it is far more important whether the plane is at full throttle or idle, whether it has a jet or a piston engine, and so forth.

It is necessary to make this point here, since some readers of early drafts of my argument, perhaps beguiled by the simplicity of the explanation, have treated all other explanations of the same phenomena as wrong, or explicitly have supposed that the argument here said everything that needed to be said about the phenomena. Nothing could be farther from my intention than to provide a monocausal or complete explanation of social and economic phenomena, or even the particular historical phenomena analyzed here. At most—at the very most—the aspiration is to provide the equivalent of Sherlock Holmes's observation of the dog that didn't bark: to provide a missing clue that gives us a better understanding of the whole story.

Since no monocausal explanation is offered, one well-known test of validity is not applicable. It is often said in methodological discussions that every meaningful scientific theory must specify one or more possible events or observations, or experimental results, which would, if they occurred, refute the theory. This rule has no applicability to multicausal conceptions unless a perfect experiment is performed, or one so nearly perfect that we could be certain that it was the error in the theory rather than the flaw in the experiment that accounted for the result. In view of the limited possibilities for experiments in economics and other social sciences, the impossibility of controlled experiments on historical events, and the extreme improbability that nature or history will on its own provide anything resembling a perfect natural experiment, a search for a single decisive refutation is futile. I am told by some philosophers of science that even in the physical and natural sciences the rejection of theories usually occurs not because of a single negative experiment, but more often from a series of anomalous observations combined with the emergence of a better alternative theory. What we should demand of a theory or hypothesis, then, is that it be clear about what observations would increase the probability that it was false and what observations would tend to increase the probability that there was some truth in it. The theory set out in the next two chapters is clear in this sense: even though it is hard to foresee any one observation that would definitively refute it, it will be evident whether an observation tends to call the theory into question, and what types of observations in the aggregate would convince us it was false.

With multicausality, it is also conceivable that all (or almost all) of the facts that appear to corroborate the theory offered in this book could actually be due to a diversity of other causes. A number of other causes could, by coincidence, have produced the intricate patterns that the theory here predicts. The theory is evidently so consilient and powerful, and at the same time so parsimonious, that the chances of this are remote. Still, it is a possibility we should never forget.

Since the multiplicity of causal forces can make a false theory seem true or a true theory seem false, any single test of the theory may be weak, or far from decisive. Some of the tests of the theory offered here are weak, and the reader will be able to think of diverse causes that could have generated the observed results. At the same time, essentially all of the tests point in the same direction, so the results in the aggregate are incomparably stronger than the individual results. If, when we wake in the morning, we are surprised to see a patch or two of white outside, there could perhaps be uncertainty about the cause, but if every twig and piece of ground is freshly white, we know it snowed last night.

We turn now to the most crucial chapter in the book, which develops the logic needed to derive all the results and to make the rest of the book comprehensible.

The Logic

2

The argument of this book begins with a paradox in the behavior of groups. It has often been taken for granted that if everyone in a group of individuals or firms had some interest in common, then there would be a tendency for the group to seek to further this interest. Thus many students of politics in the United States for a long time supposed that citizens with a common political interest would organize and lobby to serve that interest. Each individual in the population would be in one or more groups and the vector of pressures of these competing groups explained the outcomes of the political process. Similarly, it was often supposed that if workers, farmers, or consumers faced monopolies harmful to their interests, they would eventually attain countervailing power through organizations such as labor unions or farm organizations that obtained market power and protective government action. On a larger scale, huge social classes are often expected to act in the interest of their members; the unalloyed form of this belief is, of course, the Marxian contention that in capitalist societies the bourgeois class runs the government to serve its own interests, and that once the exploitation of the proletariat goes far enough and "false consciousness" has disappeared, the working class will in its own interest revolt and establish a dictatorship of the proletariat. In general, if the individuals in some category or class had a sufficient degree of self-interest and if they all agreed on some common interest, then the group would to some extent also act in a self-interested or group-interested manner.

If we ponder the logic of the familiar assumption described in the preceding paragraph, we can see that it is fundamentally and indisputably faulty. Consider those consumers who agree that they pay higher prices for a product because of some objectionable monopoly or tariff, or those workers who agree that their skill deserves a higher wage. Let us now ask what would be the expedient course of action for an individual consumer who would like to see a boycott to combat a monopoly or a lobby to repeal the tariff, or for an individual worker who would like a strike threat or a minimum wage law that could bring higher wages. If the consumer or worker contributes a few days and a few dollars to organize a boycott or a union or to lobby for favorable legislation, he or she will have sacrificed time and money. What will this sacrifice obtain? The individual will at best succeed in advancing the cause to a small (often imperceptible) degree. In any case he will get only a minute share of the gain from his action. The very fact that the objective or interest is common to or shared by the group entails that the gain from any sacrifice an individual makes to serve this common purpose is shared with everyone in the group. The successful boycott or strike or lobbying action will bring the better price or wage for everyone in the relevant category, so the individual in any large group with a common interest will reap only a minute share of the gains from whatever sacrifices the individual makes to achieve this common interest. Since any gain goes to everyone in the group, those who contribute nothing to the effort will get just as much as those who made a contribution. It pays to "let George do it," but George has little or no incentive to do anything in the group interest either, so (in the absence of factors that are completely left out of the conceptions mentioned in the first paragraph) there will be little, if any, group action. The paradox, then, is that (in the absence of special arrangements or circumstances to which we shall turn later) large groups, at least if they are composed of rational individuals, will *not* act in their group interest.

This paradox is elaborated and set out in a way that lets the reader check every step of the logic in a book I wrote entitled *The Logic of Collective Action*.[1] That book also shows that the evidence in the United States, the only country in which all powerful interest groups were considered, systematically supported the argument, and that the scattered evidence that I was aware of from other countries was also consistent with it. Since the present book is an outgrowth of *The Logic of Collective Action* and in large part even an application of the argument in it, the most serious critics or students of the present book should have read that one. For the many readers who naturally would not want to invest the time needed to do so without knowing what might be gained, and for those with a more casual interest, the first part of this chapter will explain a few features of the argument in *The Logic* that are needed to understand the rest of the present volume. Other parts of the chapter, however, should not involve any repetition.

II

One finding in *The Logic* is that the services of associations like labor unions, professional associations, farm organizations, cartels, lobbies (and even collusive groups without formal organization) resemble the basic services of the state in one utterly fundamental respect. The services of such associations, like the elemental services or "public goods" provided by governments, if provided to anyone, go to everyone in some category or group. Just as the law and order, defense, or pollution abatement brought about by government accrue to everyone in some country or geographic area, so the tariff obtained by a farm organization's lobbying effort raises the price to all producers of the relevant commodity. Similarly, as I argued earlier, the higher wage won by a union applies to all employees in the pertinent category. More generally, every lobby obtaining a general change in legislation or regulation thereby obtains a public or collective good for everyone who benefits from that change, and every combination—that is, every "cartel"—using market or industrial action to get a higher price or wage must, when it restricts the quantity supplied, raise the price for every seller, thereby creating a collective good for all sellers.

   If governments, on the one hand, and combinations exploiting their political or market power, on the other, produce public or collective goods that inevitably go to everyone in some group or category, then both are subject to the paradoxical logic set out above: that is, the individuals and firms they serve have in general no incentive voluntarily to contribute to their support.[2] It follows that if there is only voluntary and rational individual behavior,* then for the most part neither govern-

---

Rational need not imply *self-interested*. The argument in the text can hold even when there is altruistic behavior, although if particular types of altruistic behavior are strong enough it will not hold. Consider first altruistic attitudes about observable outcomes or results—suppose an individual would be willing to sacrifice some leisure or other personal consumption to obtain some amount of a collective good because of an altruistic concern that others should have this collective good. In other words, the individual's preference ordering takes account of the collective good obtained by others as

ments nor lobbies and cartels will exist, unless individuals support them for some reason *other* than the collective goods they provide. Of course, governments exist virtually everywhere and often there are lobbies and cartelistic organizations as well. If the argument so far is right, it follows that something *other* than the collective goods that governments and other organizations provide accounts for their existence.**

In the case of governments, the answer was explained before *The Logic of Collective Action* was written; governments are obviously supported by compulsory taxation. Sometimes there is little objection to this compulsion, presumably because many people intuitively understand that public goods cannot be sold in the marketplace or financed by

---

well as personal consumption. This assumption of altruism does not imply irrationality, or a tendency to make choices that are inconsistent with the maximal satisfaction of the values or preferences the individual has. Altruism also does not call into question the normal diminishing marginal rates of substitution between any pair of goods or objectives; as more of any good or objective (selfish or altruistic) is attained, other things being equal, the extent to which other goods or objectives (selfish or altruistic) will be given up to attain more of that good or objective will diminish.

A typical altruistic and rational individual of the sort described will not make any substantial voluntary contributions to obtain a collective good for a large group. The reason is that in a sufficiently large group the individual's contribution will make only a small and perhaps imperceptible difference to the amount of collective good the group obtains, whereas at the same time every contribution reduces dollar-for-dollar the amount of personal consumption and private-good charity, and the diminishing marginal rates of substitution entail that these sacrifices become progressively more onerous. In equilibrium in large groups there is accordingly little or no voluntary contribution by the rational altruist to the provision of a collective good.

Jarring as it is to the common-sense notion of rationality, let us now make the special assumption that the altruist gets satisfaction not from observably better outcomes for others, but rather from his or her own sacrifices for them. On this assumption we can secure voluntary provision of collective goods even in the largest groups. Here each dollar of personal consumption that is sacrificed can bring a significant return in moral satisfaction, and the problem that substantial personal sacrifices bring little or no perceptible change in the level of public good provided is no longer relevant. Even though this latter participatory or "Kantian" altruism is presumably not the usual form of altruism, I think it does exist and helps to account for some observations of voluntary contributions to large groups. (Yet another possibility is that the altruist is result-oriented but neglects the observable levels of the public good, simply assuming that his or her sacrifices of personal consumption increase the utility of others enough to justify the personal sacrifice.) My own thinking on this issue has been clarified by reading Howard Margolis, *Selfishness, Altruism, and Rationality* (Cambridge: At the University Press, 1982).

**This argument need not apply to small groups, which are discussed later in the chapter.

any voluntary mechanism; as I have already argued, each individual would get only a minute share of any governmental services he or she paid for and would get whatever level of services was provided by others in any event.

In the case of organizations that provide collective goods to their client groups through political or market action, the answer has not been obvious, but it is no less clear-cut. Organizations of this kind, at least when they represent large groups, are again not supported because of the collective goods they provide, but rather because they have been fortunate enough to find what I have called *selective incentives*. A selective incentive is one that applies selectively to the individuals depending on whether they do or do not contribute to the provision of the collective good.

A selective incentive can be either negative or positive; it can, for example, be a loss or punishment imposed only on those who do *not* help provide the collective good. Tax payments are, of course, obtained with the help of negative selective incentives, since those who are found not to have paid their taxes must then suffer both taxes and penalties. The best-known type of organized interest group in modern democratic societies, the labor union, is also usually supported, in part, through negative selective incentives. Most of the dues in strong unions are obtained through union shop, closed shop, or agency shop arrangements which make dues paying more or less compulsory and automatic. There are often also informal arrangements with the same effect; David McDonald, former president of the United Steel Workers of America, describes one of these arrangements used in the early history of that union. It was, he writes, a technique

> which we called . . . visual education, which was a high-sounding label for a practice much more accurately described as dues picket-ing. It worked very simply. A group of dues-paying members, selected by the district director (usually more for their size than their tact) would stand at the plant gate with pick handles or base-ball bats in hand and confront each worker as he arrived for his shift.[3]

As McDonald's "dues picketing" analogy suggests, picketing during strikes is another negative selective incentive that unions sometimes need; although picketing in industries with established and stable unions is usually peaceful, this is because the union's capacity to close down an enterprise against which it has called a strike is clear to all; the early phase of unionization often involves a great deal of violence on the part of both unions and anti-union employers and scabs.* Some opponents of labor unions argue that, since many of the members of labor unions join only through the processes McDonald described or through legally enforced union-shop arrangements, most of the relevant workers do not want to be unionized. The Taft-Hartley Act provided that impartial governmentally administered elections should be held to determine whether workers did in fact want to belong to unions. As the collective-good logic set out here suggests, the same workers who had to be coerced to pay union dues voted for the unions with compulsory dues (and normally by overwhelming margins), so that this feature of the Taft-Hartley Act was soon abandoned as pointless.[4] The workers who as individuals tried to avoid paying union dues at the same time that they voted to force themselves all to pay dues are no different from taxpayers who vote, in effect, for high levels of taxation, yet try to arrange their private affairs in ways that avoid taxes. Because of the same logic, many professional associations also get members through covert or overt coercion (for example, lawyers in those states with a "closed bar"). So do lobbies and cartels of several other types; some of the contributions by corporate officials, for instance, to politicians useful to the corporation are also the result of subtle forms of coercion.[5]

*The references to the often violent interaction between employers and employees in the early stages of unionization should not obscure the consensual and informal "unionization" that also sometimes occurs because of employers' initiatives. This sort of labor organization or collusion arises because some types of production require that workers collaborate effectively. When this is the case, the employer may find it profitable to encourage team spirit and social interaction among employees. Staff conferences and work-group meetings, newsletters for employees, firm-sponsored employee athletic teams, employer-financed office parties, and the like are partly explained by this consideration. In firms that have the same employment pattern for some time, the networks for employee interaction that the employer created to encourage effective cooperation at work may evolve into informal collusions, or occasionally even unions, of workers, and tacitly or openly force the employer to deal with his employees as a cartelized group. This evolution is unlikely when employees are, for example, day laborers or consultants, but when stable patterns of active cooperation are important to production, the employer may gain more from the extra production that this cooperation brings about than he loses from the informal or formal cartelization that he helps to create. The evolution of this type of informal unionization implies that there is more organization of labor than the statistics imply, and that the differences between some ostensibly unorganized firms and unionized firms are not as great as might appear on the surface.

Positive selective incentives, although easily overlooked, are also commonplace, as diverse examples in *The Logic* demonstrate.[6] American farm organizations offer prototypical examples. Many of the members of the stronger American farm organizations are members because their dues payments are automatically deducted from the "patronage dividends" of farm cooperatives or are included in the insurance premiums paid to mutual insurance companies associated with the farm organizations. Any number of organizations with urban clients also provide similar positive selective incentives in the form of insurance policies, publications, group air fares, and other private goods made available only to members. The grievance procedures of labor unions usually also offer selective incentives, since the grievances of active members often get most of the attention. The symbiosis between the political power of a lobbying organization and the business institutions associated with it often yields tax or other advantages for the business institution, and the publicity and other information flowing out of the political arm of a movement often generates patterns of preference or trust that make the business activities of the movement more remunerative. The surpluses obtained in such ways in turn provide positive selective incentives that recruit participants for the lobbying efforts.

III

Small groups, or occasionally large "federal" groups that are made up of many small groups of socially interactive members, have an additional source of both negative and positive selective incentives. Clearly most people value the companionship and respect of those with whom they interact. In modern societies solitary confinement is, apart from the rare death penalty, the harshest legal punishment. The censure or even ostracism of those who fail to bear a share of the burdens of collective action can sometimes be an important selective incentive. An extreme example of this occurs when British unionists refuse to speak to uncooperative colleagues, that is, "send them to Coventry." Similarly, those in a socially interactive group seeking a collective good can give special respect or honor to those who distinguish themselves by their sacrifices in the interest of the group and thereby offer them a positive selective incentive. Since most people apparently prefer relatively like-minded or agreeable and respectable company, and often prefer to associate with those whom they especially admire, they may find it costless to shun those who shirk the collective action and to favor those who oversubscribe.

Social selective incentives can be powerful and inexpensive, but they are available only in certain situations. As I have already indicated, they have little applicability to large groups, except in those cases in which the large groups can be federations of small groups that are capable of social interaction. It also is not possible to organize most large groups in need of a collective good into small, socially interactive subgroups, since most individuals do not have the time needed to maintain a huge number of friends and acquaintances.

The availability of social selective incentives is also limited by the social heterogeneity of some of the groups or categories that would benefit from a collective good. Everyday observation reveals that most socially interactive groups are fairly homogeneous and that many people resist extensive social interaction with those they deem to have lower status or greatly different tastes. Even Bohemian or other nonconformist groups often are made up of individuals who are similar to one another, however much they differ from the rest of society. Since some of the categories of individuals who would benefit from a collective good are socially heterogeneous, the social interaction needed for selective incentives sometimes cannot be arranged even when the number of individuals involved is small.

Another problem in organizing and maintaining socially heterogeneous groups is that they are less likely to agree on the exact nature of whatever collective good is at issue or on how much of it is worth buying. All the arguments showing the difficulty of collective action mentioned so far in this chapter hold even when there is perfect consensus about the collective good that is desired, the amount that is wanted, and the best way to obtain the good. But if anything, such as social heterogeneity, reduces consensus, collective action can become still less likely. And if there is nonetheless collective action, it incurs the extra cost (especially for the leaders of whatever organization or collusion is at issue) of accommodating and compromising the different views. The situation is slightly different in the very small groups to which we shall turn shortly. In such groups differences of opinion can sometimes provide a bit of an incentive to join an organization seeking a collective good, since joining might give the individual a significant influence over the organization's policy and the nature of any collective good it would obtain. But this consideration is not relevant to any group that is large enough so that a single individual cannot expect to affect the outcome.

Consensus is especially difficult where collective goods are concerned because the defining characteristic of collective goods—that they go to everyone in some group or category if they are provided at all—also entails that everyone in the relevant group gets more or less of the collective good together, and that they all have to accept whatever level and type of public good is provided. A country can have only one foreign and defense policy, however diverse the preferences and incomes of its citizenry, and (except in the rarely attainable case of a "Lindahl equilibrium")[7] there will not be agreement within a country on how much should be spent to carry out the foreign and defense policy. This is a clear implication of the arguments for "fiscal equivalence"[8] and of the rigorous models of "optimal segregation"[9] and "fiscal federalism."[10] Heterogeneous clients with diverse demands for collective goods can pose an even greater problem for private associations, which not only must deal with the disagreements but also must find selective incentives strong enough to hold dissatisfied clients.

In short, the political entrepreneurs who attempt to organize collective action will accordingly be more likely to succeed if they strive to organize relatively homogeneous groups. The political managers whose task it is to maintain organized or collusive action similarly will be motivated to use indoctrination and selective recruitment to increase the homogeneity of their client groups. This is true in part because social selective incentives are more likely to be available to the more nearly homogeneous groups, and in part because homogeneity will help achieve consensus.

IV

Information and calculation about a collective good is often itself a collective good. Consider a typical member of a large organization who is deciding how much time to devote to studying the policies or leadership of the organization. The more time the member devotes to this matter, the greater the likelihood that his or her voting and advocacy will favor effective policies and leadership for the organization. This typical member will, however, get only a small share of the gain from the more effective policies and leadership: in the aggregate, the other members will get almost all the gains, so that the individual member does not have an incentive to devote nearly as much time to fact-finding and thinking about the organization as would be in the group interest. Each of the members of the group would be better off if they all could be coerced into spending more time finding out how to vote to make the organization best further their interests. This is dramatically evident in the case of the typical voter in a national election in a large country. The gain to such a voter from studying issues and candidates until it is clear what vote is truly in his or her interest is given by the difference in the value to the individual of the "right" election outcome as compared with the "wrong" outcome, *multiplied by the probability a change in the individual's vote will alter the outcome of the election.* Since the probability that a typical voter will change the outcome of the election is vanishingly small, the typical citizen is usually "rationally ignorant" about public affairs.[11] Often, information about public affairs is so interesting or entertaining that it pays to acquire it for these reasons alone—this appears to be the single most important source of exceptions to the generalization that *typical* citizens are rationally ignorant about public affairs.

Individuals in a few special vocations can receive considerable rewards in private goods if they acquire exceptional knowledge of public goods. Politicians, lobbyists, journalists, and social scientists, for example, may earn more money, power, or prestige from knowledge of this or that public business. Occasionally, exceptional knowledge of public policy can generate exceptional profits in stock exchanges or other markets. Withal, the typical citizen will find that his or her income and life chances will not be improved by zealous study of public affairs, or even of any single collective good.

The limited knowledge of public affairs is in turn necessary to explain the effectiveness of lobbying. If all citizens had obtained and digested all pertinent information, they could not then be swayed by advertising or other persuasion. With perfectly informed citizens, elected officials would not be subject to the blandishments of lobbyists, since the constituents would then know if their interests were betrayed and defeat the unfaithful representative at the next election. Just as lobbies provide collective goods to special-interest groups, so their effectiveness is explained by the imperfect knowledge of citizens, and this in turn is due mainly to the fact that information and calculation about collective goods is also a collective good.

This fact—that the benefits of individual enlightenment about public goods are usually dispersed throughout a group or nation, rather than concentrated upon the individual who bears the costs of becoming enlightened—explains many other phenomena as well. It explains, for example, the "man bites dog" criterion of what is newsworthy. If the television newscasts were watched or newspapers were read solely to obtain the most important information about public affairs, aberrant events of little public importance would be ignored and typical patterns of quantitative significance would be emphasized; when the news is, by contrast, for most people largely an alternative to other forms of diversion or entertainment, intriguing oddities and human-interest items are in demand. Similarly, events that unfold in a suspenseful way or sex scandals among public figures are fully covered by the media, whereas the complexities of economic policy or quantitative analyses of public problems receive only minimal attention. Public officals, often able to thrive without giving the citizens good value for their tax monies, may fall over an exceptional mistake striking enough to be newsworthy. Extravagant statements, picturesque protests, and unruly demonstrations that offend much of the public they are designed to influence are also explicable in this way: they make diverting news and thus call attention to interests and arguments that might otherwise be ignored. Even some isolated acts of terrorism that are described as "senseless" can, from this perspective, be explained as effective means of obtaining the riveted attention of a public that otherwise would remain rationally ignorant.

This argument also helps us to understand certain apparent inconsistencies in the behavior of modern democracies. The arrangement of the income-tax brackets in all the major developed democracies is distinctly progressive, whereas the loopholes are more often tilted toward a minority of more prosperous taxpayers. Since both are the results of the same democratic institutions, why do they not have the same incidence? As I see it, the progression of the income tax is a matter of such salience and political controversy that much of the electorate knows about it, so populist and majoritarian considerations dictate a considerable degree of progression. The details of tax laws are far less widely known, and they often reflect the interests of small numbers of organized and usually more prosperous taxpayers. Several of the developed democracies similarly have adopted programs such as Medicare and Medicaid that are obviously inspired by the concerns about the cost of medical care to those with low or middle incomes, yet implemented or administered these programs in ways that resulted in large increases in income for prosperous physicians and other providers of medical care. Again, these diverse consequences seem to be explained by the fact that conspicuous and controversial choices of overall policies become known to the majorities who consume health care, whereas the many smaller choices needed to implement these programs are influenced primarily by a minority of organized providers of health care.

The fact that the typical individual does not have an incentive to spend much time studying many of his choices concerning collective goods also helps to explain some otherwise inexplicable individual contributions toward the provision of collective goods. The logic of collective action that has been described in this chapter is not immediately apparent to those who have never studied it; if it were, there would be nothing paradoxical in the argument with which this chapter opened, and students to whom the argument is explained would not react with initial skepticism.[12] No doubt the practical implications of this logic for the individual's own choices were often discerned before the logic was ever set out in print, but this does not mean that they were always understood even at the intuitive and practical level. In particular, when the costs of individual contributions to collective action are very small, the individual has little incentive to investigate whether or not to make a contribution or even to exercise intuition. If the individual knows the costs of a contribution to collective action in the interest of a group of which he is a part are trivially small, he may rationally not take the trouble to consider whether the gains are smaller still. This is particularly the case since the size of these gains and the policies that would maximize them are matters about which it is usually not rational for him to investigate.

This consideration of the costs and benefits of calculation about public goods leads to the testable prediction that voluntary contributions toward the provision of collective goods for large groups without selective incentives will often occur when the costs of the individual contributions are negligible, but that they will *not* often occur when the costs of the individual contributions are considerable. In other words, when the costs of individual action to help to obtain a desired collective good are small enough, the result is indeterminate and sometimes goes one way and sometimes the other, but when the costs get larger this indeterminacy disappears. We should accordingly find that more than a few people are willing to take the moment of time needed to sign petitions for causes they support, or to express their opinions in the course of discussion, or to vote for the candidate or party they prefer. Similarly, if the argument here is correct, we should not find many instances where individuals voluntarily contribute substantial sums of resources year after year for the purpose of obtaining some collective good for some large group of which they are a part. Before parting with a large amount of money or time, and particularly before doing so repeatedly, the rational individual will reflect on what this considerable sacrifice will accomplish. If the individual is a typical individual in a large group that would benefit from a collective good, his contribution will not make a perceptible difference in the amount that is provided. The theory here predicts that such contributions become less likely the larger the contribution at issue.[13]

V

Even when contributions are costly enough to elicit rational calculation, there is still one set of circumstances in which collective action can occur without selective incentives. This set of circumstances becomes evident the moment we think of situations in which there are only a few individuals or firms that would benefit from collective action. Suppose there are two firms of equal size in an industry and no other firms can enter the industry. It still will be the case that a higher price for the industry's product will benefit both firms and that legislation favorable to the industry will help both firms. The higher price and the favorable legislation are then collective goods to this "oligopolistic" industry, even though there are only two in the group that benefit from the collective goods. Obviously, each of the oligopolists is in a situation in which if it restricts output to raise the industry price, or lobbies for favorable legislation for the industry, it will tend to get half of the benefit. And the cost-benefit ratio of action in the common interest easily could be so favorable that, even though a firm bears the whole cost of its action and gets only half the benefit of this action, it could still profit from acting in the common interest. Thus if the group that would benefit from collective action is sufficiently small and the cost-benefit ratio of collective action for the group sufficiently favorable, there may well be calculated action in the collective interest even without selective incentives.

When there are only a few members in the group, there is also the possibility that they will bargain with one another and agree on collective action—then the action of each can have a perceptible effect on the interests and the expedient courses of action of others, so that each has an incentive to act strategically, that is, in ways that take into account the effect of the individual's choices on the choices of others. This interdependence of individual firms or persons in the group can give them an incentive to bargain with one another for their mutual advantage. Indeed, if bargaining costs were negligible, they would have an incentive to continue bargaining with one another until group gains were maximized, that is, until what we shall term a *group-optimal outcome* (or what economists sometimes call a "Pareto-optimal" outcome for the group) is achieved. One way the two firms mentioned in the previous paragraph could obtain such an outcome is by agreeing that each will bear half the costs of any collective action; each firm would then bear half the cost of its action in the common interest and receive half the benefits. It therefore would have an incentive to continue action in the collective interest until the aggregate gains of collective action were maximized. In any bargaining, however, each party has an incentive to seek the largest possible share of the group gain for itself, and usually also an incentive to threaten to block or undermine the collective action—that is, to be a "holdout"—if it does not get its preferred share of the group gains. Thus the bargaining may very well not succeed in achieving a group-optimal outcome and may also fail to achieve agreement on any collective action at all. The upshot of all this, as I explain elsewhere,[14] is that "small" groups can often engage in collective action without selective incentives. In certain small groups ("privileged groups") there is actually a presumption that some of the collective good will be provided. Nonetheless, even in the best of circumstances collective action is problematic and the outcomes in particular cases are indeterminate.

Although some aspects of the matter are complex and indeterminate, the essence of the relationship between the size of the group that would benefit from collective action and the extent of collective action is beautifully simple—yet somehow not widely understood. Consider again our two firms and suppose that they have *not* worked out any agreement to maximize their aggregate gains or to coordinate their actions in any way. Each firm will still get half the gains of any action it takes in the interest of the group, and thus it may have a substantial incentive to act in the group interest even when it is acting unilaterally.

There is, of course, also a *group external economy*, or gain to the group for which the firm acting unilaterally is not compensated, of 50 percent, so unilateral behavior does not achieve a group-optimal outcome.[15] Now suppose there were a third firm of the same size—the group external economy would then be two thirds, and the individual firm would get only a third of the gain from any independent action it took in the group interest. Of course, if there were a hundred such firms, the group external economy would be 99 percent, and the individual firm would get only 1 percent of the gain from any action in the group interest. Obviously, when we get to large groups measured in millions or even thousands, the incentive for group-oriented behavior in the absence of selective incentives becomes insignificant and even imperceptible.

Untypical as my example of equal-sized firms may be, it makes the general point intuitively obvious: other things being equal, *the larger the number of individuals or firms that would benefit from a collective good, the smaller the share of the gains from action in the group interest that will accrue to the individual or firm that undertakes the action. Thus, in the absence of selective incentives, the incentive for group action diminishes as group size increases, so that large groups are less able to act in their common interest than small ones.* If an additional individual or firm that would value the collective good enters the scene, then the share of the gains from group-oriented action that anyone already in the group might take must diminish. This holds true whatever the relative sizes or valuations of the collective good in the group.

There is a clear demonstration of this point in *The Logic of Collective Action,* a small part of which is included in the footnote to this sentence.* The fuller argument will make clear that the assumption in

---

*The cost (C) of a collective good is a function of the level (T) at which it is provided, i.e., $C = f(T)$. The value of the good to the group, V_g, depends not only on T but also on the "size," S_g, of the group, which in turn depends on the number in the group and the value they place on the good; $V_g = TS_g$. The value to an individual i of the good is V_i, and the "fraction," F_i, of the group value that this individual enjoys is V_i/V_g, and this must also equal F_iS_gT. The net advantage, A_i, that individual i obtains from purchasing an amount of the collective good is given by its value to him minus the cost, i.e., $A_i = V_i - C$, which changes with the level of T his expenditure obtains, so

$$dA_i/dT = dV_i/dT - dC/dT.$$

At a maximum $dA_i/dT = 0$. Because $V_i = F_iS_gT$ and F_i and S_g are constants

the preceding paragraphs of firms of equal size is unnecessary to the conclusion (though it is, I hope, helpful in obtaining a quick intuitive sense of the matter). Differences in size, or more precisely in the amount the different firms or individuals would be willing to pay for marginal amounts of the collective good, are of great importance and explain paradoxical phenomena like the "exploitation of the great by the small,"[16] but they are not essential to the argument in this book.

The number of people who must bargain if a group-optimal amount of a collective good is to be obtained, and thus the costs of bargaining, must rise with the size of the group. This consideration reinforces the point just made. Indeed, both everyday observation and the logic of the matter suggest that for genuinely large groups, bargaining among all members to obtain agreement on the provision of a collective good is out of the question.[17] The consideration mentioned earlier in this chapter, that social selective incentives are available only to small groups and (tenuously) to those larger groups that are federations of small groups, also suggests that small groups are more likely to organize than large ones.

The significance of the logic that has just been set out can best be seen by comparing groups that would have the same net gain from collective action, if they could engage in it, but that vary in size. Suppose there are a million individuals who would gain a thousand dollars each, or a billion in the aggregate, if they were to organize effectively and engage in collective action that had a total cost of a hundred million. If the logic set out above is right, they could not organize or engage in effective collective action without selective incen-

---

$d(F_i S_g T)/dT - dC/dT = 0$
$F_i S_g - dC/dT = 0.$

This gives the amount of the collective good that a unilateral maximizer would buy. This point can be given a common-sense meaning. Since the optimum is found when

$dA_i/dT = dV_i/dT - dC/dT = 0,$

and since $dV_i/dT = F_i(dV_g/dT)$

$F_i(dV_g/dT) - dC/dT = 0,$
$F_i(dV_g/dT) = dC/dT.$

Thus the optimal amount of the collective good for an individual to obtain occurs when the rate of gain to the group (dV_g/dT) exceeds the rate of increase in cost (dC/dT) by the same multiple by which the group gain exceeds the gain to the individual ($1/F_i = V_g/V_i$). In other words, the smaller F_i is, the less the individual will take, and (other things being equal) F_i must of course diminish as entry makes the group larger.

tives. Now suppose that, although the total gain of a billion dollars from collective action and the aggregate cost of a hundred million remain the same, the group is composed instead of five big corporations or five organized municipalities, each of which would gain two hundred million. Collective action is not an absolute certainty even in this case, since each of the five could conceivably expect others to put up the hundred million and hope to gain the collective good worth two hundred million at no cost at all. Yet collective action, perhaps after some delays due to bargaining, seems very likely indeed. In this case any one of the five would gain a hundred million from providing the collective good even if it had to pay the whole cost itself; and the costs of bargaining among five would not be great, so they would sooner or later probably work out an agreement providing for the collective action. The numbers in this example are arbitrary, but roughly similar situations occur often in reality, and the contrast between "small" and "large" groups could be illustrated with an infinite number of diverse examples.

The significance of this argument shows up in a second way if one compares the operations of lobbies or cartels within jurisdictions of vastly different scale, such as a modest municipality on the one hand and a big country on the other. Within the town, the mayor or city council may be influenced by, say, a score of petitioners or a lobbying budget of a thousand dollars. A particular line of business may be in the hands of only a few firms, and if the town is distant enough from other markets only these few would need to agree to create a cartel. In a big country, the resources needed to influence the national government are likely to be much more substantial, and unless the firms are (as they sometimes are) gigantic, many of them would have to cooperate to create an effective cartel. Now suppose that the million individuals in our large group in the previous paragraph were spread out over a hundred thousand towns or jurisdictions, so that each jurisdiction had ten of them, along with the same proportion of citizens in other categories as before. Suppose also that the cost-benefit ratios remained the same, so that there was still a billion dollars to gain across all jurisdictions or ten thousand in each, and that it would still cost a hundred million dollars across all jurisdictions or a thousand in each. It no longer seems out of the question that in many jurisdictions the groups of ten, or subsets of them, would put up the thousand-dollar total needed to get the thousand for each individual. Thus we see that, if all else were equal, small jurisdictions would have more collective action per capita than large ones.

Differences in intensities of preference generate a third type of illustration of the logic at issue. A small number of zealots anxious for a particular collective good are more likely to act collectively to obtain that good than a larger number with the same aggregate willingness to pay. Suppose there are twenty-five individuals, each of whom finds a given collective good worth a thousand dollars in one case, whereas in another there are five thousand, each of whom finds the collective good worth five dollars. Obviously, the argument indicates that there would be a greater likelihood of collective action in the former case than in the latter, even though the aggregate demand for the collective good is the same in both. The great historical significance of small groups of fanatics no doubt owes something to this consideration.

VI

The argument in this chapter predicts that those groups that have access to selective incentives will be more likely to act collectively to obtain collective goods than those that do not, and that smaller groups will have a greater likelihood of engaging in collective action than larger ones. The empirical portions of *The Logic* show that this prediction has been correct for the United States. More study will be needed before we can be utterly certain that the argument also holds for other countries, but the more prominent features of the organizational landscape of other countries certainly do fit the theory. In no major country are large groups without access to selective incentives generally organized—the masses of consumers are not in consumers' organizations, the millions of taxpayers are not in taxpayers' organizations, the vast number of those with relatively low incomes are not in organizations for the poor, and the sometimes substantial numbers of unemployed have no organized voice. These groups are so dispersed that it is not feasible for any nongovernmental organization to coerce them; in this they differ dramatically from those, like workers in large factories or mines, who are susceptible to coercion through picketing. Neither does there appear to be any source of the positive selective incentives that might give individuals in these categories an incentive to cooperate with the many others with whom they share common interests.* By contrast, almost

---

*Even groups or causes that are so large or popular that they encompass almost everyone in the society cannot generate very substantial organizations. Consider those concerned about the quality of the environment. Although environmental extremists are a

everywhere the social prestige of the learned professions and the limited numbers of practitioners of each profession in each community has helped them to organize. The professions have also been helped to organize by the distinctive susceptibility of the public to the assertion that a professional organization, with the backing of government, ought to be able to determine who is "qualified" to practice the profession, and thereby to control a decisive selective incentive. The small groups of (often large) firms in industry after industry, in country after country, are similarly often organized in trade associations or organizations or collusions of one kind or another. So, frequently, are the small groups of (usually smaller) businesses in particular towns or communities.

Even though the groups that the theory says cannot be organized do not appear to be organized anywhere, there are still substantial differences across societies and historical periods in the extent to which the groups that our logic says *could* be organized *are* organized. This, we shall argue, is a matter of surpassing importance for the nations involved, and it is to this that we now turn.

---

small minority, almost everyone is interested in a wholesome environment, and poll results suggest that in the United States, for example, there are tens of millions of citizens who think more ought to be done to protect the environment. In the late 1960s and early 1970s, certainly, environmentalism was faddish as well. Despite this, and despite subsidized postal rates for nonprofit organizations and reductions in the cost of direct mail solicitation due to computers, relatively few people pay dues each year to environmental organizations. The major environmental organizations in the United States have memberships measured in the tens or hundreds of thousands, with at least the larger (such as the Audubon Society, with its products for bird-watchers) plainly owing much of their membership to selective incentives. There are surely more than 50 million Americans who value a wholesome environment, but in a typical year probably fewer than one in a hundred pays dues to any organization whose main activity is lobbying for a better environment. The proportion of physicians in the American Medical Association, or automobile workers in the United Automobile Workers union, or farmers in the Farm Bureau, or manufacturers in trade associations is incomparably greater.

3 | The Implications

Although some of the implications of the logic in the preceding chapter were set out in that chapter, they were only the immediate implications of that logic alone. When we combine the argument in chapter 2 with some other logic and facts, and in particular with some standard findings from economics, we obtain a further set of implications. These second-level implications tell us what we should expect in certain types of societies and historical conditions if the theory we are now constructing is correct.

The validity or invalidity of our argument depends not only on the correctness of the preceding chapter, but also on what will be added. Fortunately, most of the economics we shall use is well-established; it is mainly the widely tested "microeconomic theory" of individual firms, consumers, and industries. Many laymen suppose that economists disagree about everything, but in fact this part of economics is mainly acceptable to almost all skilled economists, be they left-wing or right-wing, Keynesian or monetarist. To this we must add the less formal but invaluable "Schumpeterian" insight into innovation and entrepreneurship, which is also rather widely accepted, and a brief extension I have to the economist's usual analysis of the role of entry of outside firms into unusually profitable industries.

Unfortunately, it will not be possible to see how the further implications or theory we shall develop here relate to concrete problems in particular countries until we have first gone through the mildly abstract argument in this chapter—the rest of the book is not comprehensible by itself. Logical arguments that are not immediately related to practical experience do not seem important to some people, so there may understandably be readers who will wonder whether the abstract arguments of

36

this chapter and the last one are of much practical significance. I can, without any fear of ultimate disagreement, promise the reader that, *if* the argument in this chapter and the preceding one is largely correct, it is indisputably of great practical importance.

Our initial second-level implication has to do with whether a society could achieve a rational or efficient economy through bargaining among organized groups. The last chapter pointed out that a small group of individuals or firms interested in a public good would have an incentive to continue bargaining with one another until they had maximized aggregate gains. There can be no confidence that bargaining even in a small group will work, much less have the complete success that is needed for group-optimality. But such an outcome is clearly a prominent possibility, and if everyone has participated in the bargaining the result might even be deemed fair to some degree. This reminds us to ask whether whole societies could achieve efficient results through comprehensive bargaining by leaders of all the groups in the society.

If the logic set out in the previous chapter is correct, a society that would achieve either efficiency or equity through comprehensive bargaining is out of the question. Some groups such as consumers, taxpayers, the unemployed, and the poor do not have either the selective incentives or the small numbers needed to organize, so they would be left out of the bargaining. It would be in the interest of those groups that are organized to increase their own gains by whatever means possible. This would include choosing policies that, though inefficient for the society as a whole, were advantageous for the organized groups because the costs of the policies fell disproportionately on the unorganized. (In the language of the game theorist, the society would not achieve a "core" or Pareto-efficient allocation because some of the groups were by virtue of their lack of organization unable to block changes detrimental to them or to work out mutually advantageous bargains with others.) With some groups left out of the bargaining, there is also no reason to suppose that the results have any appeal on grounds of fairness. On top of this there is the likelihood that the costs of bargaining and slow decision-making would make a society that made decisions by group bargaining inefficient in any case. Thus our first implication on this level is:

1. *There will be no countries that attain symmetrical organization of all groups with a common interest and thereby attain optimal outcomes through comprehensive bargaining.*

If such countries should emerge, that would mean that the argument in this book is probably wrong.

II

Our second implication relates to the emergence of organizations for collective action over time. The last chapter argued that collective action is difficult and problematical. In addition, there are normally some special start-up costs in creating any organization or new pattern of cooperation, including the fear of and resistance to the unfamiliar; as Machiavelli pointed out in another context, "There is nothing more difficult to arrange, more doubtful of success, and more dangerous to carry through, than to initiate a new order of things. . . . Men are generally incredulous, never really trusting new things unless they have tested them by experience."[1] Thus even those groups that are in situations in which they may be able to organize or collude, because their members are small or because some selective incentive could in principle be worked out, may not be able to organize until favorable circumstances emerge. Even in small groups there will often be difficulties in working out bargains for collective action; each party wants to bear the lowest possible share of the costs and in bargaining has an incentive to hold out, sometimes for an indefinitely long time. Thus some of the collective action that is attainable through bargaining in small groups will not be attained until some time has passed.

In larger groups, where collective action is attainable only through selective incentives, even greater difficulties must be overcome. If coercion is the selective incentive, the coercive force has to be arranged, and since people do not like to be coerced there is difficulty and even danger in this. Strong leadership and favorable circumstances will usually be required. The beginning of the union career of Jimmy Hoffa illustrates this. The young Hoffa was one of the workers in an unorganized warehouse in Detroit. On a hot summer day a large shipment of strawberries that would soon spoil arrived, and Hoffa then persuaded his coworkers to strike. The employer found it better to accept Hoffa's demands than to lose his perishable cargo. Usually the circumstances are not so favorable, and leaders with the cunning, courage, and lack of inhibition that characterized Jimmy Hoffa are not often on the scene.

When social pressure and social rewards are the selective incentives, there are also difficulties and delays. When a group that is already socially interactive needs a collective good, the problem may not be so difficult, although even here the social interaction must generate a sufficient surplus for the participants that they are willing to maintain it even after they are taxed for the cost of the collective good. Creating new patterns of social interaction is more difficult and surely time-consuming as well. Some late nineteenth-century American farm organizations, such as the Grange, managed to do this particularly well with relatively isolated farm families in recently settled areas, but attracting members away from previously established social networks, when possible at all, is likely to take exceptional leadership, and even then to evolve only over a considerable amount of time.

Positive selective incentives of a more tangible and material kind can also be found, if at all, only after a great deal of effort. Generating a surplus that can finance provision of a collective good or induce others to provide it is inherently chancy—there are failures as well as successes among those who attempt to create new businesses. And entrepreneurs who make money naturally often keep it for themselves. Thus usually some complementarity between the activity that can provide a collective good and that which produces income must be found or exploited; any lobbying power must be used in part to get favorable governmental treatment of the business activity, for example, or the reputation and trust of the lobbying organization among its beneficiaries must be exploited by the associated business activity. Even when such complementarities can be exploited, they may be discovered or worked out only after some time, and then only if there are imaginative leaders.

Scattered observation, at least, supports the hypothesis that organization for collective action takes a good deal of time to emerge. Though there was some earlier collective action by workers, it was not until 1851, or nearly a century after the start of the Industrial Revolution, that the first sustainable modern trade union emerged, the Amalgamated Society of Engineers in Great Britain. Though there was legal repression of combinations of workers at times during the Industrial Revolution, this cannot explain why unions did not become the norm in Britain until the decades just before World War I. Elsewhere unionization took place even later. In the United States a number of unions were established in the last half of the nineteenth century, but the fastest growth of union membership was in the period from 1937 to 1945, long after the country achieved the industrialized condition most favorable to unions. A study of unionization, industry by industry, in France similarly reveals ''a lag between the initial appearance of an industry and the time its workers acquire an organizational capacity for collective action.''[2] Farm organizations have taken even longer to develop. In the United States there was some farm organization in the second half of the nineteenth century, but it was not until the organization of the Farm Bureau (by the government-funded Agricultural Extension Service) after World War I that there was any really large or stable farm organization. Yet American farmers had significant common interests from the founding of the American republic. Many similar examples could be cited for other countries and other types of organizations.

The other side of the matter is that those organizations that have secured selective incentives to maintain themselves will often survive as organizations even if the collective good they once provided is no longer needed. As the sociologist Max Weber pointed out long ago,[3] the leader who is making a living out of an organization may keep it alive even after its original purpose has disappeared; an organization set up to represent the drivers of teams of horses, for example, will take on the task of representing drivers of trucks, and an organization set up to help the veterans of one war will outlive these veterans by representing veterans of subsequent wars. Selective incentives make indefinite survival feasible. Thus those organizations for collective action, at least for large groups, that can emerge often take a long time to emerge, but once established they usually survive until there is a social upheaval or some other form of violence or instability.[4]

If organizations and collusions for collective action usually emerge only in favorable circumstances and develop strength over time, a stable society will see more organization for collective action as time passes (unless, of course, constitutional and legal constraints on collective action, or on the changes in public policies lobbying is permitted to bring about, should leave little scope for such organizations). The more time that passes, the larger the number of those groups that are in situations in which collective action is a possibility will have enjoyed the favorable circumstances and innovative political leadership that they need to organize, and the greater the likelihood that the organizations that have been created will have achieved their potential. This, in combination with the fact that organizations with selective incentives in stable societies normally survive indefinitely, leads to our second implication:

2. *Stable societies with unchanged boundaries* tend to accumulate more collusions and organizations for collective action over time.*

III

The third implication is perhaps the hardest to relate to casual observation, so its meaning may not be clear until later. The source of this implication is, however, obvious: it is the finding in the last chapter that oligopolists and other small groups have a greater likelihood of being able to organize for collective action, and can usually organize with less delay, than large groups. It follows that the small groups in a society will usually have more lobbying and cartelistic power per capita (or even per dollar of aggregate income) than the large groups. The fact that small groups can usually organize with less delay than large ones implies that this disproportion will tend to be greatest in the societies that have enjoyed only a brief period of stability and least great in those societies that have been stable for a long time. Accordingly, our third implication is:

3. *Members of "small" groups have disproportionate organizational power for collective action, and this disproportion diminishes but does not disappear over time in stable societies.*

The reader may find it helpful to give this implication a skeptical examination after it has been put to practical use later in the book.

IV

If the extent and type of organization for collective action varies across societies and historical periods, then it is important to determine what impact such organization has on the efficiency and rate of economic growth of a society. Normally all such organizations, whatever their scale or form, have reason to want economic efficiency and growth, and good fortune generally, for the society in which they operate. Whatever type of goods or labor the members of an organization sell, normally the demand for it will be greater the more prosperous the society (there are

---

*The meaning and significance of the reference to "unchanged boundaries" will be made clear in a later chapter.

"inferior" goods on which more is spent if income falls, but they are exceptional). Similarly, the available technology will generally be better and the goods (though not the labor) that the members of the organization buy will generally be cheaper if they live in a more productive society. It might seem that one logical possibility, then, is that such organizations could in some circumstances serve their members' interests by helping to make the society in which they operate more productive.

Except for a special case we shall deal with later, the only other way in which such an organization could serve its members' interests is by obtaining a larger share of the society's production for the organization's members. In other words, the organization can in principle serve its members either by making the pie the society produces larger, so that its members would get larger slices even with the same shares as before, or alternatively by obtaining larger shares or slices of the social pie for its members. Our intuition tells us that the first method will rarely be chosen, but it is important to figure out exactly why this is so.

It will normally cost an organization something to make the society of which it is a part more efficient. Suppose a lobbying organization were to strive to eliminate the losses in economic efficiency that arise because of differential rates of tax on income from different sources (tax loopholes), or to attempt to reduce the losses from monopoly in the society. An effective campaign to achieve such goals would have significant costs that the organization sponsoring the campaign would have to bear. But the members of the organization would get only a part of the benefits that would result if they made the society as a whole more efficient; they would share in the lower prices or lower taxes or other gains from greater efficiency in the society, but so would most of the rest of society. This is important because in most cases each organization of the kind we are considering represents only a minute percentage of the population or other resources of a society. The typical trade association for an industry represents a small number of firms which, even though they may be large, own only a tiny share of the productive assets in a country; the typical labor union, even if it has tens or hundreds of thousands of members, includes only a minute percentage of the labor force of a country, and so forth. (There are exceptionally encompassing organizations for collective action in a few countries, and these are considered separately below.)

Suppose, for the sake of illustration, that an organization represents workers or firms that have 1 percent of the income-earning capacity in the country. This organization will have to bear the cost of whatever campaign it mounts to make the society more efficient, but its members will tend, on average, to get only about 1 percent of the resulting gain to the society. The organization's members would, on average, profit from devoting their resources to making the society more efficient only if those resources produced social gains one hundred times or more larger than the cost of obtaining those gains. (More generally, in the symbolic language of the footnote on page 31 in chapter 2, the benefit-cost ratio of the activity to make the society more efficient must equal or exceed $1/F_i$, or the reciprocal of the fraction of the income-earning capacity of the society that the organization represents.)

Thus there is a parallel between the individual in a group that would gain from provision of a collective good and the organization for collective action within the society. The organization that acts to provide some benefit for the society as a whole is, in effect, providing a public good for the whole society, and it is accordingly in the same position as an individual who contributes to the provision of a collective good for a group of which he or she is a part. In each case the actor gets only a part (and often only a tiny part) of the benefits of its action, yet bears the whole cost of that action.

Now suppose that our illustrative organization that represents 1 percent of the income-earning capacity in the country attempts to serve its members by getting a larger slice of the social pie. The resources that are diverted to seizing a larger share of the society's output will not, of course, produce the social output they produced in their previous employments, so this will reduce social output to some extent. More important, the pattern of incentives in the society will be changed by the redistribution, and (as we shall see) in ways that can vastly reduce the level of production. On the other hand, the members of the organization are part of the society, so they will also share in the loss of social output that results from the redistribution toward themselves. Self-interest alone will make them take these losses into account along with the gains from the redistribution to themselves. *But it will pay to go ahead with the redistribution, unless the reduction in the value of the society's output is a hundred or more times larger than the amount won by the organization's clients in the distributional struggle.* Exactly the same logic we have used all along suggests that the typical organization for collective action will do nothing to eliminate the social loss or "public bad" its effort to get a larger share of the social output brings about. The familiar image of the slicing of the social pie does not really capture the essence of the situation; it is perhaps better to think of wrestlers struggling over the contents of a china shop.

In short, the typical organization for collective action within a society will, at least if it represents only a narrow segment of the society, have little or no incentive to make any significant sacrifices in the interest of the society; it can best serve its members' interests by striving to seize a larger share of a society's production for them. This will be expedient, moreover, even if the social costs of the change in the distribution exceed the amount redistributed by a huge multiple; *there is for practical purposes no constraint on the social cost such an organization will find it expedient to impose on the society in the course of obtaining a larger share of the social output for itself.* (The ratio of the social cost or excess burden to the amount redistributed must equal or exceed $1/F_i$ before it will constrain the organization.) The organizations for collective action within societies that we are considering are therefore overwhelmingly oriented to struggles over the distribution of income and wealth rather than to the production of additional output— they are "distributional coalitions" (or organizations that engage in what, in one valuable line of literature, is called "rent seeking").[5]

There has long been some intuitive apprehension of this, if not of the extent of social losses that it would pay such organizations to impose on society in efforts to get a larger share of social output. This intuitive apprehension is perhaps suggested by the *special-interest group* label sometimes used for such organizations. Now that the incentives such organizations face have been set out starkly, I shall sometimes use the expression special-interest group as a synonym for distributional coalition, even though that expression has, as we shall see later, a somewhat narrower connotation in everyday language than is appropriate here. These coalitions may be cartels as well as lobbies and are often both. Any combination of individuals or firms for collusive action in the marketplace, whether a professional association, a labor union, a trade association, or an oligopolistic collusive group, will here be called a cartel, whatever term may be used to describe it in everyday language.

One of the obvious ways in which a special-interest group can increase the income of its members while reducing the efficiency and output of the society is by lobbying for legislation to raise some price or wage or to tax some types of income at lower rates than other income.

Although the effects may be different under certain initial conditions (because of "second-best" problems),[6] in general measures of this sort will not only increase the income of those favored by the legislation but also reduce efficiency. There will be an incentive for additional resources to move into the industry or activity that is favored by the higher price or lower tax, and this shift of resources will continue until the private post-tax returns are the same in the favored area as in the rest of the economy. But if the price is higher or the tax lower in the favored area simply because of special-interest legislation, then the extra resources that have been diverted into the favored area will be adding less to the value of society's output than they did in their previous employments. Whenever resources are free to move into the favored area, the private returns will eventually be the same in the favored area as in the rest of the economy, and this tends to make the gain to the special-interest group very small in relation to the cost to society. In this type of case the only gain to the clients of the distributional coalition is the capital gain on those assets that are specialized to the favored industry plus transitional profits during the time it takes other resources to move into the area. The situation is different if entry is not allowed into the favored area, but as I shall later show, barriers to entry usually impose substantial social costs of other kinds. The argument we have just used is extremely simple and leaves aside many fascinating questions, both technical and social.[7] The argument also has only a lesser applicability to any country in which constitutional and structural factors constrain the number and power of lobbying organizations, as appears to be the case in Switzerland. Nonetheless, as later parts of this book should show, the basic point that it makes is widely applicable and enormously important.

Another way in which a special-interest organization can increase the income of its members while reducing society's output is through cartelization—the members can agree to reduce output as a single monopolist would have done and thereby enjoy a higher price. The gains from cartelization and monopoly arise because less is sold to obtain a higher price, so naturally there is (in the absence of other distortions)[8] a reduction in social output; in general, the society will get a mix of goods that contains an inefficiently small proportion of those goods sold at a monopoly price and an inefficiently large proportion of those goods sold at a competitive price. Effective cartels must always block entry into the line of business in which they have raised the price, so the process described in the preceding paragraph, which made the coalition's gain small in relation to the cost to society, does not work in the same way. But the ubiquitous barriers to entry will make certain other social costs (which we shall examine later) even greater.

There is an interesting literature in economics, stemming mainly from a seminal article by Arnold Harberger,[9] suggesting that the social losses from monopoly and (as others have argued) from tariffs and certain other distortions of the price system are relatively small in relation to the national income. Later I will endeavor to show that these losses can sometimes be colossal, but for the moment it may be sufficient to point out that the foregoing analysis of the incentives faced by special-interest groups could make them impose very large costs indeed on the society as a whole. And, as the international trade theorist Jagdish Bhagwati has pointed out,[10] there is, alas, nothing in the laws of economics that requires that, if a society is inefficient, it must be inefficient in a small way.

One consideration that does limit the losses from distributional coalitions to some extent, however, is that occasionally some of them will nullify or offset the effects of others. A farmers' lobby may win the repeal of a tariff on farm machinery or automobile manufacturers may limit the protection given the steel industry. Note that, in cases such as these, the effort of the special-interest group can lead to an increase in the efficiency and income of the society, but that the gains are not diffused through the society so that the special-interest group gets a share approximated by the proportion of the income-earning capacity of the society it represents—instead, those in the special-interest group get a substantial share of the total social gain from their activity. Occasionally there are other types of situations in which the constituents of special-interest organizations seek to increase social efficiency because they would get a lion's share of the gain in output; this occurs when the special-interest organization provides a collective good to its members that increases their productive efficiency and also when it gets the government to provide some public good that generates more income than costs, yet mainly benefits those in the special-interest group. It certainly is not easy to find any significant percentage of special-interest organizations whose principal objective is some policy that has the special property that it will mainly benefit the clients of the organization and at the same time increase the efficiency and aggregate income of the society. Yet multiple causation and mixed motivation are usually evident in any area, including that of special-interest groups, so it is important not to lose sight of organizations or situations of this type. The largest proportion of the cases that this researcher has been able to find appear to consist of organizations whose clients suffer disproportionately from inefficiencies obtained by other distributional coalitions and who therefore oppose those inefficiencies. If the first of the implications in this chapter—that there is not and will not be a symmetrically organized society—is wrong, this situation is not or will no longer be a special case. But if, as the findings in later parts of this book and elsewhere suggest, that implication is true, then the great majority of special-interest organizations redistribute income rather than create it, and in ways that reduce social efficiency and output.

In addition, this focus on distribution makes the significance of distributional issues in political life relatively greater and the significance of widespread common interests in political life relatively smaller. The common interests that all or most of the people in a nation or other jurisdiction share can draw them together, as they are drawn together when they perceive a common interest in repelling aggression. In distributional struggles, by contrast, none can gain without others losing as much or (normally) more, and this can generate resentment. Thus when special-interest groups become more important and distributional issues accordingly more significant, political life tends to be more divisive. Moreover, as Dennis Mueller,[11] building on the work of Kenneth Arrow,[12] has shown, the increased emphasis on distributional issues due to accumulations of special-interest groups can also increase the likelihood that a democratic political system can repudiate its prior choices, even if all the individuals in the electorate have the same preferences as before—it can (for some reasons that cannot be explained briefly or without technical language) encourage intransitive or irrational and cyclical political choices. The divisiveness of distributional issues, and the fact that they may make relatively lasting or stable political choices less likely, can even make societies ungovernable.

Thus we have our fourth implication:

4. On balance, special-interest organizations and collusions reduce efficiency and aggregate income in the societies in which they operate and make political life more divisive.

V

There are also, in some countries, special-interest organizations that encompass a substantial portion of the societies of which they are a part.

A labor union that includes most of the manual workers in a country, for example, represents a large proportion of the income-earning capacity of that country. So does a lobbying organization that includes all the major firms in an industrialized country. How might the policies of such encompassing or inclusive organizations differ from the more common narrow special-interest groups discussed in the preceding section?

The incentives facing an encompassing special-interest organization are dramatically different from those facing an organization that represents only a narrow segment of society. If an organization represents, say, a third of the income-producing capacity of a country, its members will, on average, obtain about a third of the benefit from any effort to make the society more productive. The organization will therefore have an incentive to make sacrifices up to a point for policies and activities that are sufficiently rewarding for the society as a whole. The members of the highly encompassing organization own so much of the society that they have an important incentive to be actively concerned about how productive it is; they are in the same position as a partner in a firm that has only a few partners. Moreover, the organization whose clients own a third of the income-earning potential of the society will, on average, bear about a third of any loss in the society's output that results from the policies it obtains. Thus any effort to obtain a larger share of the national income for the clients of such an encompassing organization could not make sense if it reduced the national income by an amount three or more times as great as the amount shifted to its members. As the discussion in the previous section would suggest, the argument here is that this can be a constraint of great practical importance. Clearly the encompassing organization, if it has rational leadership, will care about the excess burden arising from distributional policies favorable to its members and will out of sheer self-interest strive to make the excess burden as small as possible.

The illustrative assumption that an encompassing interest group represents a third of the society is admittedly favorable to the distinction that has been drawn. But contrast an organization that represents even a tenth of the income-earning capacity of a country with one that represents, as most special-interest organizations do, only a minuscule segment of the whole society. The former sort of organization has not only an incentive at least to consider the effect of its policies on the efficiency of the society, but also an incentive to bargain with other substantial organized groups in the interest of a more productive society. The really narrow special-interest group usually does not have an incentive to do even that.

A special-interest organization that is minuscule in relation to a country may, however, be encompassing in relation to a particular firm or industry. Consider a labor union that represents all the workers in some firm (an "enterprise union," such as is common in Japan), or alternatively a union that represents all the workers in each of the firms in one industry. Such a union could be small in relation to society as a whole, but if (as is typical) about two-thirds of the value added of each firm is devoted to the wage bill, then the union is relatively encompassing in relation respectively to the firm or the industry. It is true that in principle greater prosperity for firms is supposed to result in higher profits, whereas the wages of labor in the firm are supposed to be explained instead by the general state of the labor market; if this is the whole story, a union has no reason to care whether its firm or industry is especially prosperous. But if the union has any real bargaining strength, it can force the unusually prosperous firms to raise wages well above the market level, whereas no amount of bargaining power can force a firm in a desperate financial situation to do this. Some of the workers may, moreover, have skills that are specific to the firm or industry for which they work, and the market value of these skills may rise if the firm or industry is profitable enough to expand. Thus a union that is encompassing in relation to the firm or industry for which its members work has a reason to help the host firm or industry prosper and expand. Contrast this with the situation of a craft union that controls the supply of some specialized skill a firm or industry needs, but controls only a minute percentage of the relevant employees. Such a union would have only a minute influence on the profitability of any firm and accordingly would have little incentive to avoid inefficient practices or to help the employer or industry in any other ways.

The foregoing logic therefore suggests that the efficiency of firms and industries can be influenced by whether or not the relevant institutions for collective action are encompassing in relation to them. It implies, for example, that enterprise and industry unions should usually agree to more efficient work practices than the narrower craft unions; the anecdotal evidence suggests that this is the case.

It would be a mistake, however, to suppose that any increase in the extent to which a special-interest organization is encompassing is necessarily desirable. The degree of monopoly power often increases as an organization becomes more encompassing. If an enterprise union becomes an industry-wide union, for example, it may, by striking against any firms in the industry that do not cooperate, make it easier for the firms to have an effective cartel, and thereby maximize the joint monopoly gain of the firms and the workers. The competition among firms also limits the premium that any one firm can pay its unionized workers, so the gains from monopolizing the supply of labor will usually be less for an enterprise union than for one that controls the labor force in the whole industry. There is, in addition, little or no gain in concern for the society as a whole when a special-interest organization expands from, say, firm to industry size; it is likely to be so small in relation to the society even after the expansion that it will not take account of its impact on the efficiency of the society. The circumstance in which an increase in the extent to which a special-interest organization is encompassing is likely to be most constructive is when it is already so substantial that it encompasses many different industries. At that stage further expansion may not affect the market or industrial action of the organization, but it would create an incentive to give greater weight to the organization's impact on social efficiency.

In the same way national confederations of business or labor organizations can also introduce a more nearly national perspective on political issues without affecting the degree of monopoly. These organizations, which political scientists sometimes call *peak associations,* frequently lack the unity needed to have any great influence on public policy, or even coherent and specific policies. Nonetheless, peak associations should on average take a somewhat less parochial view than the narrow associations of which they are composed, and this offers one way of empirically testing the argument that has just been put forth. The Norwegian sociologist Gudmund Hernes has found, in connection with some collaborative research he and I are doing on encompassing organizations in Scandinavia (where such organizations are unusually important), that Norwegian peak associations at least appear to fit the theoretical prediction very well.

The logic of the distinction between narrow and encompassing interests is not limited to special-interest groups. This is evident, for example, from an inference many political scientists have drawn from the observation of American politics. This is the inference that the United States would gain from stronger and more responsible political parties.[13] These political scientists observe that individual members of Congress are overwhelmingly influenced by the parochial interests of their particular districts and by special-interest lobbies, and that incoherent national policies are often the result. The leadership of whatever party is perceived to be in control usually is to some extent concerned about the aggregate national consequences of the policies chosen, since there is some connection between the state of the nation and the election prospects of the party deemed to be in control. Party discipline, however, is so weak that the influence of the party leadership and the concern about the party's fate in the next election exert only a marginal influence. The conclusion is that if party discipline could be strengthened and each party be held responsible for the policies it chose and their outcome, then national policies would tend to improve.

The logic set out in this book can help to explain and justify the political scientists' argument, if it is combined with an analysis of the electoral system. The United States does not use proportional representation or any other electoral system that gives candidates or parties that come in second, third, or worse in a general election some portion of the power; the winner in any given general election wins it all. Thus it does not make any sense to have a political party in the United States that would over the long run expect to get, say, a fourth of the votes in a presidential election; parties that expected to come in second or lower, however, could gain something by combining if that gave them a chance of winning. Thus the electoral system in the United States encourages a two-party system (as do some other factors that need not be discussed here). Given that, each of the parties will be quite encompassing; each will attempt to represent a majority of the electorate. A party whose clients comprise half or more of the society naturally is concerned about the efficiency and welfare of the society as a whole, particularly in comparison with lobbies for special-interest groups and congressmen accountable only to small districts. It is accordingly not surprising that systematic observers should note that American political parties were, on balance, more concerned about the welfare of the nation than were special-interest groups or individual congressmen, and therefore would favor stronger political parties.

The same logic shows up in a comparison of the behavior of congressmen and presidents over pork-barrel legislation, for example. A congressional district that contains about 1/435th of the United States will tend to gain from any project for the district financed with federal taxes, so long as the costs are not 435 or more times greater than the benefits. Obviously, congressmen are aware of this. A president, by contrast, will stand a much better chance of being able to win reelection on the ground that the voters never had it so good if he can reserve the public monies for undertakings with better cost-benefit ratios. Thus, year after year, with presidents and with congressmen of both party affiliations, we see presidents trying to limit pork-barrel projects and congressmen trying to promote them.

The applications of this logic naturally vary from country to country. In some countries with many small political parties, the logic is revealed in neglect of broad conceptions of the national interest by not-very-encompassing parties and disjointed policies of coalition governments. In other countries one sometimes sees labor or socialist parties that emerged from trade unions, but with leaders that sometimes take a less parochial view than the parent unions, presumably because the party leader has a more encompassing constituency. There are also parallel cases of conservative parties that draw their core support from business and professional associations, yet sometimes withhold certain favors from these lobbies in the interest of a thriving national constituency.

The occurrence of fragile coalition governments composed partly or wholly of many small parties, or of governments that are precarious for other reasons, also reminds us that the power of special-interest groups cannot be defined solely in terms of their organizational strength but should, strictly speaking, be defined in terms of a ratio of their power to that of more encompassing structures such as presidents or political parties. This nicety can probably be neglected in most cases, but it may be of decisive importance in understanding some countries with fragile governments.

Even though more encompassing organizations and institutions for collective action are systematically less likely to have an incentive to act in an antisocial way, it would be too hasty to conclude that more encompassing institutions should always be preferred. As I pointed out in the last chapter, information about collective goods is itself a collective good and accordingly there is normally little of it. When ignorance is often a rational strategy for constituents, there is a substantial possibility that an interest group or a political leader will not act in accord with the interest of constituents. If a political system is composed only of highly encompassing organizations and institutions, there also may be less diversity of advocacy, opinion, and policy, and fewer checks to erroneous ideas and policies. Encompassing organizations and institutions may therefore perform unusually badly in some cases or periods and unusually effectively in others. Accordingly, the idea of encompassing organizations and institutions is not necessarily always a guide for reform, but it is essential to a complete understanding of many important organizations and institutions.

So long as it is clear that our fifth implication refers to the incentives that face encompassing organizations rather than to their choices in particular cases, there should be no confusion. Thus:

> 5. *Encompassing organizations have some incentive to make the society in which they operate more prosperous, and an incentive to redistribute income to their members with as little excess burden as possible, and to cease such redistribution unless the amount redistributed is substantial in relation to the social cost of the redistribution.*

VI

We must now develop a point that may at first seem unimportant, and that in any case is obvious to anyone who has endured a committee meeting where it took a long time to make (or fail to make) a decision. The point is that special-interest organizations and collusions tend to make decisions more slowly than the firms or individuals of which they are composed. We shall see later that this trait is crucial to understanding phenomena as important as the business cycle and the rate of adoption of new technologies, and that the reasons for this slowness of decision-making are also very much worthy of our attention. The two main reasons why special-interest groups make decisions more slowly than the individuals or firms of which they are constituted is that they must use either *consensual bargaining* or *constitutional procedures,* or both of these methods, to make decisions.

Consensual bargaining is simply an expression to remind us that members of smaller groups who may hope to act collectively without selective incentives must bargain until they agree on a joint course of action and on how the costs of this action are to be shared. As the argument in the last chapter made clear, a group cannot achieve a group-optimal level of provision of a collective good through voluntary action unless everyone who would benefit from the collective good contributes to the marginal cost of providing it, so group-optimal provision requires unanimity, or what we have just called consensual bargaining.

In the case of collective action in the marketplace, this collective action normally requires consensus even if it does not reach a group-optimal level. Collusion among oligopolists to achieve a higher price entails an agreement to reduce the quantity sold so that a higher price can be achieved. If some of the firms in an industry, or even all but one of the firms, agree to restrict their sales in the interest of a higher price, then obviously whatever firm or firms are outside the agreement can gain by selling more than before, and normally so much more that the price will be driven down to a competitive level, so that the subset of firms that agreed to curtail sales is left with a competitive price and an unprofitably small quantity sold. There can be exceptional circumstances where this does not occur, as when the firm or firms outside the agreement lack the productive capacity to take full advantage in the short run of the cutbacks by other firms, but in general collusion to obtain a higher price will not work without consensus among the sellers.

The unanimous consent is made more difficult to achieve because the parties have a direct conflict of interest about how the costs of the collective action should be shared. In the case of firms agreeing on a higher price, there must be some agreement or arrangement that determines what cutback will be required of each firm. The consensus that is required also implies that it can be a rational strategy for each prospective participant to demand an altogether disproportionate share of the gains from the collective action in return for his indispensable cooperation. Threats to be a holdout in turn will not be credible unless they are sometimes carried out, and this means that it can take an extraordinary amount of time to achieve the necessary unanimity. The problem of resolving the conflict of interest about the costs of collective action naturally applies whatever the method of decision-making, so we shall need to return to this after considering decision-making by constitutional procedures.

When there are so many participants that bargaining is not feasible, collective action will require some decision-making rules or by-laws, which I call *constitutional procedures*. Groups that are small enough so that bargaining is feasible may also agree to some constitutional procedures on the ground that the individual members find it expedient to agree not to use their capacity to block unanimous action in return for the savings in bargaining costs and the greater likelihood of continuing collective action. Decision-making under constitutional procedures also takes time, especially in larger groups. Decisions may have to wait until everyone is talked out, or until the next board meeting or the next annual meeting, or even until those who favor a change in policy force out those officials who prefer the old policy. There is also the possibility that once decisions are made, they may be unmade or replaced by different decisions, even if none of the members has had a change of heart. That is, for reasons that were first fully explained by Kenneth Arrow[14] and that I discussed when showing that distributional coalitions could help to make societies ungovernable, there may be voting cycles, or situations in which an organization's democratic choices are intransitive or unstable. In my judgment, there probably is not as much instability in democratic choices as some students of voting cycles claim, partly because the typical procedural rules of democratic bodies tend to discourage reversals and to give the status quo an advantage over alternatives. But the very procedures that limit the extent to which democratic bodies reverse themselves, and especially the advantage given the status quo, tend to make democratic organizations slower in deciding how to adapt to new circumstances than their individual members are. Moreover, since the choices made by majority rule, elected leaders, or other devices for collective decisions may be harmful to some of those involved, participants often insist upon safeguards that protect them from arbitrary decisions by elected officers, or even by majorities, even though these safeguards slow decision-making further. The provision in the constitutions of some unions that a decision to strike, or to accept a contract, can be taken only by a vote (and sometimes more than a majority vote) of the membership or of some large representative body is an example of such a safeguard.

Whenever an organization for collective action is large, and sometimes even when it is not, it will have many different decisions to make. The combination of slow decision-making and multiple decisions usually leads to a crowded agenda. Everyday experience, even in organizations as small as departments in universities, suggests that some matters wait a long while to receive attention and that some never get on the agenda at all. Crowded agendas often delay decisions further. The importance of this phenomenon is also evident from the creation of committees and subcommittees, which are used mainly to relieve crowded agendas. Even the committees and subcommittees can have crowded agendas. When decisions are made by consensual bargaining, the word *agenda* is not usually used, but there is the same problem if a multiplicity of matters needs to be dealt with. Some matters may get on the bargaining table only after much delay and others not at all. Some agreements or contracts may be left unchanged, even when new circumstances make them no longer optimal, because of a concern about the time, trouble, and uncertainty involved in working out a new deal.

There are dramatic examples of this. In a study of some legal agreements to fix prices in Denmark, Bjarke Fog found an extreme case in which the price of a product was unchanged for a decade, despite rising costs and disappearing profits.[15] Similarly, F. M. Scherer has pointed out that for a considerable time the International Air Transport Association was able to change decisions only on relatively peripheral matters such as jet surcharges, motion picture fees, and the definition of a sandwich: ''Since the Association by-laws require that fare changes be approved unanimously, the result . . . was a perpetuation of the status quo.''[16]

When there are crowded agendas or cluttered bargaining tables, resolving the conflict of interest about how to share the costs of collective action is even more difficult. This difficulty encourages organizations and collusions for collective action to seek impartial outsiders, simple formulas, or seniority rules that can apportion the costs of collective action among the participants. If there is a substantial reward to a group for collective action in the first place, then there is a likelihood that each prospective participant will gain from the collective action under a variety of reasonable rules or decisions about the allocation of costs, so there may be an incentive for each of the parties to agree to an impartial arrangement for decisions about the allocation of costs, rather than risk losing all the gains that the collective action is expected to bring.

Some observers of OPEC, for example, claim that the degree of collusion it occasionally achieved was due in part to the fact that the competition among the big international companies provided an approximate allocation of the costs of restriction of oil output among member nations. The OPEC nations could then agree on a price per barrel, and the amount that each nation could sell at that price was then the result of the relative success of the oil company or companies that pumped each nation's oil.[17] Similarly, labor unions usually stipulate that seniority rules, or even decisions by the employer, determine who gets the benefit of the higher wage the union negotiates, partly to insure that the union members do not have to fight as much about who has to work less, or who loses a job, because the employer now has an incentive to use less labor. Naturally, the favoritism to senior workers—and the neglect of the interests of potential entrants who are not hired because of the higher wage—also reflects the normally greater influence of senior workers in the union and the absence of any vote at all for potential entrants. Nonetheless, a seniority rule enables a union to settle the troublesome issue of how to allocate the benefits of the higher wage with one relatively straightforward vote.

It is partly because of this conflict of interest over the sharing of costs that a majority of cartels and lobbies seek to fix prices or wages, rather than the quantity that can be sold. Since the amount offered for sale determines the price or wage, a union or a cartel of firms can obtain whatever price it finds optimal, of course, simply by a sufficient restriction on the quantity that will be sold. Although other factors (like the greater ease in some cases of detecting cheating on price agreements than on quantity agreements) are also involved, one reason why prices and wages are fixed more often than quantities is surely that this makes it easier to leave the decision about the allocation of the costs to the market or to other impartial forces. At times, outside or impartial mechanisms will work in ways that are very harmful to dominant interests in the distributional coalition, and they then may be abandoned. If under a seniority rule, for example, a substantial majority of the workers would be laid off, there would naturally be pressure for job sharing, wage reductions, or other alternatives. In still other cases, entry restriction would be feasible but price-fixing would not be; there would be more resistance to increases in physicians' charges than to an increase in the qualifications demanded of entering physicians, even though these two measures would have similar effects.

After taking the time needed to arrive at their own decisions, cartels and lobbies sometimes then need more time to deal with their partners and antagonists. A labor union, for example, has to bargain with the employer as well as decide on its own policy. The lobbying organization must, besides agreeing on its own policies, go through the compromises and procedures needed to change government policy. All this makes decision-making still slower.

The combination of all the factors slowing decisions and the special-interest groups' typical preference for price-fixing rather than quantity-fixing results in relatively sticky or inflexible prices and wages in sectors where special-interest organization or collusion is important. If special-interest organizations usually specified the quantity that is made available, the prices and wages would vary with market conditions and the quantity sold would be given in the intervals between decisions. When they specify the price or wage, it remains unchanged over the intervals between decisions and the quantity then varies.

The foregoing considerations taken together provide the sixth implication:

> 6. *Distributional coalitions make decisions more slowly than the individuals and firms of which they are comprised, tend to have crowded agendas and bargaining tables, and more often fix prices than quantities.*

VII

If the environment in which the special-interest organization operates never changes, then the slow decision-making does not make much difference; once an optimal policy for the coalition is chosen, it will serve indefinitely. But the economic situation is changing all the time. Nowadays the most important source of change is perhaps the advance of scientific knowledge. The opportunities open even to the least dynamic economies in modern times are constantly changing, since they have access to a stream of innovations from abroad and from basic scientific discoveries. There are also changes in consumer tastes, resource discoveries, and even changes in the weather, to which an economy must adapt if it is to maintain its efficiency and exploit the opportunities for growth.

The environment in which special-interest groups operate also changes because of the incentives to innovate that face the firms in the economy, and particularly those firms in sectors that are not affected by cartels or lobbies. However, we cannot go very far into the incentives facing firms in the absence of special-interest groups without getting into old material that would already be familiar to economists, at least. An analysis of the incentives facing firms (or consumers) in the absence of special-interest groups would take us into the theory of unconstrained markets, which, as we know, is more than two hundred years old. And if such an analysis were to be complete, it would require a book far longer than this one. So I shall include only a few casual, impressionistic paragraphs on the effect of the incentives in unconstrained markets and how this in turn helps to change the environment in which special-interest groups operate. These paragraphs will focus on those respects in which my perspective on unconstrained markets differs a little from that of most other economists.

In this book, I do not assume there is perfect competition, even in the absence of special-interest groups. There are, of course, some purely competitive markets, particularly in agriculture. The perfectly competitive model admittedly also has a remarkable "robustness" (or capacity to generate valid predictions in many cases even when some of its assumptions are not satisfied). Nonetheless, the assumption here is that in most markets firms can choose the price at which they will sell their outputs, and that the quantity they sell will vary inversely with the price they charge—that is, that there are normally elements of monopoly power. This assumption is in accord with everyday observation of most firms and is also, unlike any straightforward model of perfect competition, consistent with a firm's decision to advertise. My argument, accordingly, does not imply that a market system in the absence of special-interest organization and collusion is ideally (Pareto) efficient. Neither does it assume the market system is static, as do most formal perfectly competitive and general-equilibrium models.

The assumption that drives the argument about unconstrained markets in this book is that, in the absence of cartelization or government intervention due to lobbies or other causes, there is normally no barrier to entry into any industry or line of economic activity and also no barrier to imitation of any profitable pattern of activity. This assumption is staggeringly powerful. If there are more than normal profits or returns of any kind in an industry or line of activity, there will be an incentive to enter that line of activity, and that incentive will remain until enough resources have moved into the area that profits are no longer above normal. In no area, in the absence of institutions such as those that this book examines, can abnormal profits or returns be secure in the long run. Free entry also entails that no firm has any shelter from a Darwinian struggle for survival, so none can remain lethargic or inefficient and survive. Free entry eventually eliminates all shelter and monopoly profits, but it need not bring about perfect competition (product differentiation may remain) nor does it ensure perfect (Pareto) efficiency. But the absence of barriers to entry and imitation does ensure that any product or service that generates abnormal profits will invite entry or imitation, so that there will be at least close substitutes for this good or service, and with close substitutes the degree of monopoly (the extent to which the demand curve is less than infinitely elastic) and the extent of any inefficiency in resource allocation will be limited.

It is sometimes supposed that the amount of capital needed to enter the industries in which there are giant companies is so great that these firms are protected against entry. This overlooks the desire for profits of other giant firms (and the imperial aspirations of some of their managers); these firms have the access to capital needed to enter any industry, and the prevalence of multiproduct and even conglomerate firms owes something to this willingness to enter industries with supranormal profits. In some smaller and medium-sized countries, especially less developed ones, it is said that there are only a few firms with the resources to enter certain industries, so entry is then not likely. But this argument depends on the tariffs and restrictions on foreign firms that organizations and domestic firms have normally obtained. In the absence of these restrictions there would be entry into areas of excessive profit by multinational firms. There are some markets in which the demand is small in relation to the scale at which a firm in that market must operate to be efficient, so that the industry can accommodate only a few firms, or even (as in the "natural monopoly" case) only one firm. But these markets are the exception rather than the rule, and (contrary to what economists used to believe) there is also the danger of entry in these markets;* they are also "contestable," to use an apt term borrowed from William Baumol et al.[18]

---

*In other words, even if only one or two firms can survive in the industry and these one or two could earn supranormal profits if assured there would be no entry, it does not follow that there will be no entry. If the established firm or firms make abnormal profits or become slack through lack of competition, another firm may still have an incentive to enter the industry; the entrant in this case must replace an existing firm, since the industry will not support them all, and this means increased risk for the entrant. But the established firm or firms in the industry also know that any entrant could lead to their own demise and are well advised to keep this in mind before seeking conspicuously large profits or letting their firm become lethargic. A few economists, perhaps too anxious to show the virtues of laissez faire, assume that there never can be abnormal profits even in the natural monopoly; but this goes too far, at least in cases where a great deal of fixed capital is needed to produce the good in question, because, among other reasons, the established firm might even build a plant of a size designed to discourage entry, rather than one that would maximize profits in the absence of entry.[19] The safer conclusion is that, in the absence of distributional coalitions, abnormal profits will eventually induce entry in the overwhelming majority of markets, and that even in markets that can support only one or two firms the existing firms are constrained to a significant extent by the possibility of entry.[20]

In the short run, and sometimes in the not-so-short run, there are often supranormal (and sometimes even colossal) rates of profit for some firms even with free entry. The reason is that it can take some time before the opportunity to get supranormal profits by entry or imitation is noticed, and still more time to learn the tricks of a new line of activity and to purchase or construct the capital needed for it. This is a matter that needs more research, but my judgment of the evidence is that temporarily supranormal profits (sometimes accompanied by high, if temporary, degrees of monopoly power) are very common indeed, so common that some readers may question the importance of the free entry condition. But what gives rise to these temporary profits? Most notably, innovations of one kind or another—discoveries of new technologies, previously unsatisfied demands of consumers, lower-cost methods of production, and so on. And the greater the extent of the profits due to difficulties of entry and imitation, the greater the reward to the innovations that mainly explain economic growth and progress!* Indeed, the rate of economic growth that can result from these incentives to innovate in an unconstrained economy is sometimes so rapid that, as I have argued in other publications,[21] there may be certain costs of social disruption. That is, however, a separate and complicated matter that will not substantially alter any conclusions in this book, so I will not go into it here.

VIII

It is at this point essential to remind ourselves that there are some factors that, in contrast to the incentives to innovate that have just been discussed, can affect the efficiency of an economy but *not* its rate of

---

*This account of the reward to innovation owes a great deal to the now-standard Schumpeterian analysis of innovation and entrepreneurship, but it differs in one respect. The Schumpeterian analysis emphasized that temporary monopoly was the reward to the entrepreneurs who introduced successful innovations. The rewards due to the delays in entry and imitation that are emphasized may, but need not, entail monopoly. Suppose that a farmer or a firm in any purely competitive industry discovers a new method of production that is significantly less expensive than any previously known, but suppose also that increasing costs, as the scale of the enterprise increases, ensure that the innovator will not take over the industry. The innovative firm then has no monopoly power—no capacity to influence the price of what it sells—but until others can successfully imitate the innovation it has supranormal profits. So it is disequilibrium rather than monopoly itself that is emphasized here as the reward to innovation.

growth. This seems counterintuitive to some people, so it will be necessary to compare two hypothetical economies that are identical in all but one respect. Suppose that the first of these economies had no distributional coalitions, but that the second had a large number that had obtained a larger share of that economy's output for their constituents by methods that greatly reduced that output. If the distributional coalitions reduced the second economy's output by a constant proportion in each period, this economy would have a lower per capita income but need *not* have a lower rate of growth. If special-interest groups did not interfere with the second economy's adaptation to change or its generation of new innovations, but simply kept it at all times a constant percentage below the income it would achieve without such groups, then this economy could grow just as fast as the first economy. Thus the argument that led up to our Implication 4, taken by itself, shows that special-interest groups lower the level of efficiency and per capita income, but it does not necessarily show that the rate of change of per capita income would be different. The gradual accumulation of such groups explained in Implication 2 would lower the rate of growth, but that is another matter.

In fact, as I implied in the discussion of barriers to entry, the distributional coalitions do interfere with an economy's capacity to adapt to change and to generate new innovations and therefore do reduce the rate of growth. A labor union, for example, sometimes has an incentive to repress a labor-saving innovation that would reduce the demand for the workers it represents, or to demand featherbedding or overmanning. Similarly, whenever a firm in a collusive group develops a product or productive process that its competitors cannot immediately copy, the other firms in the group have an incentive to use the collusive power to block or delay the innovation. Since a major technological advance will normally change the optimal policy for a cartelistic organization and the relative strength of its members, it will normally require difficult new rounds of bargaining which the special-interest organization or collusion might not survive. This in turn makes cartelistic groups cautious about innovation and change. When an industry is nationalized, regulated as a public utility, or for other reasons subject to political dictation, the pertinent lobbies may veto changes, or simply require consultation about them, and innovations and investments will take place less often and more slowly. In some cases even straightforward adaptations to new patterns of demand and the adoption of new machinery can be delayed, sometimes for generations, as the example of American railroads illustrates, so that a configuration of practices that might once have been optimal diverges ever farther from the current ideal arrangement.

The slow decision-making and crowded agendas and bargaining tables of distributional coalitions are important to understanding the delays in adapting to new technologies and other changes. If the required bargaining and consultation took place instantaneously, there might not be any delay. If a cost-saving innovation becomes available to a firm, the use of that innovation will mean that the difference between revenues and production costs will be greater, so that there is more money to divide between the firm and the workers; a sufficiently powerful union will therefore be able to get more for its members than if the firm did not adopt the innovation[22] (the firm and the union have an incentive to bargain with one another until they maximize the joint surplus, which is essentially the difference between revenues net of non-labor costs and the opportunity costs in the form of leisure and alternative employment of the workers). Of course, things do not always work out this way in practice. When there is one big innovation and no other changes to consider, there may be an agreement to use the new technology. When, as is more commonly the case, there are many changes and innovations, large and small, that must be adopted in each period to maximize efficiency, it is much less likely that there will be prompt agreement to adopt all of the efficient changes. The slowness of decision-making and the crowded agendas and bargaining tables prevent rapid adaptation, and the rational ignorance of constituents about collective action by the union makes matters worse. Whereas delays in adaptation involving labor unions are better known, the above logic applies also to lobbies and cartels of firms. Colluding firms, for example, sometimes obtain monopoly rights under public utility regulation which they are loathe to lose, even though the system of regulation and collusion is so slow-moving that there is not efficient adaptation to changing conditions. Trucking, railroads, and airlines in modern American economic history offer many examples of this.

Special-interest groups also slow growth by reducing the rate at which resources are reallocated from one activity or industry to another in response to new technologies or conditions. One obvious way in which they do so is by lobbying for bail-outs of failing firms, thereby delaying or preventing the shift of resources to areas where they would have a greater productivity. Some other policies that slow the rate of reallocation of resources are perhaps not so obvious. Consider a situation in which there is, for any reason, a large increase in the demand for labor in some industry or profession and where the labor is controlled by a single union or professional association. The cartelistic organization will be able to demand a higher rate of pay because of the shift in demand, and the new higher monopoly wage will reduce the amount of labor purchased by the booming sector and thereby reduce growth and efficiency.

Moreover, the movement of labor into the cartelized area may be restricted to a greater extent than would be supposed from the fact that there would be a rise in the monopoly wage. If there is a large upward shift in the demand for labor in the booming sector, those in the cartel may not want to supply as much extra labor as is wanted; the higher wage will increase the incentive to work, but the extra income it brings also means that the workers can afford to take more leisure, so at best there will be only a limited increase in the hours of work. Although there is a "need" for much more labor than those already in the cartel can provide, this need may not be met. Except for one special case,[23] adding additional members to the cartel would make the marginal product and wage of the old members lower than it would otherwise have been, so no additional members may be admitted. The movement into the booming area may, in other words, not only be constrained by the increase in the monopoly price, but even in some cases essentially limited to the amount the previous workers wish to supply.*

*An economist who neglects the effects of decision-making costs and delays might argue that there was a gain to be made from bringing extra labor into the sector and suppose that the cartel would bring in the labor to secure the gain; he might point out that, in the circumstances described, there would be a difference between the wage that suitable laborers outside the cartel would be willing to accept and the monopoly wage (marginal revenue) that the cartel could obtain from selling the outside labor to employers, so that the cartel would hire or admit additional workers, and the old members would pocket the difference between the wage paid to the newcomers and the marginal revenue obtained from selling this labor to the employers. Needless to say, this sequence is not usually observed. Decision-making costs and delays make it difficult for a cartelistic organization to buy and sell labor or to deal with different classes of membership. The cartel might let the employers hire the extra labor and pay the cartel members part of the profits obtained by doing so, but that would undercut the cartel's monopoly, so it happens only rarely, and then normally on a temporary basis. The argument that has just been put forth also makes it clear that the growth forgone because of increased monopoly prices in areas favored by rises in demand is not necessarily offset by decreased monopoly prices in the cartelized areas suffering from adverse shifts in demand.

Some economists have supposed that a given level of barriers to the reallocation of resources would reduce the level but not the rate of growth of income. In fact, as Sir John Hicks has rigorously proved in a paper that responded to an earlier version of my argument,[24] barriers to resource reallocation will in general also reduce the growth rate. Any increases in productivity in the different industries will normally change relative prices as well as income levels. There is the possibility that expenditures on each product, despite the income and price changes, might by chance be at just the level that induced all resources to remain in exactly the same employments. Unless expenditures happen to be at this special level, the increases in productivity will entail that resources must be reallocated if economic efficiency is to be maintained and the society is to take full advantage of the increases in productivity. The required resource reallocations will be prevented or delayed by the barriers to entry. Hicks has further demonstrated that the magnitude of the reduction in the growth rate will vary with the extent to which the new pattern of expenditures deviates from the old and on the size of the industries in which resources are wasted because of the changes growing out of the increases in productivity.[25] We can conclude that, even if there should be no accumulation of special-interest groups over time, the barriers to resource reallocation that such groups create would lower the rate of growth as well as the absolute level of income.

The argument that led to our fourth implication showed that, when there were lobby-induced price changes or other subsidies and no barriers to entry into the favored area, the gains to the special-interest group could be small in relation to the loss to society. We now see that when there are barriers to entry this slows the resource reallocations needed for rapid economic growth. When the slower adoption of new technologies resulting from special-interest groups is also taken into account, the reduction in growth rates can be considerable. The slower adoption of new technologies and barriers to entry can subtract many times more from the society's output than the special-interest group obtains, particularly over the long run.

So we now have the seventh implication, the dynamic or growth-oriented counterpart to the fourth implication about static efficiency:

> 7. *Distributional coalitions slow down a society's capacity to adopt new technologies and to reallocate resources in response to changing conditions, and thereby reduce the rate of economic growth.*

IX

At least after they reach a certain point, distributional coalitions have an incentive to be exclusive. In the case of collusive oligopolists or others that operate in the marketplace, the reason is simply that whatever quantity an entrant would sell must either drive down the price received by those already in the cartel, or alternatively force existing members to restrict their sales further.[26] When it is created, the cartel must, for reasons explained above, normally enlist all the sellers in the market if it is to succeed, but once it has done this there is a compelling incentive to exclude any entrant. Indeed, existing members even have a reason to hope that some of their number die or depart so that those who remain can each sell more at the monopoly price.[27]

If the number of physicians increases, for example, the earnings of physicians must decline if other things are equal, and in country after country one finds that the professional organizations representing physicians work to limit entry into the profession. As the high income-levels of physicians in many countries testify, these efforts often succeed. The educational credentials and qualifying examinations usually required of those who would enter the practice of medicine are, of course, explained as necessary to protect the patient against incompetence. But note that the examinations are almost always imposed only on entrants. If the limits were mainly motivated by the interest of patients, older physicians would also be required to pass periodic qualifying examinations to demonstrate that they have kept their medical knowledge up-to-date. Among lawyers and other professionals in many countries there are similar limitations on entry. In legal systems without much limitation on the initiation of litigation, however, additional lawyers can raise the demand for their colleagues by increasing the likelihood of legal disputes, and this makes control of entry less important.

In the case of those distributional coalitions that seek their objectives by political action, the reason for exclusion is that there will be more to distribute to each member of the coalition if it is a minimum winning coalition. A lobby, or even a military alliance seeking spoils, will have less to distribute to each member if it admits more members than are necessary for success. Just as a cartel must include all of the sellers, so the coalition operating politically or militarily must include enough members to win. In a world of uncertainty, the size of the minimum winning coalition may not be known in advance, in which case the coalition must, over a range, trade off lower payoffs per member against greater probabilities of success. There will nonetheless always be some point beyond which it must be in the interest of the existing members to exclude new entrants. In the terms of the dichotomy introduced in *The Logic of Collective Action,* distributionally oriented lobbies as well as cartels must be *exclusive* instead of *inclusive* groups.

A governing aristocracy or oligarchy can provide an interesting illustration of the exclusivity of special-interest groups that use political or military methods. Imagine a country or historical period in which some subset of the population, such as the nobility or the oligarchy, dominates the political system. This subset has an incentive to choose public policies that distribute more of the social output to its own members. Except in the case where the aristocracy or oligarchy would increase its security if new members (for example, powerful rivals) were added, it will be exclusive: every unnecessary entrant into the favored subset reduces what is left for the rest. The relevance of this argument is evident from the exclusiveness of governing nobilities throughout history. Any number of devices and emblems have been used to mark off ruling aristocracies from the rest of the population with the utmost clarity. The exclusivity is perhaps most dramatically evident when a ruling group is secure enough to pass its powers on to its descendants. In these cases there is, of course, great resistance to admitting anyone other than the children of the nobility or ruling group into the ruling group. Such exclusivity is so general that some people think of it as only "natural," and find *any* explanation of it unsatisfying.

Let us nonetheless ask what institutions for marriage or childrearing we would expect to emerge. If the sons and daughters of the ruling group marry outsiders, and both the sons and daughters and the spouses of these sons and daughters are in the ruling group in the next generation, the ruling nobility will tend to double in size in the next generation. In the next generation there will then tend to be half as much for each member. One possible solution is to allow only descendants of one sex and their families to be in the ruling class in the next generation, and probably some discriminatory rules against women in certain societies are explained in this way. But those members of the ruling group that have only or mainly daughters have reason to oppose such rules; even apart from natural concern about their daughters, they would lose their share of the future receipts of their ruling group. So how can all families in the ruling group bequeath their share of the group's entitlement to descendants without making the value of a share in the entitlement decline by half or more with each successive generation?

They can do this through rules or social pressures that enforce endogamy: if the sons and daughters of the ruling group are induced to marry one another, the growth of the ruling group can be constrained in ways that preserve a legacy for all the families in it. Again, the evidence that nobilities and aristocracies have resisted marriages to commoners and lower ranks generally is abundant, and from many diverse societies. In a similar spirit, the abhorrence in earlier times of royalty marrying commoners can be understood as a rule that helped to limit the losses that a multinational class such as European royalty would have suffered had their numbers expanded exponentially.

Of course, there are other factors that can encourage endogamy and one must be careful not to push the foregoing argument too far.[28] Yet later parts of this book do, I think, strongly suggest that we cannot ignore the logic that has just been set forth. We cannot conclude that endogamy is simply the result of general difficulties of marriages and other close social relationships among people of different backgrounds—that the nobility marry nobility and royalty marry royalty because they would not know how to get along with others. The disproportionate intermarriage within social groups of all kinds suggests there is something in this—that very often nobility would have married nobility, and so forth, even in the absence of any rules or mores that suggested that this was expected. But it still does not adequately explain legal or social condemnation of marriages of royalty and nobility to commoners; if the arrangement was uncomfortable for the couple, we still need to explain why *others* were so concerned. The rule of thumb that, in most cases, a person will be better off if married to someone of a similar background is not what is at issue. The mother from a family of average means who advises her daughter to marry within their social group does not usually want the daughter to discriminate against millionaires. Whatever might work out best in most cases, the individual has an interest in being able to follow the rule or not as circumstances dictate. Thus it is comprehensible that some noble families short on money should violate the mores of their group by marrying daughters of rich merchants. What needs explanation are legal and social rules that say a marriage outside the ruling group is to be condemned *by others* as a violation of *principle*. Such rules must be explained, as they are here, at least partly in terms of the interest of the group. Whatever may be the reaction to the possibly uncomfortable illustration that has been offered, the logic behind exclusion in distributional coalitions remains clear.

Both in cartels and in special-interest organizations focused on the polity there are the further considerations mentioned in the last chapter. Collective action will be easier if the group is socially interactive, so there are social selective incentives. The fact that everyone in the relevant group gets a uniform amount and type of the collective good and must put up with the same group policies also argues that groups of similar incomes and values are more likely to agree. Thus our eighth implication:

> 8. *Distributional coalitions, once big enough to succeed, are exclusive and seek to limit the diversity of incomes and values of their membership.*

X

To achieve their objectives, distributional coalitions must use their lobbying power to influence governmental policy or their collusive power to influence the market. These two influences affect not only efficiency, economic growth, and exclusion of entrants in a society, but also the relative importance of different institutions and activities. Lobbying increases the complexity of regulation and the scope of government, and collusion and organizational activity in markets increase the extent of bargaining and what I call *complex understandings*. An increase in the payoffs from lobbying and cartel activity, as compared with the payoffs from production, means more resources are devoted to politics and cartel activity and fewer resources are devoted to production. This in turn influences the attitudes and culture that evolve in the society.

Lobbying increases the complexity of regulation and the scope of government by creating special provisions and exceptions. A lobby that wins a tax reduction for income of a certain source or type makes the tax code longer and more complicated; a lobby that gets a tariff increase for the producers of a particular commodity makes trade regulation more complex than if there were a uniform tariff on all imports and much more complex than it would be with no tariff at all. The limited incentive the typical citizen has to monitor public policy also implies that lobbies for special interests can sometimes succeed where matters are detailed or complex but not when they are general and simple, and this increases complexity still further.

The regulatory complexity that derives from lobbies is magnified by a dynamic process that Charles Schultze has described.[29] When regulations are established through lobbying or other measures, there is an incentive for ingenious lawyers and others to find ways of getting around the regulations or ways of profiting from them in unexpected ways. The interests behind the regulations and the officials who administer the regulations will often amend or extend the regulation to close the loophole and prevent the unexpected use of the regulation, but this will make the regulation still more complex. It does not, of course, follow that the more complex regulations cannot also be exploited. Indeed, the possibility of evasion and unintended consequences may sometimes even increase as the regulations become more complicated. So, as Schultze pointed out, there can be an unending process of loophole discoveries and closures with the complexity and cost of regulation continually increasing.

The more elaborate the regulation, the greater the need for specialists to deal with these regulations, such as lawyers, accountants, or other consultants on this or that aspect of governmental relations. When these specialists become significant enough, there is even the possibility that the specialists with a vested interest in the complex regulations will collude or lobby against simplification or elimination of the regulation. As the general argument here emphasizes, there is nothing easy, prompt, or automatic about the emergence of lobbies, but sometimes they will in time emerge. When lobbies of this kind emerge, the effects they have are aptly illustrated by the successful opposition of trial lawyers in many American states to ''no-fault'' automobile insurance laws that would greatly reduce the extent of litigation about automobile accidents. In the political system in the United States, at least, there is a sense in which even legislators can come to have a vested interest in the complexity of regulations, as Morris Fiorina and Roger Noll pointed out.[30] Congressmen and senators can gain exceptional support by helping constituents to obtain particular services or exceptions from the government, since the legislator is obviously linked more closely with these favors than with general legislation that can pass only if many legislators voted affirmatively. For this reason, Fiorina and Noll have argued, legislators seek more bureaucratic or manipulatable legislation that further increases the importance of the constituent services that help them to be re-elected. Interestingly, the proportion of incumbents getting re-elected has increased over time. I recall, in support of the Fiorina–Noll hypothesis, that when I was an official in the U.S. Department of Health, Education and Welfare, then-President Lyndon Johnson placed a general moratorium on a class of construction projects particularly favored by the Congress, allegedly in an attempt to pressure the Congress into supporting administration legislation. According to reports I heard, congressmen often privately were pleased with the moratorium, apparently because those exceptions to it that they were able to obtain brought them substantial credit with constituents.

Someone has to administer the increasingly complex regulations that result from the lobbying and the related processes that have been described. This increases the scale of bureaucracy and government. Lobbying obviously also adds in another way to the scope of government when it leads to government expenditures and programs to serve special-interest groups. Although lobbying on the whole undoubtedly tends to increase the extent of government activity, it would probably be claiming too much for the present argument to attribute most of the increase in the role of government around the world in the last generation or so to the growth of special-interest groups. The interwar depression, World War II, and other developments led to profound ideological changes that increased the scope of government, and developments like the cold war and pollution, to mention only two, also increased the demands upon governments. A great many factors have to be taken into account to explain the growth of government, and all that is asserted here is that the accumulation of special-interest organizations is one of these factors.

The increase of collusion and cartelistic organization similarly increases the amount of bargaining and organizational activity in the marketplace. There must be transactions between buyers and sellers in any market, but cartelization, as was argued earlier, also requires either a demanding type of bargaining or constitutional procedures for associational politics. The cartelistic organizations and collusions must sometimes also bargain with each other, as happens when there are negotiations between organizations of employers and labor unions. Given the slow decision-making, crowded agendas, and cluttered bargaining tables, it takes some time before negotiators agree on anything. But once agreements are reached, the same considerations suggest that they should not be changed without compelling reason. Thus, in time, work rules, customary market shares, or established ways of doing things emerge that cannot easily be changed. As time goes on, these arrangements often become rather complex. The complexity can be codified in legal contracts, as is often the case in labor-management bargains in the United States, or embodied in a network of customs, understandings, and habits, as is commonly the case in British industrial relations and in collusive activities among oligopolistic firms. Whether the agreements or understandings are written or not, they become more elaborate over time, and this is what is meant by increasingly complex understandings. Increasing complexity of understandings implies, for example, that employers dealing with labor unions would sometimes want to move to new locations, even if they would confront other equally powerful and aggressive unions in the new situations, because they would not there be hindered by a heritage of complex and out-of-date understandings.

The growth of coalitions with an incentive to try to capture a larger share of the national income, the increase in regulatory complexity and governmental action that lobbying coalitions encourage, and the increasing bargaining and complexity of understanding that cartels create alter the pattern of incentives and the direction of evolution in a society. The incentive to produce is diminished; the incentive to seek a larger share of what is produced increases. The reward for pleasing those to whom we sell our goods or labor declines, while the reward for evading or exploiting regulations, politics, and bureaucracy and for asserting our rights through bargaining or the complex understandings becomes greater.

These changes in the patterns of incentives in turn deflect the direction of a society's evolution. Some observers might suppose that the accumulation of distributional coalitions would make societies evolve in ways that favor the less talented, the weak, and the poor, but this is wrong. In every environment, those who are best fitted for that environment are most likely to thrive, survive, and multiply. There is evolution in the zoo as there is in the jungle, as those animals that are able to adapt to cages and keepers outlast those that cannot. So also with cultural evolution and evolution in human societies. Every society, whatever its institutions and governing ideology, gives greater rewards to the fittest—the fittest for *that* society. What it takes to be favored varies from society to society, but no society rewards those who are least fit to thrive under its arrangements.

If a society mainly rewards production or the capacity to satisfy those with whom one engages in free exchange, it stimulates the development of productive traits. It does this particularly through cultural or Lamarckian evolution, whereby learned or acquired behavior can be passed on to descendants. If the accumulation of distributional coalitions increases the incentive for distributional struggle, augments regulatory complexity, encourages the dominance of politics, stimulates bargaining, and increases the complexity of understandings, this encourages the development of different attitudes and attributes. What we loosely call intelligence, or aptitude for education, will probably be favored as much as or more than before because the articulate and educated have a comparative advantage in regulation, politics, and complex understandings. This, in turn, probably limits the extent to which intellectuals oppose their elaboration.

The competition is not any gentler because it takes a different form. The gang fight is fully as rough as the individual duel, and the struggle of special-interest groups generates no magnanimity or altruism. Competition about the division of income is not any nicer than competition to produce or to please customers. The new competition is, in part, less individualistic, so in certain areas the rewards to individual effort are diminished and the relative attractiveness of leisure enhanced. But the weaker groups still suffer. The poor and the unemployed have no selective incentives to enable them to organize, whereas small groups of great firms or wealthy individuals can organize with relative ease. Thus life is not any gentler because of special-interest groups, but it is less productive, especially in the long run.

So, with thanks to the reader for patiently waiting until the next chapter before getting to the main practical applications of the argument, we come finally to the ninth and last implication.

9. *The accumulation of distributional coalitions increases the complexity of regulation, the role of government, and the complexity of understandings, and changes the direction of social evolution.*

To make later reference to them more convenient, all of the implications are listed on the next page.

Implications

1. There will be no countries that attain symmetrical organization of all groups with a common interest and thereby attain optimal outcomes through comprehensive bargaining.

2. Stable societies with unchanged boundaries tend to accumulate more collusions and organizations for collective action over time.

3. Members of "small" groups have disproportionate organizational power for collective action, and this disproportion diminishes but does not disappear over time in stable societies.

4. On balance, special-interest organizations and collusions reduce efficiency and aggregate income in the societies in which they operate and make political life more divisive.

5. Encompassing organizations have some incentive to make the society in which they operate more prosperous, and an incentive to redistribute income to their members with as little excess burden as possible, and to cease such redistribution unless the amount redistributed is substantial in relation to the social cost of the redistribution.

6. Distributional coalitions make decisions more slowly than the individuals and firms of which they are comprised, tend to have crowded agendas and bargaining tables, and more often fix prices than quantities.

7. Distributional coalitions slow down a society's capacity to adopt new technologies and to reallocate resources in response to changing conditions, and thereby reduce the rate of economic growth.

8. Distributional coalitions, once big enough to succeed, are exclusive, and seek to limit the diversity of incomes and values of their membership.

9. The accumulation of distributional coalitions increases the complexity of regulation, the role of government, and the complexity of understandings, and changes the direction of social evolution.

The Developed Democracies Since World War II

4

In the preceding chapters I have argued, among other things, that associations to provide collective goods are for the most fundamental reasons difficult to establish, and that therefore even those groups that are in situations where there is a potential for organization usually will be able to organize only in favorable circumstances. As time goes on, more groups will have enjoyed favorable circumstances and overcome difficulties of collective action. The interest of organizational leaders insures that few organizations for collective action in stable societies will dissolve, so these societies accumulate special-interest organizations and collusions over time (Implication 2). These organizations, at least if they are small in relation to the society, have little incentive to make their societies more productive, but they have powerful incentives to seek a larger share of the national income even when this greatly reduces social output (Implication 4). The barriers to entry established by these distributional coalitions and their slowness in making decisions and mutually efficient bargains reduces an economy's dynamism and rate of growth (Implication 7). Distributional coalitions also increase regulation, bureaucracy, and political intervention in markets (Implication 9).

If the argument so far is correct, it follows that countries whose distributional coalitions have been emasculated or abolished by totalitarian government or foreign occupation should grow relatively quickly after a free and stable legal order is established. This can explain the postwar "economic miracles" in the nations that were defeated in World War II, particularly those in Japan and West Germany. The everyday use of the word *miracle* to describe the rapid economic growth in these countries testifies that this growth was not only unexpected, but also outside the range of known laws and experience. In Japan and West Germany, totalitarian governments were followed by Allied occupiers determined to promote institutional change and to ensure that institutional life would start almost anew. In Germany, Hitler had done away with independent unions as well as all other dissenting groups, whereas the Allies, through measures such as the decartelization decrees of 1947 and denazification programs, had emasculated cartels and organizations with right-wing backgrounds.[1] In Japan, the militaristic regime had kept down left-wing organizations, and the Supreme Commander of the Allied Powers imposed the antimonopoly law of 1947 and purged many hundreds of officers of zaibatsu and other organizations for their wartime activities.[2] (In Italy, the institutional destruction from totalitarianism, war, and Allied occupation was less severe and the postwar growth "miracle" correspondingly shorter, but this case is more complex and will be discussed separately.)* The theory here predicts that with continued stability the Germans and Japanese will accumulate more distributional coalitions, which will have an adverse influence on their growth rates.

Moreover, the special-interest organizations established after World War II in Germany and Japan were, for the most part, highly encompassing. This is true of the postwar labor union structure of West Germany, for example, and of the business organization, Keidanren, that has played a dominant role in economic policymaking in Japan. The high growth rates of these two countries also owe something to the relatively encompassing character of some of the special-interest organizations they did have (and this organizational inclusiveness in turn was sometimes due to promotion by occupation authorities).[3] At least in the first two decades after the war, the Japanese and West Germans had not developed the degree of regulatory complexity and scale of government that characterized more stable societies.

The theory also offers a new perspective on French growth experience.[4] Why has France had relatively good growth performance for much of the postwar period (achieving by about 1970 levels of income

---

*In Italy the evolution of political competition since World War II appears to have resulted in progressively weaker governments and less stable governing coalitions. Thus, apart from the growing strength of distributional coalitions, the *ratio* of the strength of these coalitions to that of the government appears to have increased. Another element of the Italian postwar experience is mentioned in the next chapter.

broadly comparable with other advanced countries) when its investment climate has often been so inclement? The foreign invasions and political instability that have hindered capital accumulation have also disrupted the development of special-interest organizations and collusions. The divisions in French ideological life must have deepened as one upheaval after another called into question the country's basic political and economic system. The intensity of these ideological divisions must have further impaired the development of at least the larger special-interest organizations in that country. Most notably, the development of French labor unions has been set back by periods of repression and disruption and by ideological fissures that divide the French labor movement into competing communist, socialist, and catholic unions. The competition among these semideveloped unions, often in the same workplaces, in most cases prevents any union from having an effective monopoly of the relevant work force. French unions accordingly have only a limited capacity to determine work rules or wage levels (or to make union membership compulsory, with the result that most French union members do not pay dues). Smaller groups such as trade associations and the alumni of prestigious schools (as Implication 3 predicts) have been better able to organize. But their effects on growth rates in the last two decades have been limited by considerations discussed in the next chapter, which will develop another reason why the French economy has performed better in the 1960s than its troubled history would lead us to expect.[5] The foregoing argument about France has some applicability to other continental countries as well.

II

The logic of the argument implies that countries that have had democratic freedom of organization without upheaval or invasion the longest will suffer the most from growth-repressing organizations and combinations. This helps to explain why Great Britain, the major nation with the longest immunity from dictatorship, invasion, and revolution, has had in this century a lower rate of growth than other large, developed democracies. Britain has precisely the powerful network of special-interest organizations that the argument developed here would lead us to expect in a country with its record of military security and democratic stability. The number and power of its trade unions need no description. The venerability and power of its professional associations is also striking. Consider the distinction between solicitors and barristers, which could not possibly have emerged in a free market innocent of professional associations or government regulations of the sort they often obtain; solicitors in Britain have a legal monopoly in assisting individuals making conveyances of real estate and barristers a monopoly of the right to serve as counsel in the more important court cases. Britain also has a strong farmers' organization and a great many trade associations. In short, with age British society has acquired so many strong organizations and collusions that it suffers from an institutional sclerosis that slows its adaptation to changing circumstances and technologies.

Admittedly, lobbying in Britain is not as blatant as in the United States, but it is pervasive and often involves discreet efforts to influence civil servants as well as ministers and other politicians. Moreover, the word *establishment* acquired its modern meaning there and, however often that word may be overused, it still suggests a substantial degree of informal organization that could emerge only gradually in a stable society. Many of the powerful special-interest organizations in Britain are, in addition, narrow rather than encompassing. For example, in a single factory there are often many different trade unions, each with a monopoly over a different craft or category of workers, and no one union encompasses a substantial fraction of the working population of the country. Britain is also often used as an example of ungovernability. In view of the long and illustrious tradition of democracy in Britain and the renowned orderliness of the British people, this is remarkable, but it is what the theory here predicts.

This explanation of Britain's relatively slow postwar growth, unlike many other explanations, is consistent with the fact that for nearly a century, from just after the middle of the eighteenth century until nearly the middle of the nineteenth, Britain was evidently the country with the *fastest* rate of economic growth. Indeed, during their Industrial Revolution the British invented modern economic growth. This means that no explanation of Britain's relatively slow growth in recent times that revolves around some supposedly inherent or permanent feature of British character or society can possibly be correct, because it is contradicted by Britain's long period with the fastest economic growth. Any valid explanation of Britain's relatively slow growth now must also take into account the *gradual* emergence of the ''British disease.'' Britain began to fall behind in relative growth rates in the last decades of the nineteenth century,[6] and this problem has become especially notable since World War II. Most other explanations of Britain's relatively slow growth in recent times do not imply a temporal pattern that is consistent with Britain's historical experience with dramatically different relative growth rates,[7] but the theory offered here, with its emphasis on the gradual accumulation of distributional coalitions (Implication 2), does.

III

There cannot be much doubt that totalitarianism, instability, and war reduced special-interest organizations in Germany, Japan, and France, and that stability and the absence of invasion allowed continued development of such organizations in the United Kingdom. My colleague Peter Murrell systematically recorded the dates of formation of those associations recorded in *Internationales Verzeichnis der Wirtschaftsverbande*.[8] This is, to be sure, an incomplete source, and is perhaps flawed also in other ways, but it was published in 1973 and thus cannot have been the result of any favoritism toward the present argument. Murrell found from this source that whereas 51 percent of the associations existing in 1971 in the United Kingdom were founded before 1939, only 37 percent of the French, 24 percent of the West German, and 19 percent of the Japanese associations were. Naturally, Britain also had a smaller proportion of its interest groups founded after 1949—29 percent, contrasted with 45 percent for France and 52 percent for Germany and for Japan. Britain also has a much larger number of associations than France, Germany, or Japan, and is exceeded in this category only by the far larger United States. Of course, we ought to have indexes that weight each organization by its strength and its membership, but I know of none.

Murrell also worked out an ingenious set of tests of the hypothesis that the special-interest groups in Britain reduced that country's rate of growth in comparison with West Germany's. If the special-interest groups were in fact causally connected with Britain's slower growth, Murrell reasoned, this should put old British industries at a particular disadvantage in comparison with their West German counterparts, whereas in new industries where there may not yet have been time enough for special-interest organizations to emerge in either country, British and West German performance should be more nearly comparable. Thus, Murrell argued, the *ratio* of the rate of growth of new British industry to old British industry should be higher than the corresponding *ratio* for West Germany. There are formidable difficulties of definition and measurement, and alternative definitions and measures had to be used. Taking all of these results together, it is clear that they support the hypothesis that new British industries did relatively better in relation to old British industries than new German industries did in relation to old German industries. In most cases the results almost certainly could not have been due to chance, that is, they were statistically significant. Moreover, Murrell found that in heavy industry, where both industrial concentration and unionization are usually greater than in light industry, the results were strongest, which also supports the theory.[9]

IV

Of the many alternative explanations, most are ad hoc. Some economists have attributed the speed of the recoveries of the vanquished countries to the importance of human capital compared with the physical capital destroyed by bombardment, but this cannot be a sufficient explanation, since the war killed many of the youngest and best-trained adults and interrupted education and work experience for many others. Knowledge of productive techniques, however, had not been destroyed by the war, and to the extent that the defeated nations were at a lower-than-prewar level of income and needed to replace destroyed buildings or equipment, they would tend to have an above-average growth rate. But this cannot explain why these economies grew more rapidly than others after they had reached their prewar level of income and even after they had surpassed the British level of per capita income.[10]

Another commonplace ad hoc explanation is that the British, or perhaps only those in the working classes, do not work as hard as people in other countries. Others lay the unusually rapid growth of Germany and Japan to the special industriousness of their peoples. Taken literally, this type of explanation is unquestionably unsatisfactory. The rate of economic growth is the rate of *increase* of national income, and although this logically could be due to an *increase* in the industriousness of a people, it could not, in the direct and simple way implied in the familiar argument, be explained by their normal level of effort, which is relevant instead to their *absolute* level of income. Admittedly, when the industriousness of those who innovate is considered, or when possible connections between level of effort and the amount of saving are taken

PENTICTON PUBLIC LIBRARY
Receipt
2022-01-10 14:35
Items Out

THE RISE AND DECLINE OF
NATIONS - INTERLIBRARY
LOAN
33074003830334
Due date: 2022-01-24

The wealth and poverty of nations
33074000740650
Due date: 2022-01-23

Total Items Out: 2

You saved $39.99 by using the
library today!

News

into account,[11] there could be some connection between industriousness and growth. But even if the differences in willingness to work are part of the explanation, why are those in the fast-growing countries zealous and those in the slow-growing countries lazy? And since many countries have changed relative position in the race for higher growth rates, the timing of the waves of effort also needs explaining. If industriousness is the explanation, why were the British so hard-working during the Industrial Revolution? And by this work-effort theory the Germans evidently must have been lazy in the first half of the nineteenth century when they were relatively poor, and the impoverished Japanese quite lethargic when Admiral Perry arrived.

One plausible possibility is that industriousness varies with the incentive to work to which individuals in different countries have become accustomed. These incentives, in turn, are strikingly influenced, whether for manual workers, professionals, or entrepreneurs, by the extent to which special-interest groups reduce the rewards to productive work and thus increase the relative attractiveness of leisure. The search for the causes of differences in the willingness to work, and in particular the question of why shirking should be thought to be present during Britain's period of slower-than-average growth but not when it had the fastest rate of growth, brings us to economic institutions and policies, and to the more fundamental explanation of differences in growth rates being offered in this book.

V

Some observers endeavor to explain the anomalous growth rates in terms of alleged national economic ideologies and the extent of government involvement in economic life. The "British disease" especially is attributed to the unusually large role that the British government has allegedly played in economic life. There is certainly no difficulty in finding examples of harmful economic intervention in postwar Britain. Nonetheless, as Samuel Brittan has convincingly demonstrated in an article in the *Journal of Law and Economics*,[12] this explanation is unsatisfactory. First, it is by no means clear that the government's role in economic life has been significantly larger than in the average developed democracy; in the proportion of gross domestic product accounted for by government spending, the United Kingdom has been at the middle, rather than at the top, of the league, and it has been also in about the middle, at roughly the same levels as Germany and France, in the percentage of income taken in taxes and social insurance.[13] Perhaps in certain respects or certain years the case that the British government was unusually interventionist can be sustained, but there is no escaping Brittan's second point: that the relatively slow British growth rate goes back about a hundred years, to a period when governmental economic activity was very limited (especially, we might add, in Great Britain).

Some economists have argued that when we look at the developed democracies as a group, we seem to see a negative correlation between the size of government and the rate of growth.[14] This more general approach is much superior to the ad hoc style of explanation, so statistical tests along these lines must be welcomed. But the results so far are weak, showing at best only a tenuous and uncertain connection between larger governments and slower growth, with such strength as this relationship possesses due in good part to Japan, which has had both the fastest growth rate and the smallest government of the major developed democracies. A weak or moderate negative relationship between the relative role of government and the rate of growth is predicted by Implication 9.

VI

One well-known ad hoc explanation of the slow British growth focuses on a class consciousness that allegedly reduces social mobility, fosters exclusive and traditionalist attitudes that discourage entrants and innovators, and maintains medieval prejudices against commercial pursuits. Since Britain had the fastest rate of growth in the world for nearly a century, we know that its slow growth now cannot be due to any *inherent* traits of the British character. There is, in fact, some evidence that at the time of the Industrial Revolution Britain did not have the reputation for class differences that it has now. It is a commonplace among economic historians of the Industrial Revolution that at that time Britain, in relation to comparable parts of the Continent, had unusual social mobility, relatively little class consciousness, and a concern in all social classes about commerce, production, and financial gain that was sometimes notorious to its neighbors:

> More than any other in Europe, probably, British society was open. Not only was income more evenly distributed than across the

Channel, but the barriers to mobility were lower, the definitions of status looser. . . .

It seems clear that British commerce of the eighteenth century was, by comparison with that of the Continent, impressively energetic, pushful, and open to innovation. . . . No state was more responsive to the desires of its mercantile classes. . . . Nowhere did entrepreneurial decisions less reflect non-rational considerations of prestige and habit. . . . Talent was readier to go into business, projecting, and invention. . . .

This was a people fascinated by wealth and commerce, collectively and individually. . . . Business interests promoted a degree of intercourse between people of different stations and walks of life that had no parallel on the Continent.

The flow of entrepreneurship within business was freer, the allocation of resources more responsive than in other economies. Where the traditional sacro-sanctity of occupational exclusiveness continued to prevail across the Channel . . . the British cobbler would not stick to his last nor the merchant to his trade. . . .

Far more than in Britain, continental business enterprise was a class activity, recruiting practitioners from a group limited by custom and law. In France, commercial enterprise had traditionally entailed derogation from noble status.[15]

It is not surprising that Napoleon once derided Britain as a "nation of shopkeepers" and that even Adam Smith found it expedient to use this phrase in his criticism of Britain's mercantilistic policies.[16]

The ubiquitous observations suggesting that the Continent's class structures have by now become in some respects more flexible than Britain's would hint that we should look for processes that might have broken down class barriers more rapidly on the Continent than in Great Britain, or for processes that might have raised or erected more new class barriers in Britain than on the Continent, or for both.

VII

One reason that only remnants of the Continent's medieval structures remain today is that they are entirely out of congruity with the technology and ideas now common in the developed world. But there is another, more pertinent reason: revolution and occupation, Napoleonism and totalitarianism, have utterly demolished most feudal structures on the Continent and many of the cultural attitudes they sustained. The new

families and firms that rose to wealth and power often were not successful in holding their gains; new instabilities curtailed the development of
new organizations and collusions that could have protected them and
their descendants against still newer entrants. To be sure, fragments of
the Middle Ages and chunks of the great fortunes of the nineteenth
century still remain on the Continent; but, like the castles crumbling in
the countryside, they do not greatly hamper the work and opportunities
of the average citizen.

The institutions of medieval Britain, and even the great family-
oriented industrial and commercial enterprises of more recent centuries,
are similarly out of accord with the twentieth century and have in part
crumbled, too. But would they not have been pulverized far more finely
if Britain had gone through anything like the French Revolution, if a
dictator had destroyed its public schools, if it had suffered occupation
by a foreign power or fallen prey to totalitarian regimes determined to
destroy any organizations independent of the regime itself? The importance of the House of Lords, the established church, and the ancient
colleges of Oxford and Cambridge has no doubt often been grossly
exaggerated. But they are symbols of Britain's legacy from the preindustrial past or (more precisely) of the unique degree to which it has
been preserved. There was extraordinary turmoil until a generation or
two before the Industrial Revolution[17] (and this probably played a role
in opening British society to new talent and enterprise), but since then
Britain has not suffered the institutional destruction, or the forcible
replacement of elites, or the decimation of social classes, that its Continental counterparts have experienced. The same stability and immunity
from invasion have also made it easier for the firms and families that
advanced in the Industrial Revolution and the nineteenth century to
organize or collude to protect their interests.

Here the argument in this book is particularly likely to be misun-
derstood. This is partly because the word *class* is an extraordinarily
loose, emotive, and misleadingly aggregative term that has unfortunately been reified over generations of ideological debate. There are, of
course, no clearly delineated and widely separated groups such as the
middle class or the working class, but rather a large number of groups of
diverse situations and occupations, some of which differ greatly and
some of which differ slightly if at all in income and status. Even if such
a differentiated grouping as the British middle class could be precisely
delineated, it would be a logical error to suppose that such a large group

as the British middle class could voluntarily collude to exclude others or to achieve any common interest.[18] The theory does suggest that the unique stability of British life since the early eighteenth century must have affected social structure, social mobility, and cultural attitudes, but *not* through class conspiracies or coordinated action by any large class or group. The process is far subtler and must be studied at a less aggregative level.

We can see this process from a new perspective if we remember that concerted action usually requires selective incentives, that social pressure can often be an effective selective incentive, and that individuals of similar incomes and values are more likely to agree on what amount and type of collective good to purchase. Social incentives will not be very effective unless the group that values the collective good at issue interacts socially or is composed of subgroups that do. If the group does have its own social life, the desire for the companionship and esteem of colleagues and the fear of being slighted or even ostracized can at little cost provide a powerful incentive for concerted action. The organizational entrepreneurs who succeed in promoting special-interest groups, and the managers who maintain them, must therefore focus disproportionately on groups that already interact socially or that can be induced to do so. This means that these groups tend to have socially homogeneous memberships and that the organization will have an interest in using some of its resources to preserve this homogeneity. The fact that everyone in the pertinent group gets the same amount and type of a collective good also means, as we know from the theories of fiscal equivalence and optimal segregation,[19] that there will be less conflict (and perhaps welfare gains as well) if those who are in the same jurisdiction or organization have similar incomes and values. The forces just mentioned, operating simultaneously in thousands of professions, crafts, clubs, and communities, would, by themselves, explain a degree of class consciousness. This in turn helps to generate cultural caution about the incursions of the entrepreneur and the fluctuating profits and status of businessmen, and also helps to preserve and expand aristocratic and feudal prejudices against commerce and industry. There is massive if unsystematic evidence of the effects of the foregoing processes, such as that in Martin Wiener's book on *English Culture and the Decline of the Industrial Spirit, 1850–1980.*[20]

Unfortunately, the processes that have been described do not operate by themselves; they resonate with the fact that every distributional coalition must restrict entry (Implication 8). As we know, there is no way a group can obtain more than the free market price unless it can keep outsiders from taking advantage of the higher price, and organizations designed to redistribute income through lobbying have an incentive to be minimum winning coalitions. Social barriers could not exist unless there were some groups capable of concerted action that had an interest in erecting them. We can see now that the special-interest organizations or collusions seeking advantage in either the market or the polity have precisely this interest.

In addition to controlling entry, the successful coalition must, we recall, have or generate a degree of consensus about its policies. The cartelistic coalition must also limit the output or labor of its own members; it must make all the members conform to some plan for restricting the amount sold, however much this limitation and conformity might limit innovation. As time goes on, custom and habit play a larger role. The special-interest organizations use their resources to argue that what they do is what in justice ought to be done. The more often pushy entrants and nonconforming innovators are repressed, the rarer they become, and what is not customary is "not done."

Nothing about this process should make it work differently at different levels of income or social status. As Josiah Tucker remarked in the eighteenth century, "All men would be monopolists if they could." This process may, however, proceed more rapidly in the professions, where public concern about unscrupulous or incompetent practitioners provides an ideal cover for policies that would in other contexts be described as monopoly or "greedy unionism."[21] The process takes place among the workers as well as the lords; some of the first craft unions were in fact organized in pubs.

There is a temptation to conclude dramatically that this involutional process has turned a nation of shopkeepers into a land of clubs and pubs. But this facile conclusion is too simple. Countervailing factors are also at work and may have greater quantitative significance. The rapid rate of scientific and technological advance in recent times has encouraged continuing reallocations of resources and brought about considerable occupational, social, and geographical mobility even in relatively sclerotic societies.[22]

In addition, there is another aspect of the process by which social status is transmitted to descendants that is relatively independent of the present theory. Prosperous and well-educated parents usually are able through education and upbringing to provide larger legacies of human as well as tangible capital to their children than are deprived families. Although apparently the children of high-ranking families occasionally are enfeebled by undemanding and overindulgent environments, or even neglected by parents obsessed with careers or personal concerns, there is every reason to suppose that, on average, the more successful families pass on the larger legacies of human and physical capital to their children. This presumably accounts for some of the modest correlation observed between the incomes and social positions of parents and those that their children eventually attain. The adoption of free public education and reasonably impartial scholarship systems in Britain in more recent times has disproportionately increased the amount of human capital passed on to children from poor families and thereby has tended to increase social mobility. Thus there are important aspects of social mobility that the theory offered in this book does not claim to explain and that can countervail those it does explain.

I must once again emphasize multiple causation and point out that there is no presumption that the process described in this book has brought *increasing* class consciousness, traditionalism, or antagonism to entrepreneurship. The contrary forces may overwhelm the involution even when no upheavals or invasions destroy the institutions that sustain it. The only hypothesis on this point that can reasonably be derived from the theory is that, of two societies that were in other respects equal, the one with the longer history of stability, security, and freedom of association would have more institutions that limit entry and innovation, that these institutions would encourage more social interaction and homogeneity among their members, and that what is said and done by these institutions would have at least some influence on what people in that society find customary and fitting.[23]

VIII

The evidence that has already been presented is sufficient to provoke some readers to ask rhetorically what the policy implications of the argument might be and to answer that a country ought to seek a revolution, or even provoke a war in which it would be defeated. Of course, this policy recommendation makes no more (or less) sense than the suggestion that one ought to welcome pestilence as a cure for overpopulation. In addition to being silly, the rhetorical recommendation obscures the true principal policy implications of the logic that has been developed here (which will be discussed later). Those readers who believe that the main policy implication of the present theory is that a nation should casually engage in revolutions or unsuccessful wars should read the remaining chapters of the book, for some of the further implications of the logic that has already been set out are sure to surprise them.

This is really too early in the argument to consider policy implications. There is much more evidence to consider. Let us proceed, as the lovely expression used by Mao Tse Tung's more pragmatic successors says, "to seek truth from facts," and to do so without the preconceptions that a prior knowledge of policy implications sometimes can generate. Let us look first at the other developed democracies that, although lacking as long a history of stability and immunity from invasion as Britain, have nonetheless enjoyed relatively long periods of stability and security—namely, Switzerland, Sweden, and the United States.

As a glance at table 1.1 reveals, Switzerland has been one of the slowest growing of the developed democracies in the postwar period; it has grown more slowly than Great Britain. Such slow growth in a long-stable country certainly is consistent with the theory. We should not, however, jump to the conclusion that Switzerland necessarily corroborates the argument I have offered, because Switzerland for some time has had a higher per capita income than most other European countries and therefore has enjoyed less "catch-up" growth. Those countries that had relatively low per capita incomes in the early postwar period presumably had more opportunities to grow than Switzerland had, so probably we should make an honorary addition to Switzerland's growth rate to obtain a fairer comparison. Even though no one knows just what size this honorary addition should be, possibly it would be large enough to classify Switzerland as having a relatively successful postwar growth performance. This is, in effect, the assumption made in "Pressure Politics and Economic Growth: Olson's Theory and the Swiss Experience" by Franz Lehner,[24] a native of Switzerland who is a professor of political science at the University of Bochum in Germany. Lehner shows that the exceptionally restrictive constitutional arrangements in Switzerland make it extremely difficult to pass new legislation. This makes it difficult for lobbies to get their way and thus greatly limits Switzerland's losses from special-interest legislation. The high per capita income that the Swiss have achieved is then, by Lehner's argument, evidence in favor of the present theory.

Since cartelistic action sometimes requires government enforcement, the Swiss constitutional limitations undoubtedly also limit the losses from cartelization. On the other hand, there can also be cartelistic action without government connivance, and so I would hypothesize that Switzerland ought to have accumulated some degree of cartelistic organization. The extraordinary Swiss reliance on guest workers from other countries for a considerable period would suggest that this cartelization mainly would not involve the unskilled or semi-skilled manual workers that are strongly unionized in some other countries, but rather business enterprises and the professions. The theory here also would predict that, by now, stable Switzerland would have acquired at least a few rigidities in its social structure. The private cartelization and some attendant class stratification should have offset to at least a slight extent some of the growth Switzerland has enjoyed from the limitations on the predations of lobbies and governmentally enforced cartels. Another consideration is that Switzerland has enjoyed not only the normal encouragement for long-run investment that stability provides but also the special gains that accrue from its history as a haven of stability and its permissive banking laws in a historically unstable and restrictive continent. Just as Las Vegas and Monaco profit more from gambling than they would if similar gambling were legal everywhere, so Switzerland has profited more from its stability and permissiveness than it would have if its neighbors had enjoyed a similar tranquility and liberalism. If there had not been capital flights and fears about the stability and economic controls of other continental countries, Switzerland would not have received so much capital or had such an impressive role in international banking. Of course, this factor must not be exaggerated; Britain has profited from being a center of international finance for much the same reasons. When all these factors, and another factor that will emerge in a later chapter, are taken into account, it is difficult to be utterly certain how the theory fares in the test against Swiss experience. The hope must be that the example of Lehner's useful study will stimulate additional expert investigations of the matter.

IX

If we also make a large enough honorary addition to Sweden's growth rate to adjust for its relatively high per capita income, that country then seems at first sight to contradict the theory. Although it industrialized late, Sweden has enjoyed freedom of organization and immunity from invasion for a long time, and it does not have the constitutional obstacles to the passage of special-interest legislation that Switzerland has. The strength and coverage of special-interest organizations in Sweden are what our model would predict. Why then did Sweden (at some times during the postwar period, at least) achieve respectable growth even though it already had a high standard of living? In particular, why (despite some severe recent reverses) has Sweden's economic performance been superior to Britain's when its special-interest organizations are also uncommonly strong? Similarly, why has neighboring Norway done as well as it has? Even though Norway's stability was interrupted briefly by Nazi occupation during World War II, it has relatively strong special-interest organizations. Does the experience of these two countries argue against our theory?

Not at all. The theory lets us see this experience from a new perspective. As we recall from chapter 3, the basic logic of the theory implies that encompassing organizations face very different incentives than do narrow special-interest organizations (Implication 5). Sufficiently encompassing or inclusive special-interest organizations will internalize much of the cost of inefficient policies and accordingly have an incentive to redistribute income to themselves with the least possible social cost, and to give some weight to economic growth and to the interests of society as a whole. Sweden's and Norway's main special-interest organizations are highly encompassing, especially in comparison with those in Great Britain and the United States, and probably are more encompassing than those in any other developed democracies. For most of the postwar period, for example, practically all unionized manual workers in each of these countries have belonged to one great labor organization. The employers' organizations are similarly inclusive. As our theory predicts, Swedish labor leaders, at least, at times have been distinguished from their counterparts in many other countries by their advocacy of various growth-increasing policies, such as subsidies to labor mobility and retraining rather than subsidies to maintain employment in unprofitable firms, and by their tolerance of market forces.[25] Organized business in Sweden and Norway has apparently sought and certainly obtained fewer tariffs than its counterparts in many other developed countries. It is even conceivable that the partial integration for part of the postwar period of the Norwegian and Swedish labor organizations with the even more encompassing labor parties (on a basis that contrasts with corresponding situations in Great Britain) has at times accentuated the incentive to protect efficiency and growth,[26] although any definite statement here must await further research.

Why Sweden and Norway have especially encompassing organizations also needs to be explained. This task will in part be left for another publication,[27] but one hypothesis follows immediately from my basic theory: smaller groups are much more likely to organize spontaneously than large ones (Implication 3). This suggests that many relatively small special-interest organizations (for example, British and American craft unions) would be a legacy of early industrialization,[28] whereas special-interest organizations that are established later, partly in emulation of the experience of countries that had previously industrialized, could be as large as their sponsors or promoters could make them.[29] The improvement over time in transportation and communication and in the skills needed for large-scale organization could also make it feasible to organize larger organizations in more recent than in earlier times. Small and relatively homogeneous societies obviously would be more likely to have organizations that are relatively encompassing in relation to the society than would large and diverse societies.

It might seem that the gains from encompassing—as compared with narrow special-interest—organizations would ensure that there would be a tendency for such organizations to merge in every society, in much the way large firms come to dominate those industries in which large-scale production is most efficient. This is not necessarily the case. When there are large economies of scale, the owners of small firms usually can get more money by selling out to or merging with a larger firm and thereby can capture some of the gains from creating a firm of a more efficient scale. The leaders of a special-interest organization, by contrast, cannot get any of the gains that might result from the mergers that could create a more encompassing organization by "selling" their organization; a merger is indeed even likely to result in the elimination or demotion of some of the relevant leaders. There is, accordingly, no inexorable tendency for encompassing organizations to replace narrow ones.

Inclusive special-interest organizations, however, sometimes can break apart. There are significant conflicts of interest in any large group in any society. For example, these arise among firms in different industries or situations over government policies that harm some firms while helping others, or between strategically placed or powerful groups of workers and groups of workers with less independent bargaining power when uniform wage increases (or diminished wage differentials) are sought by an encompassing union.

As the discussion of Implication 5 pointed out, the extent to which a special-interest organization is encompassing affects the incentives it faces when seeking redistributions to its clients and when deciding whether to seek improvements in the efficiency of the society; but the link between incentives and policies is not perfect. A special-interest organization's leaders may be mistaken about what policies will best serve their clients; they may not immediately see the gains their clients will obtain from more rapid economic growth, for example, or may be mistaken about what policies will achieve such growth. Since, as chapter 2 pointed out, information about collective goods is itself a collective good, the chances of mistakes about such matters are perhaps greater than they are for firms or individuals dealing with private goods. And even if most of the firms in a market make mistaken decisions, one or more may make correct ones and these will accordingly profit, expand, and be imitated, so the errors before very long will be corrected. In a society with encompassing special-interest organizations, by contrast, there are not many entities making choices, and these may be *sui generis* organizations without direct competitors, so there may be no corrective mechanism apart from the reaction to the setbacks the society suffers. Thus there is no guarantee that encompassing organizations will always operate in ways consistent with the well-being of their societies, or that the societies with such organizations will necessarily always prosper.

Nonetheless, the society with encompassing special-interest organizations does have institutions that have some incentive to take the interest of society into account, so there is the possibility and perhaps the presumption that these institutions in fact generally do so. Sweden and Norway (and sometimes other countries, such as Austria) at times have been the beneficiaries of such behavior. There is not even the possibility that such behavior can be general among the narrow special-interest organizations and collusions that prevail in some other countries.

X

Since it achieved its independence, the United States has never been occupied by a foreign power. It has lived under the same democratic constitution for nearly two hundred years. Its special-interest organizations, moreover, are possibly less encompassing in relation to the economy as a whole than those in any other country. The United States has also been since World War II one of the slowest growing of the developed democracies.

In view of these facts, it is tempting to conclude that the experience of the United States provides additional evidence for the theory offered here. This conclusion is, however, premature, and probably also too simple. Different parts of the United States were settled at very different times, and thus some have had a much longer time to accumulate special-interest organizations than others. Some parts of the United States have enjoyed political stability and security from invasion for almost two centuries. By contrast, the South was not only defeated and devastated in the Civil War—and then subjected to federal occupation and "carpet-bagging"—but for a century had no definitive outcome to the struggle over racial policy that had been an ultimate cause of that war.

There are other complications that make it more difficult to see how well aggregate U.S. experience fits the theory offered here. The United States, like the other societies of recent settlement, has no direct legacy from the Middle Ages. The feudal pattern that seems to have left less of a mark on the chaotic Continent than on stable Britain has never even existed in the United States, or in most of the other societies settled in postmedieval times. Few of the earliest immigrants from Britain to the thirteen colonies were people of high social status, and it was often impossible to enforce feudal patterns of subordination, or to enforce contracts with indentured servants, on a frontier that sometimes offered a better livelihood to those who abandoned their masters. The social and cultural consequences of the non-feudal origins of American society were presumably enhanced by the relatively egalitarian initial distribution of income and wealth (except, of course, in the areas with slavery), which in turn must have owed something to the abundance of unused land. A vast variety of foreign observers, of whom Tocqueville is the best known, testified to this greater equality, and there is quantitative evidence as well that the inequality of wealth was less in the American colonies than in Britain.[30] This point has not been seriously disputed by historians (though there has been a good deal of disagreement about the timing and extent of the apparent increase in inequality sometime during the nineteenth century and about the estimates showing some reduction in inequality since the late 1920s).[31] The implication of the absence of a direct feudal inheritance and the unusually egalitarian beginnings of much of American society, according to the model developed earlier, is that the United States (and any areas of recent settlement with similar origins) should be predicted to be less class-conscious and less condescending toward business pursuits than are societies with a direct feudal inheritance, or at any event less than those with a feudal tradition and a long history of institutional stability.

Obviously, the United States and comparable countries can have no special-interest organizations or institutions with medieval origins. The theory predicts that countries that were settled after the medieval period, and that have enjoyed substantial periods of stability and immunity from invasion, would more nearly resemble Great Britain in their labor unions and in modern types of lobbying organizations than in any structural or cultural characteristics that had had medieval origins. It would also suggest that, other things being equal, the societies of recent settlement would have levels of income or rates of growth at least a trifle above those that would be predicted using only the length of time they had enjoyed political stability and immunity from invasion.

Just as it is hard to say exactly what growth performance the theory offered here would predict for the United States, so it is also difficult to say exactly how bad or good the country's growth performance has been. In at least most of the postwar period, the United States has had the highest per capita income of all major nations, partly because (at least in the earlier decades) it had a higher level of technology than other countries. This means that, at least for part of the postwar period, other countries have had the opportunity to catch up by adopting superior technologies used for some time in the United States, as well as the opportunity to adopt those developed in the current period, whereas in most industries in the United States any technical improvements could be only of the latter variety. Thus the U.S. growth rate should probably be adjusted upward for a fair test of the model offered here, but no one knows by just how much.

XI

The very fact that the United States is a large federation composed of different states, often with different histories and policies, makes it possible to test the theory against the experience of the separate states.

It is indeed doubly fortunate that such a test is possible, because it helps compensate for the fact there are only a handful of developed democracies with distinctive growth rates. As we shall see later, the theory offered here explains at least the most strikingly anomalous growth rates among the developed democracies, and no competing theory developed so far can do this. Although this is an important argument in favor of the present theory, my impression is that many readers of early drafts of the argument have been too easily convinced by it. Intellectual history tells us that there is a considerable susceptibility to new theories when the old ones are manifestly inadequate, and this is as it should be. Yet, just as it is understandable that a drowning man should grab at a straw, so it is also unhelpful. We should look skeptically at the theory offered here, however it may compare with the available alternatives. This skepticism is all the more important because of the aforementioned small number of developed democracies with distinctive growth rates. When the number of observations or data points is so small, it is always possible that the relative growth rates are what they are because of a series of special circumstances, and that these special circumstances have, simply by chance, produced a configuration of results that is in accord with what the theory predicts. The timing and gradual emergence of Britain's relatively low ranking in growth rates is somewhat reassuring, because special circumstances are unlikely to have generated the particular profile of relative growth rates observed over such a long period. So are Murrell's results in his comparison of old and new British and West German industries; since he compared so many industries, his results are almost certainly not due to chance. Nonetheless, there are so many ways in which the facts can mislead us that it is important to remain skeptical and to be thankful for the additional observations that can be obtained from the separate states (and from the other countries and developments to be considered in later chapters).

The number of observations is emphasized partly because it is so often neglected. It is neglected both by those who draw strong generalizations out of a few observations (for example, those who write of the "lessons" drawn from only one or two historical experiences), and also by those whose beliefs remain unaltered by even massive statistical evidence (for example, those who still doubt the compelling statistical evidence on the harmful effects of smoking). If prior reactions to earlier drafts are any guide, this book will probably illustrate both problems—a small number of dramatic illustrations will generate more belief in the theory than is warranted, whereas the statistical evidence will generate less conviction than it should. Psychologists have also shown through experiments that vivid or dramatic examples tend to be given more weight as evidence than they deserve, whereas extensive statistical evidence tends to be given less credence than is justified.[32]

Admittedly, one reason why statistical arguments sometimes fail to persuade is that different statistical methods may produce varying results, and investigators are suspected of choosing the method most favorable to their arguments. The range of statistical techniques available to the modern econometrician is so wide that the zealous advocate can often ''torture the data until it confesses.'' But I will in the following tests use only the most obvious and elementary procedures. A rudimentary approach is appropriate as a first step and also offers the reader a small degree of protection against the selection of methods favorable to the theory offered here.

Although the statistical methods that will be used are among the simplest, they may still seem forbidding to those readers who have never studied the principles of statistical inference. Partly in the interest of those readers, and partly to provide a guide to the statistical material that follows, I shall endeavor in the next three paragraphs to offer a glimpse of the statistical tests and findings in everyday language.

The theory here cannot say very much about state-to-state variations in economic growth in earlier periods of American history. One reason is that, until more recent times, even the oldest states had not been settled long enough to accumulate a great deal of special-interest organization, so such organizations could not have caused large variations in growth rates across states. Another reason is that until fairly recently the United States had frontier areas that were growing unusually rapidly, and it would bias any tests in favor of the theory offered here if the rapid growth of these frontier areas were attributed solely, or even mainly, to their lack of distributional coalitions; through most of American history the newer, more westerly areas have tended to grow more rapidly, and the center of gravity of the American economy has moved steadily in a westerly and southwesterly direction. This is entirely consistent with the theory but is due partly to other factors. Accordingly, the theory is most appropriately tested against recent experience; the following tests consider the period since World War II, and most often the period since the mid-1960s.

The statistical tests reveal that throughout the postwar period, and especially since the early 1960s, there has been a strong and systematic relationship between the length of time a state has been settled and its rate of growth of both per capita and total income. The relationship is negative—the longer a state has been settled and the longer the time it has had to accumulate special-interest groups, the slower its rate of growth. In the formerly Confederate states, the development of many types of special-interest groups has been severely limited by defeat in the Civil War, reconstruction, and racial turmoil and discrimination (which, until recently, practically ruled out black or racially integrated groups). The theory predicts that these states should accordingly be growing more rapidly than other states, and the statistical tests systematically and strongly confirm that this is the case. The theory also predicts that the recently settled states and those that suffered defeat and turmoil should have relatively less membership in special-interest organizations, and although comprehensive data on state-by-state membership in such organizations have not been found, the most pertinent available data again strongly support the theory. Moreover, as expected, the higher the rate of special-interest organization membership, the lower the rate of growth. All of the many statistical tests showed that the relationships are not only always in the expected direction, but virtually without exception were statistically significant as well. The statistical significance means that the results almost certainly are not due to chance, but it does not rule out the possibility that some obscure factor that happens to be correlated with the predictions of the theory could have made the results spurious. There is an independent tendency for relatively poorer states to catch up with relatively more prosperous ones, but the hypothesized relationships hold even when this tendency is taken into account. A variety of tests with other familiar or plausible hypotheses about regional growth show that these other hypotheses do not explain the data nearly as well as the present theory. Strongly significant as the statistical tests are, it is nonetheless clear that many other factors also importantly influence the relative rates of growth of different states. Accordingly, the theory here is not nearly sufficient to serve as a general explanation of differences in regional growth rates. There is also a need for massive historical and statistical studies (especially on the South) that would search for heretofore unrecognized sources of variation in regional growth rates and then take them into account along with the present theory. Only then could we rule out the possibility that there are obscure but systematic factors that somehow have happened to generate the pattern of results that the theory leads one to expect.

It is possible to follow the remaining chapters of this book even if one skips the rest of this chapter, but I hope that even readers who have never studied statistical inference will persevere. They will rarely find easier or more straightforward examples of statistical tests. And the evidence is important; it is not simply the experience of one country, but of forty-eight separate jurisdictions, each of which provides additional evidence.

XII

The statistics we are about to consider lend themselves especially well to straightforward treatment. The theory specifies a connection that goes primarily or entirely in one direction: the length of time an area has had stability should affect its rate of growth, but there is (for a first approximation) not much reason to suppose that the rate of growth of a region would on the whole greatly change the rate at which it accumulates distributional coalitions. On the one hand, a booming economy may make strikes and barriers to entry more advantageous, but on the other, adversity can give a threatened group a reason to organize to protect customary levels of income. This suggests that simple and straightforward tests (nonstructural regressions) should not only be sufficient, but perhaps even better than any more subtle method (such as a simultaneous equation specification) apparent now.

Since the theory predicts that the longer an area has had stable freedom of organization the more growth-retarding organizations it will accumulate, states that have been settled and politically organized the longest ought, other things being equal, to have the lowest rates of growth, except when defeat in war and instability such as occurred in the ex-Confederate states destroyed such organizations. The length of time a state has been settled and politically organized can roughly be measured by the number of years it has enjoyed statehood. Thus, if we exclude erstwhile members of the Confederacy, a simple regression between years since statehood and rates of growth should provide a preliminary test of our model.

If carried back into the nineteenth century, however, this test might be biased in favor of the model, since some states were then still being settled. The westward-moving frontier must have created disequilibria (the California gold rush might be the most dramatic example) with unusual rates of growth of total, if not per capita, income. The frontier is generally supposed to have disappeared by the end of the nineteenth century, but where agriculture and other industries oriented to natural resources are at issue, some disequilibria may have persisted into the present century. Thus, the more recent the period, the more likely that frontier effects are no longer present. In large part for this reason, we begin by looking at the years since 1965. Great disequilibria are unlikely three-quarters of a century after the frontier closed, especially since many of the great agricultural areas in most recently settled states suffered substantial exogenous depopulations during the agricultural depression of the 1920s, the dust bowl of the 1930s, and the massive postwar migration from farms to cities. The two newest states may, however, still be enjoying frontier or similar disequilibria and thus bias the results in favor of the theory, so we shall consider only the forty-eight contiguous states.

Another reason for concentrating on relatively recent experience arises from the ease of mobility of capital and labor within the United States. If the theory offered here is correct, there ought to be some migration of both firms and workers from those states with more distributional coalitions to those with fewer. The extent of this migration should be given by the extent of the *differential* in the degree of special-interest organization across states. There could not have been any substantial differential in the earliest periods of American history, but if the theory is right there should be significant differentials in more recent times. This will be explored more specifically later, but it is already evident that the states which the theory predicts should grow most rapidly should do so in periods when the differential in levels of special-interest organization across states is greatest.

The aforementioned regressions and a variety of other statistical tests were done with my former student Kwang Choi, who has undertaken more detailed inquiries that complement the present study, and are to be published separately.[33] We found that there is the hypothesized negative relationship between the number of years since statehood for all non-Confederate states and their current rates of economic growth, and that this relationship is statistically significant. This holds true for income from manufacturing only, for private nonfarm income, for personal income, and for labor and proprietors' income from all sources.*

In a country with no barriers to migration of workers, migration should *eventually* make real per capita incomes much the same everywhere, so the regressions use measures of total rather than per capita income as dependent variables. When the corresponding measures of growth of per capita income by state are used, however, the relationship remains negative and statistically significant.** Conceivably, the duration of statehood and political stability should not be measured on a ratio scale, and nonparametric tests focusing only on rank orders should be used instead, to guard against the possibility that the result might be an artifact of states at the far ends of the distribution or of other spurious intervals. Accordingly, Choi ran nonparametric tests on the same variables, and these equally supported the hypothesis derived from the theory.[34]

Happily, there is a separate test that can provide not only additional evidence but also insight into whether it is the duration of stable freedom of organization and collusion, rather than any lingering frontier effect, that explains the results. Several of the defeated Confederate

$$*LPI = 10.896 - 0.0160 \text{ STAHOD}$$
$$(1965-80) \quad (4.02) \quad R^2 = 0.32$$
$$PN = 11.699 - 0.0218 \text{ STAHOD}$$
$$(1965-78) \quad (6.25) \quad R^2 = 0.53$$

The first dependent variable, *LPI,* is the growth rate of income (but not transfer payments) received by labor or by proprietors, irrespective of source. The other, *PN,* measures only nonfarm income from private sources. STAHOD is years since statehood. The absolute value of the t statistic is given in parentheses beneath the coefficient. Unfortunately, there are no data on what proportion of the profits of corporations operating in more than one state were generated in each state, so both measures exclude undistributed corporate profits. There are data on dividends, interest, and rents received by state, but these factor payments will often have been generated by activity in states other than states where the recipient lived—indeed, if the most profitable corporations are in the fastest growth areas and their stockholders are dispersed across states in proportion to absolute levels of income, attributing dividends or other corporate profits to the state of the stockholder's residence will tend to understate the growth of production in the rapid-growth states. Corporate profits should vary roughly in accordance with wage and proprietary income by state. Thus *LPI* should be a better measure for testing the hypothesis here than any comprehensive measure of "national income" by state that could be estimated.

$$**PCLPI = 8.538 - 0.0060 \text{ STAHOD}$$
$$(3.19) \quad R^2 = 0.22$$
$$PCPN = 9.744 - 0.0142 \text{ STAHOD}$$
$$(6.24) \quad R^2 = 0.53$$

states were among the original thirteen colonies, so they are as far from frontier status as any parts of the United States, and, of course, all the Confederate states had achieved statehood by 1860. Yet the political stability of these Deep South states was profoundly interrupted by the Civil War and its aftermath, and even at times by conflicts and uncertainties about racial policies that were settled only with the civil rights and voting rights acts of 1964 and 1965. If the model proposed here is correct, the former Confederate states should have growth rates more akin to those of the newer western states than to the older northeastern states. Although we shall soon turn to earlier periods, we shall start with the southern rates of growth since 1965. In earlier years there were episodes of instability, lynchings, and other lawlessness that complicate the picture, but after the passage of the voting rights and civil rights acts there was clearly a definitive answer to the question of whether the South could have significantly different racial policies than the rest of the nation and unambiguous stability. In earlier years there is also the greater danger of the lingering frontier effects even in the South, so including it will not serve so well as protection against the possibility of these effects in the West; there is also a lesser differential in special-interest accumulation across states, not to mention other complexities. So we briefly postpone our consideration of earlier periods and ask if the former Confederate states have a higher average growth rate than the other states in the years since 1965.

They definitely do. The exponential growth rate for the ex-Confederate states is 9.37 percent for income from labor and proprietorships (LPI), and 9.55 percent for private nonfarm income (PN), whereas the corresponding figures are 8.12 percent and 8.19 percent for the thirty-seven states that were not in the Confederacy. If variations in growth rates are normally distributed, the probabilities that these two samples are from different populations can be calculated. Choi found that the difference in growth rates on this basis was statistically significant. A nonparametric test, the Mann-Whitney U-test, also indicated that the difference in average growth rates between the South and the rest of the United States was statistically significant. Again, this result holds true whether the growth of total or per capita income is at issue. These findings obviously argue in favor of the model offered in this book and should also allay any fears that regression results involving years since statehood for the non-Confederate states were due to any western frontier settlement that might have taken place since 1965.

XIII

Because the southern and western results are essentially the same and the parametric and nonparametric tests yield about the same results, it is reasonable to consider the data on all the forty-eight states together and use only standard ordinary-least-squares regression techniques. This has been done with the few score of Choi's regressions shown in the following tables. Although more elaborate tests might possibly produce different conclusions, the results are nonetheless remarkably clear and consistent.

As the results with the separate treatment of the South and the other states suggest, any regressions that use the year of statehood for the non-Confederate states to establish the earliest possible date for special-interest groups, and *any* year after the end of the Civil War to establish when the Confederate states came to have stable freedom of organization, will provide a statistically significant explanation of growth rates by state (table 4.1). Since organizations that could most directly constrain modern urban and industrial life have had more time to develop in states that have been urbanized longer, the level of urbanization in 1880 was also used as an independent variable. This variable again tends to have a significant negative influence on current growth rates. In combination with a dummy variable for defeat in the Civil War, it explains a fair amount of the variance, but it is apparently not as significant as the duration of freedom of organization. The same patterns hold for income from manufacturing, and for all of our broader measures of income as well, and apply whether total or per capita income is at issue.

The theory predicts that distributional coalitions should be more powerful in places that have had stable freedom of organization, so we can get an additional test of its validity by looking at the spatial distribution of the memberships of such organizations. The only special-interest organizations on which we have so far found state-by-state membership statistics are labor unions. In view of the widespread neglect of the parallels between labor unions and other special-interest organizations, it is important not to attribute all the losses caused by such organizations and collusions to labor unions. They are, however, certainly the most relevant organizations for studying income from manufacturing, and for reasons that will be explained later are appropriate for tests within a country in which manufacturers are free to move to wherever costs of production are lowest. In addition, many other types of distributional

Table 4.1. Determinants of Growth since 1965

(1)	$MFG = 12.6802 - 5.5427$ STACIV1 (7.34)	$R^2 = 0.54$
(2)	$LPI = 11.227 - 3.051$ STACIV1 (4.74)	$R^2 = 0.33$
(3)	$PN = 11.988 - 4.018$ STACIV1 (7.25)	$R^2 = 0.53$
(4)	$MFG = 11.5575 - 4.3148$ STACIV2 (6.89)	$R^2 = 0.51$
(5)	$LPI = 10.742 - 2.592$ STACIV2 (5.18)	$R^2 = 0.37$
(6)	$PN = 11.248 - 3.248$ STACIV2 (7.37)	$R^2 = 0.54$
(7)	$MFG = 10.5131 - 2.9334$ STACIV3 (5.60)	$R^2 = 0.41$
(8)	$LPI = 10.172 - 1.866$ STACIV3 (4.75)	$R^2 = 0.33$
(9)	$PN = 10.493 - 2.266$ STACIV3 (6.20)	$R^2 = 0.45$
(10)	$MFG = 10.2920 - 0.0626$ UR1880 (5.89)	$R^2 = 0.43$
(11)	$LPI = 9.796 - 0.029$ UR1880 (3.27)	$R^2 = 0.19$
(12)	$PN = 10.192 - 0.042$ UR1880 (5.22)	$R^2 = 0.37$
(13)	$MFG = 10.2450 + 0.1067$ CIVWAR $- 0.0616$ UR1880 (0.21) (5.25)	$R^2 = 0.43$
(14)	$LPI = 9.545 + 0.573$ CIVWAR $- 0.023$ UR1880 (1.39) (2.45)	$R^2 = 0.22$
(15)	$PN = 10.033 + 0.363$ CIVWAR $- 0.039$ UR1880 (0.96) (4.38)	$R^2 = 0.38$
(16)	$MFG = 12.2885 - 4.0418$ STACIV1 $- 0.0284$ UR1880 (4.17) (2.32)	$R^2 = 0.59$
(17)	$LPI = 11.141 - 2.722$ STACIV1 $- 0.006$ UR1880 (3.12) (0.56)	$R^2 = 0.33$
(18)	$PN = 11.776 - 3.206$ STACIV1 $- 0.015$ UR1880 (4.39) (1.66)	$R^2 = 0.56$
(19)	$MFG = 10.6865 - 1.6460$ STACIV3 $- 0.0397$ UR1880 (2.51) (2.92)	$R^2 = 0.50$

(*continued*)

Table 4.1. (*Continued*)

$$(20) \quad LPI = 10.198 \quad - \; 1.674 \; STACIV3 \; - \; 0.006 \; UR1880$$
$$(3.13) \qquad\qquad (0.53) \qquad R^2 = 0.33$$

$$(21) \quad PN = 10.581 \quad - \; 1.620 \; STACIV3 \; - \; 0.020 \; UR1880$$
$$(3.38) \qquad\qquad (2.01) \qquad R^2 = 0.50$$

$$(22) \; PCMFG = 10.7060 \; - \; 4.2147 \; STACIV1$$
$$(6.06) \qquad\qquad\qquad R^2 = 0.44$$

$$(23) \quad PCLPI = \; 8.833 \quad - \; 1.129 \; STACIV1$$
$$(3.95) \qquad\qquad\qquad R^2 = 0.25$$

$$(24) \quad PCPN = 10.014 \quad - \; 2.690 \; STACIV1$$
$$(7.02) \qquad\qquad\qquad R^2 = 0.52$$

$$(25) \; PCMFG = \; 9.0864 \; - \; 2.2829 \; STACIV3$$
$$(4.97) \qquad\qquad\qquad R^2 = 0.35$$

$$(26) \quad PCLPI = \; 8.495 \quad - \; 0.987 \; STACIV3$$
$$(5.50) \qquad\qquad\qquad R^2 = 0.40$$

$$(27) \quad PCPN = \; 9.067 \quad - \; 1.616 \; STACIV3$$
$$(6.79) \qquad\qquad\qquad R^2 = 0.50$$

$$(28) \; PCMFG = \; 9.0063 \; - \; 0.0529 \; UR1880$$
$$(5.96) \qquad\qquad\qquad R^2 = 0.44$$

$$(29) \quad PCLPI = \; 8.314 \quad - \; 0.016 \quad UR1880$$
$$(3.92) \qquad\qquad\qquad R^2 = 0.25$$

$$(30) \quad PCPN = \; 8.907 \quad - \; 0.033 \quad UR1880$$
$$(6.49) \qquad\qquad\qquad R^2 = 0.48$$

$$(31) \; PCMFG = \; 8.9810 \; + \; 0.0575 \; CIVWAR \; - \; 0.0523 \; UR1880$$
$$(0.14) \qquad\qquad (5.33) \qquad R^2 = 0.44$$

$$(32) \quad PCLPI = \; 8.103 \quad + \; 0.481 \; CIVWAR \; - \; 0.012 \; UR1880$$
$$(2.64) \qquad\qquad (2.74) \qquad R^2 = 0.35$$

$$(33) \quad PCPN = \; 8.769 \quad + \; 0.314 \; CIVWAR \; - \; 0.030 \; UR1880$$
$$(1.35) \qquad\qquad (5.44) \qquad R^2 = 0.50$$

NOTE: Explanation of and for the Variables Used in the Regressions

The absolute values of the *t* statistic are given in parentheses beneath the coefficients.

Statehood, Civil War, Length of Time:

CIVWAR: Dummy variable 1 for defeated (Confederate) states and 0 for non-Confederate states

YEAR: For Confederate—100

For non-Confederate—length of time since statehood

YEAR2: For Confederate—50

For non-Confederate—length of time since statehood

YEAR3: For Confederate—0

For non-Confederate—length of time since statehood

STACIV1 = YEAR/178   STACIV2 = YEAR2/178   STACIV3 = YEAR3/178

Table 4.1. (*Continued*)

178   = 1965–1787 (earliest year of statehood)
STAHOD: Years since statehood

SOURCE: Date of Statehood: Council of State Governors, *The Book of the States*, 1976; Civil War Information: Peter J. Parish, *The American Civil War* (New York: Holmes and Meier, 1975).

Growth Rates of Income:
  MFG: Exponential rate of growth of manufacturing income during 1965–1978
  LPI: Exponential rate of growth of income of labor and proprietors during 1965–80
  PN: Exponential rate of growth of private nonfarm income during 1965–1978
  PCLPI: Exponential rate of growth of per capita labor and proprietors' income during 1965–1980
  PCPN: Exponential rate of growth of per capita private nonfarm income during 1965–1978

SOURCE: Information from the Regional Economic Information System Branch, Bureau of Economic Analysis, U.S. Department of Commerce. These data have income by state of employment rather than state of residence, which is better for present purposes. Essentially the same results were obtained using published data on personal income from the *Survey of Current Business* and the *Statistical Abstract*.

Urbanization: UR1880 and UR1970: the percentage of people who resided in cities in the corresponding year.
SOURCE: U.S. Department of Commerce, Bureau of Census, *Historical Statistics of the U.S.—Colonial Times to 1970*, 1976.

coalitions, such as trade associations of manufacturers, are likely to obtain special-interest legislation or monopoly prices that can enrich the states in which they are located at the expense of the rest of the nation. Thus labor unions are the main organizations with negative effects on local growth, and their membership should also serve as a proxy measure of the strength of such other coalitions that are harmful to local growth.[35] We will nonetheless also consider the number of lawyers per 100,000 of population, on the debatable assumption that the need for lawyers would probably show *some* tendency to increase with the extent of lobbying and the complexity of legislation and regulation it brings about.

Table 4.2 suggests immediately that union membership as a percentage of nonagricultural employment is greatest in the states that have had stable freedom of organization longest. Urbanization in 1880 is also

Table 4.2. Special Interest Organizations

A. *Membership as Dependent Variable*

(1) UNON64 = 18.536 + 0.262 UR1880
               (3.64) R^2 = 0.22

(2) UNON70 = 18.842 + 0.212 UR1880
               (3.21) R^2 = 0.19

(3) UNON74 = 16.586 + 0.234 UR1880
               (3.79) R^2 = 0.24

(4) UNON64 = 9.820 + 0.223 UR1970
               (2.25) R^2 = 0.10

(5) UNON74 = 9.663 + 0.185 UR1970
               (2.16) R^2 = 0.09

(6) UNON64 = 22.924 − 9.974 CIVWAR + 0.167 UR1880
               (3.28)   (2.34) R^2 = 0.38

(7) UNON74 = 19.922 − 7.584 CIVWAR + 0.162 UR1880
               (2.82)   (2.57) R^2 = 0.35

(8) UNON64 = 17.687 − 11.780 CIVWAR + 0.143 UR1970
               (4.01)   (1.63) R^2 = 0.30

(9) UNON74 = 15.984 − 9.465 CIVWAR + 0.122 UR1970
               (1.55) R^2 = 0.29

(10) UNON64 = 12.107 + 0.104 STACIV1
               (3.06) R^2 = 0.17

(11) UNON64 = 12.178 + 0.114 STACIV2
               (4.36) R^2 = 0.32

(12) UNON64 = 15.441 + 0.094 STACIV3
               (5.19) R^2 = 0.37

(13) UNON74 = 14.044 + 0.081 STACIV3
               (5.19) R^2 = 0.37

a statistically significant predictor of union membership in the period
from 1964 on. Indeed, the crucial importance of the duration of freedom
of organization is shown by the fact that urbanization in the 1880s is a
better predictor of union membership in the 1960s and 1970s than
urbanization in 1970. The number of years of freedom of organization is
often an even better predictor. There is a similar connection between the
length of time a state has enjoyed political stability and the number of
lawyers, although this relationship is less strong and sometimes not
statistically significant.

Table 4.2. (*Continued*)

B. *Membership in Special-Interest Organizations and Growth*

(1)	MFG = 11.223	− 0.0953 UNON64		
		(4.49)		$R^2 = 0.31$
(2)	LPI = 10.420	− 0.053 UNON64		
		(3.22)		$R^2 = 0.18$
(3)	PN = 10.898	− 0.067 UNON64		
		(4.33)		$R^2 = 0.29$
(4)	MFG = 11.3033	− 0.102 UNON70		
		(4.19)		$R^2 = 0.28$
(5)	LPI = 10.525	− 0.058 UNON70		
		(3.20)		$R^2 = 0.18$
(6)	PN = 11.001	− 0.074 UNON70		
		(4.19)		$R^2 = 0.28$
(7)	PCMFG = 9.171	− 0.0773 UNON64		
		(4.28)		$R^2 = 0.29$
(8)	PCLPI = 8.703	− 0.031 UNON64		
		(4.18)		$R^2 = 0.27$
(9)	PCPN = 9.390	− 0.050 UNON64		
		(4.84)		$R^2 = 0.33$

NOTE: UNON64 and UNON70 are union memberships as a percentage of employees in nonagricultural establishments in 1964 and 1970.
SOURCE: Same as in table 4.1 and Bureau of Labor Statistics, U.S. Department of Labor, *Directory of National Unions and Employee Associations,* 1967 and 1971. Bureau of the Census, U.S. Department of Commerce, *Statistical Abstract of the United States,* 1976.

As the previous results and the theory suggest, there is also a statistically significant negative relationship between special-interest organization membership in 1964 and 1970 and rates of economic growth since 1965. This result holds for income from manufacturing and for all measures of income and for both total and per capita changes in those measures (table 4.2, part b). Thus there is not only statistically significant evidence of the connection between the duration of stable freedom of organization and growth rates predicted by our model, but also (at least as far as labor unions are concerned) distinct and statistically significant evidence that the process the model predicts is going on, that is, that the accumulation of special-interest organization is occurring, and that such organizations do, on balance, have the hypothesized negative effect on economic growth. A negative relationship between the proportion of lawyers and the rate of growth also is evident, but again this relationship is somewhat weaker.

XIV

A number of possible problems should be considered. One of these is that changing responses to climate may explain the results. The advances in airconditioning presumably have induced migration toward some of the more rapidly growing states (although other rapidly growing states in the Northwest are among the coldest in the country). Accordingly, Choi regressed the mean temperature for January for each state's principal city, and also the average temperature in the city over the entire year, against growth rates by state. These variables were positively correlated with growth rates, but usually less strongly than our measures of the length of time a state has had to acquire distributional coalitions.

Another possibility is that the rapidly growing states happened to contain the industries that have been growing most rapidly, and that such an accident of location explains our results. To test for this possibility, Choi regressed the rate of growth of ten major (one-digit) industries, and also a subclassification (two-digit) of eighteen manufacturing industries that existed in more than a score of states, against our measure of the time available in each state for the formation of special-interest groups. In all these industries but one (agricultural services, forestry, and fisheries), all or almost all of the signs were consistent with the theory, and in a large proportion of cases the results for each separate industry were statistically significant as well.[36]

A third possible problem is that the forty-eight states might be, for the purposes of the present argument, essentially three homogeneous regions—the South, the West, and the Northeast–Midwest. If that is true, we do not have forty-eight observations but only three, and thus too few for statistically significant results. To test for this possibility, Choi and I examined each of the three regions separately and also considered the thirty-seven non-Confederate states as a separate unit. The same pattern shows up within each region; the pattern is weak within the West and to some extent in the ex-Confederate states but very strong within the Northeast–Midwest region and for the thirty-seven non-Confederate states.

Still another possibility is that the results are a peculiarity of the recent past and considering a longer period would give different results. If we take the longest possible period, the whole of American history, we see a massive movement in a westerly (even somewhat southwesterly) direction. This movement has been greatly slowed at times by the rapid relative decline in agriculture (which abated only in the 1970s), but its existence and continued rapid pace long after the disappearance of the frontier is consistent with the theory.

XV

The picture in the South over the longer run, although it also appears in a general way consistent with the theory, is more complex and more difficult to sort out. If my highly preliminary investigation of southern history is at all correct, the first important special-interest coalitions that emerged in the South during and after Reconstruction were small, local, and white-only coalitions, sometimes without formal organization. All these small groups were by no means always against the advancement of the black population, but many were, and there was an undoubted susceptibility of the majority of the white southern population at that time to racist demagogues. The much weaker black population was in essence denied political organization and often the opportunity to vote through extra-legal coercion, which included at times widespread lynchings. The electoral consequence of the disproportion in organized power between the races and the susceptibility of the white population to racist appeals was the *gradual* emergence of the ''Jim Crow'' pattern of legalized segregation and racial subordination. This was apparently augmented by informal exclusion and repression by some of the white-only coalitions. Many have supposed that the segregationist patterns in the South emerged promptly after Reconstruction or even earlier, but the historian C. Vann Woodward has shown that decades passed before most of the Jim Crow legislation was passed and that it was in the twentieth century that this system reached its full severity.[37] In other words, the collective action of the white supremacists took some time to emerge in each of the many southern communities and states.

The low productivity of black sharecroppers predates the full development of the Jim Crow system and cannot be blamed entirely upon it. The causes of this low productivity and the widespread poverty of the black population after the Civil War are the subject of a vast and controversy-laden literature that this book could by no means resolve. Yet it is not on the surface astonishing that the deprivations of the black population under slavery, their lack of education and limited access to credit, and the vast and sudden change from the large-scale slave-plantation to small-scale independent sharecropping should have resulted in low productivity in black agriculture, and that this should have had adverse effects on the southern economy as a whole.

The lack of industrial development is another matter. Although I must postpone any conclusions for a separate publication that may emerge from some further research that I hope to do,[38] my very tentative hunch now is that many of the organized interests in many of the southern communities realized that any substantial outside investment or in-migration from the North would disrupt or at least endanger the Jim Crow system and the lattice of vested interests intertwined with it. There certainly was a lot of intensely agrarian, chauvinistic, anti-industrial, and anti-capitalist rhetoric for a long time in the South.[39] The large-scale efforts to attract business from afar, moreover, emerged mainly after the old system was already breaking down. Outside investors and potential in-migrants must at times also have been put off by the extra-legal violence and the uncertain stability of the system. The old pattern of coalitions in the South was eventually emasculated by New Deal and postwar federal policies, by cosmopolitan influences due to better communication and transportation, by increased black resistance, by adaptation to new technologies and methods of production, and perhaps by still other factors. These changes and a variety of favorable exogenous developments permitted rapid change and growth. A new pattern of coalitions, such as racially integrated labor unions, has begun to form in the South, but this new pattern of coalitions has been emerging only gradually, and thus has not had any massively adverse impact on economic development.

The tentative and heuristic character of the foregoing conjectures cannot be emphasized too strongly. Even if the foregoing speculation is largely correct, clearly it could be only one part of a complex and multicausal story. Another possible source, for example, of the increasing tempo of the southern (and western) growth in recent years is the growing relative importance of "footloose" industries. These industries, unlike the "resource-based" industries like iron and steel, and unlike the other heavy industries for which transportation costs are substantial, can locate in many different areas and thus can more easily avoid environments with inefficient institutional arrangements. High technology and other footloose light industries have become increasingly important in the United States in recent times. It is perhaps also significant that transportation costs have not been very significant for a long time in textiles; this was the first manufacturing industry of importance to move to the South.

As later chapters of this book should make clear, labor unions are often only a small part of the story of distributional coalitions, and sometimes not part of the story at all, but they are the most important coalitions where the migration of footloose manufacturing is concerned. The manufacturers, even if they are cartelized, will have lower profits if they face higher costs of production due to restrictive work rules or supracompetitive wages. If the theory offered in this book is right, the location of manufacturing activity, at least to the extent that the location of natural resources does not constrain it, should be influenced by differences in the strength of unions across areas. The most rapid growth of American labor unions began in 1937 and proceeded rapidly through World War II, so it is during the postwar period that differences in union strength across the states have been really important. Implication 6 suggests, moreover, that distributional coalitions cause more inefficiency when they are old than when they are first organized, because slow decision-making means that work rules become archaic after a long period of organization; only in the postwar period were there great differentials in the extent of mature unionism. A test of the present theory on the whole of the postwar experience is accordingly appropriate, especially for manufacturing output, and so we turn to this now.

The results, as we can see from table 4.3, are again strongly in favor of the theory. Separate regressions indicate that they also support the theory in each major part of the postwar period—before the mid-1960s as well as after. The relation is not as strong in early postwar years as it is later, however; it is also perhaps slightly less strong in the last few years, perhaps because the differential in union membership across states is diminishing somewhat.

XVI

The above tests focus on growth-retarding influences and assume that opportunities for growth in different states are randomly distributed.

Table 4.3. Growth Since World War II

A. *Value Added by Manufacturers, 1947–1977*

(1) VAM = 11.0097 − 4.8402 STACIV1
(7.07) $R^2 = 0.52$

(2) VAM = 10.1951 − 4.0375 STACIV2
(7.70) $R^2 = 0.56$

(3) VAM = 8.8613 − 0.0518 UR1880
(5.23) $R^2 = 0.37$

(4) VAM = 9.7758 − 0.0848 UNON64
(4.50) $R^2 = 0.31$

B. *Value Added by Manufacturers, 1947–1963*

(1) VAM = 9.5861 − 4.3589 STACIV1
(4.26) $R^2 = 0.28$

(2) VAM = 8.8401 − 3.6157 STACIV2
(4.47) $R^2 = 0.30$

(3) VAM = 7.6063 − 0.0447 UR1880
(3.24) $R^2 = 0.19$

(4) VAM = 7.9001 − 0.0528 UNON64
(1.99) $R^2 = 0.08$

C. *Total Personal Income, 1946–1978*

(1)   PI = 8.5767 − 1.8469 STACIV1
(3.25) $R^2 = 0.19$

(2)   PI = 8.3399 − 1.6609 STACIV2
(3.76) $R^2 = 0.24$

(3)   PI = 7.6575 − 0.0153 UR1880
(2.00) $R^2 = 0.08$

(4)   PI = 8.1406 − 0.0338 UNON64
(2.50) $R^2 = 0.12$

D. *Per Capita Personal Income, 1946–1978*

(1) PCPI = 8.3012 − 0.6911 STACIV1
(2.92) $R^2 = 0.16$

(2) PCPI = 8.4394 − 0.8618 STACIV2
(5.29) $R^2 = 0.38$

(3) PCPI = 8.1811 − 0.0123 UR1880
(4.52) $R^2 = 0.31$

(4) PCPI = 8.3574 − 0.0184 UNON64
(3.52) $R^2 = 0.21$

E. *Summary and Additional Regressions*

	Total Personal Income 1946–1978		Per Capita Income 1946–1978		Mfg. Value-Added 1963–1977		Mfg. Value-Added 1947–1977	
	t	R^2	t	R^2	t	R^2	t	R^2
STACIV1	3.25	0.19	2.92	0.16	6.03	0.44	7.07	0.52
STACIV2	3.76	0.24	5.29	0.38	6.54	0.48	7.70	0.56
STACIV3	3.65	0.22	6.56	0.48	5.82	0.42	6.68	0.49
UR1880	2.00	0.08	4.52	0.31	4.89	0.34	5.23	0.37
CIVWAR	1.62	0.13[a]	5.23	0.57	1.27	0.37	1.33	0.40
UR1880	1.21		3.07		3.99		4.26	
STACIV1	2.43	0.19	0.28	0.31	3.41	0.48	4.22	0.55
UR1880	0.06		3.15		1.76		1.73	
STACIV2	3.11	0.24	2.74	0.41	3.76	0.50	4.63	0.58
UR1880	0.67		1.46		1.24		1.14	
STACIV3	2.92	0.23	4.11	0.50	3.19	0.46	3.84	0.53
UR1880	0.37		1.11		1.82		1.83	
CIVWAR	3.30	0.25	7.10	0.54	5.16	0.50	6.58	0.63
STAHOD	3.02		2.15		5.72		7.05	
STAHOD	1.90	0.07	0	0	3.47	0.21	4.26	0.28
UNON64	2.50	0.12	3.52	0.21	5.87	0.43	4.50	0.31
UNON70	2.36	0.11	3.03	0.17	5.74	0.42	4.14	0.27

a. When there are two independent variables, the R^2 values appear on the lines between the two variables.

NOTE: Explanation of Variables

VAM: Exponential growth rate of value added by manufactures

PI: Exponential growth rate of total personal income

PCPI: Exponential growth rate of per capita personal income

SOURCE: Same as in table 4.1 and U.S. Department of Commerce, *Survey of Current Business,* April 1965, April 1967, and April 1981. Bureau of the Census, U.S. Department of Commerce, *1977 Census of Manufactures—General Summary,* April 1981.

There is, however, at least one systematic difference in the opportunities for growth across states. This difference arises because the economies in some states had not come close to exploiting the full potential of modern technology or of their own natural and human resources, at least at the beginning of the period of growth we are studying. The areas that have many unexploited opportunities can, other things being equal, grow faster than those that have very few, and thus we once again come upon the well-known hypothesis that poorer and technologically less advanced areas can grow faster, as they catch up, than richer and technologically more advanced areas.[40] I have argued elsewhere that the catch-up argument is a particularly congenial partner for the present theory and that there are sometimes severe specification problems if the two are not tested together.[41] Obviously the catch-up hypothesis cannot explain, for example, the differences between German and Japanese rates of growth, on the one hand, and British rates of growth, on the other. But it does not mean that the catch-up process was not operating;[42] its impact may have been obscured by stronger forces working in the opposite direction.

The forty-eight states provide a uniquely rich and comparable data base for testing the present theory and the catch-up model together. Choi has calculated how much the per capita income deviated, in terms of each of our measures of income, from the average for the forty-eight states in a given year. If the catch-up hypothesis is true, this deviation should then be negatively associated with the state's growth rate. In all the equations reported in table 4.4, the catch-up coefficient has the hypothesized negative sign, and in several regressions it has statistical significance as well. The catch-up factor appears to have less significance than the length of time a state has had to develop organizations pertinent to modern urban conditions,[43] but since the two theories are compatible, it would be absurd to reject one simply because it may have less significance than the other.

XVII

When we look at cities and metropolitan areas we see the same tendency for relative decline in the places that have had the longest time to accumulate special-interest groups. The best-known manifestation of this and of the ungovernability brought about by dense networks of such coalitions is the bankruptcy that New York City would have suffered in the absence of special loan guarantees from the federal government. Interestingly, Norman Macrae of the *Economist* was sufficiently impressed by the parallels between his own country and New York City that he wrote a section entitled "Little Britain in New York" in his book on the United States.[44] But New York is only a prototypical case.

Table 4.4. Growth with Catch-Up Variables Added

(1) MFG = 3.8973 + 9992.38 INVLPI
$\qquad$ (3.96) $\qquad$ $R^2 = 0.25$

(2) LPI = 7.03 + 4231.00 INVLPI
$\qquad$ (2.15) $\qquad$ $R^2 = 0.09$

(3) PN = 6.69 + 3848.44 INVPN
$\qquad$ (3.96) $\qquad$ $R^2 = 0.25$

(4) MFG = 8.4112 + 0.0025 DEVLPI
$\qquad$ (4.02) $\qquad$ $R^2 = 0.26$

(5) LPI = 8.92 − 0.0011 DEVLPI
$\qquad$ (2.37) $\qquad$ $R^2 = 0.11$

(6) PN = 8.83 − 0.0019 DEVPN
$\qquad$ (4.88) $\qquad$ $R^2 = 0.34$

(7) MFG = 8.8894 − 2.5009 STACIV3 + 2767.57 INVLPI
$\qquad$ (3.53) $\qquad$ (0.91) $\qquad$ $R^2 = 0.42$

(8) LPI = 11.41 − 2.196 STACIV3 − 2113.81 INVLPI
$\qquad$ (4.13) $\qquad$ (0.93) $\qquad$ $R^2 = 0.34$

(9) PN = 9.72 − 1.999 STACIV3 + 951.89 INVPN
$\qquad$ (4.20) $\qquad$ (0.88) $\qquad$ $R^2 = 0.46$

(10) MFG = 8.5228 − 0.0533 UR1880 + 3117.81 INVLPI
$\qquad$ (3.93) $\qquad$ (1.11) $\qquad$ $R^2 = 0.45$

(11) LPI = 9.37 − 0.0269 UR1880 + 746.11 INVLPI
$\qquad$ (2.34) $\qquad$ (0.31) $\qquad$ $R^2 = 0.19$

(12) PN = 9.03 − 0.0339 UR1880 + 1456.76 INVPN
$\qquad$ (3.21) $\qquad$ (1.26) $\qquad$ $R^2 = 0.39$

(13) MFG = 10.0981 − 2.4533 STACIV3 − 0.0008 DEVLPI
$\qquad$ (3.51) $\qquad$ (1.04) $\qquad$ $R^2 = 0.42$

(14) LPI = 10.34 − 2.0585 STACIV3 − 0.0003 DEVLPI
$\qquad$ (3.89) $\qquad$ (0.55) $\qquad$ $R^2 = 0.33$

(15) PN = 10.02 − 1.7219 STACIV3 − 0.0008 DEVPN
$\qquad$ (3.59) $\qquad$ (1.71) $\qquad$ $R^2 = 0.49$

(16) MFG = 9.9302 − 0.0531 UR1880 − 0.0008 DEVLPI
$\qquad$ (3.87) $\qquad$ (1.09) $\qquad$ $R^2 = 0.44$

(17) LPI = 9.65 − 0.0253 UR1880 − 0.0003 DEVLPI
$\qquad$ (2.17) $\qquad$ (0.53) $\qquad$ $R^2 = 0.19$

(18) PN = 9.63 − 0.0276 UR1880 − 0.0010 DEVPN
$\qquad$ (2.62) $\qquad$ (2.11) $\qquad$ $R^2 = 0.43$

(19) MFG = 7.9862 + 5088.80 INVLPI − 0.0671 UNON64
$\qquad$ (1.64) $\qquad$ (2.48) $\qquad$ $R^2 = 0.34$

(*continued*)

Table 4.4. (*Continued*)

(20)	LPI =	9.98	+ 687.38 INVLPI	− 0.0485 UNON64		
			(0.28)	(2.28)		$R^2 = 0.19$
(21)	PN =	8.72	+ 3421.65 INVPN	− 0.0487 UNON64		
			(1.49)	(2.43)		$R^2 = 0.32$

NOTE: Explanation of Variables

INVPN, INVLPI: Inverse of per capita private nonfarm income and labor and proprietors' income in 1965, respectively.

DEVPN, DEVLPI: Deviation of per capita private nonfarm income and labor and proprietors' income in 1965, respectively, from U.S. average in 1965.

SOURCE: Same as in table 4.1.

As Felix Rohatyn has pointed out, all the great cities to the north and east of a crescent extending from just south of Baltimore to just west of St. Louis and Milwaukee are in difficulty. In general, the newer cities of the South and the West are in incomparably better shape. Statistical tests like those used here have much the same success in explaining the relative growth of what the Census Bureau calls the "Standard Metropolitan Statistical Areas." The results also hold true when the biggest cities—which might perhaps be in decline because of crowding or lack of space—are omitted, and when the independent effect of city size is allowed for in other ways.[45]

Casual observation also suggests that the "older" manufacturing industries in the United States, such as the railway, steel, automobile, and farm machinery industries, are often in relative decline. Newer American industries, such as the computer, aircraft, and other high-technology industries, are doing much better. Because of the lack of any one unambiguous measure of industry age, statistical tests in this case are more difficult and problematic, and I have so far not attempted any. Peter Murrell, however, has looked at the pattern of exports of the United States and various other major trading countries and found that the pattern of comparative advantage exhibited by the U.S. economy resembles that of Britain more than that of Germany and Japan.[46] This is surely consistent with the hypothesis that the United States as well as Britain does relatively badly in older industries and heavy industries that are especially susceptible to oligopolistic collusion and unionization. No doubt other factors are also relevant, but the fact that wage rates in the troubled U.S. automobile and steel industries have been very much higher than the average wages in American manufacturing tends to confirm Murrell's hypothesis that the present theory is part of the explanation. I would also not be surprised if in these troubled industries there have also been excessive numbers of vice-presidents and other corporate bureaucrats with handsome perquisites.

XVIII

All the statistical tests that have been reported (and many others that have not been discussed in the interest of brevity) are consistent with the theory and almost all are statistically significant as well. In this complex, multicausal world, it is hard to see how the data could have fitted the theory much better. Still, the case is not yet compelling. Less elementary and straightforward tests, for example, might yield somewhat different results, or an alternative model that is inconsistent with the theory could produce still better results. Any alternative model should, however, also be tested against international and historical experience of the kind considered earlier in this chapter. As I argued in the first chapter, the presumption must be in favor of the theory that explains the most with the least, so a model that could not explain anything else but the growth experience of the states of the United States, or could not do so without losing its parsimony, is out of the running.

Partly because the credibility of a theory depends on how much it can explain (without losing parsimony) and partly because of its intrinsic interest, we shall present more evidence—much more. This evidence will relate to different countries and different historical periods. But the theory remains unchanged, so the later evidence will strengthen the argument made in this chapter in the same way that the evidence in this chapter adds strength to later results.

5

Jurisdictional Integration
and Foreign Trade

As we know from table 1.1, the original six members of the European
Economic Community have grown rapidly since World War II, particularly in comparison with Australia, New Zealand, the United Kingdom,
and the United States, and for some of the member countries the growth
was fastest in the 1960s when the Common Market was becoming
operational. Although I have offered some explanation of the most
anomalous or puzzling cases of rapid growth in Germany and France,
there has been no analysis of the rapid growth of the other four members
of the Six. Such an analysis is necessary not only to complete the
coverage of the developed democracies, but also to show that there was
a further factor contributing to the growth of France and Germany that
complements the explanation in the previous chapter. In addition, the
analysis of the Common Market will also help us to understand why
New Zealand's postwar growth performance has been about as poor as
that of the United Kingdom, and why Australia's growth has also been
unimpressive, especially in view of the valuable natural resources it has
discovered in the postwar period.

Looking at the timing of the growth of most of the Six, one is
tempted to conclude, as many casual observers have, that the Common
Market was responsible. This is *post hoc ergo propter hoc* reasoning
and we obviously cannot rely on it, especially in view of the fact that
most, if not all, of the careful quantitative studies indicate that the gains
from the Common Market were *very* small in relation to the increases in
income that the members enjoyed. The quantitative studies of the gains
from freer trade, like those of the losses from monopoly, usually show
far smaller effects than economists anticipated, and the calculations of

118

the gains from the Common Market fit the normal pattern. The studies of Edwin Truman and Mordechai Kreinen, for example, while maintaining that trade creation overwhelmed any trade diversion, imply that the Common Market added 2 percent or less to EEC manufacturing consumption.[1] Bela Balassa, moreover, argues that, taking economies of scale as well as other sources of gain from the Common Market into account, there was a "0.3 percentage point rise in the ratio of the annual increment of trade to that of GNP," which was probably "accompanied by a one-tenth of one percentage point increase in the growth rate. By 1965 the cumulative effect of the Common Market's establishment on the Gross National Product of the member countries would thus have reached one-half of one percent of GNP."[2] Careful studies by other skilled economists also suggest that the intuitive judgment that large customs unions can bring about substantial increases in the rate of growth is not supported by economists' typical comparative-static calculations.

II

There is a hint that there is more to the matter in the instances of remarkable economic growth in historical times discussed in chapter 1. The United States, we know, became the world's leading economy in the century or so after the adoption of its constitution. Germany similarly advanced from its status as a poor area in the first half of the nineteenth century to the point where it was, by the start of World War I, overtaking Britain, and this occurred after the formation of the Zollverein, or customs union, of most German-speaking areas and the political unification of Germany. Both situations, I shall argue, were similar to the Common Market because they shared three crucial features. These common features are sometimes overlooked because the conventional nomenclature calls attention to the differences between the formation of governments and of customs unions.

The Common Market created a large area within which there was something approaching free trade; it allowed relatively unrestricted movement of labor, capital, and firms within this larger area; and it shifted the authority for decisions about tariffs and certain other matters from the capitals of each of the six nations to the European Economic Community as a whole. When we consider these features, we immediately recognize that the creation of a new or larger country out of many smaller jurisdictions also includes each of these three fundamental features.

The establishment of the United States of America out of thirteen independent ex-colonies involved the creation of an area of free trade and factor mobility, as well as a shift in the institutions that made some of the governmental decisions. The adoption of the Constitution did, in fact, remove tariffs that New York had established against certain imports from Connecticut and New Jersey. Similarly, not only the Zollverein but also the creation of the German Reich itself included the same essential features. Until well into the nineteenth century, most of the German-speaking areas of Europe were separate principalities or city-states or other small jurisdictions with their own tariffs, barriers to mobility, and economic policies, but an expanding common market and a shift of some governmental powers resulted from the Zollverein, and even more from the formation of the German state, which was complete by 1871.

There was a much earlier development elsewhere in Europe that also created vastly larger markets, established far wider domains for factor mobility, and shifted the locus of governmental decision-making. The centralizing monarchs of England and France in the late fifteenth and sixteenth centuries tried to create nation-states out of the existing mosaic of parochial feudal fiefdoms; there had been nominal national kingdoms before, but the real power customarily rested with lords of various fiefs, or sometimes with virtually self-governing walled towns. Each of these mini-governments tended to have its own tolls and tariffs; a boat trip along the Rhine, where toll-collecting castles are sometimes only about a kilometer apart, is sufficient to remind one how numerous were local tolls in medieval Europe. The nationalizing monarchs, with their mercantilistic policies, strove to eliminate these local authorities and their restrictions and in turn imposed highly protectionist policies at the national level. In France many of the feudal tolls and restrictions to trade and factor mobility were not removed until the Revolution, but in Britain the creation of nationwide markets took place much more rapidly. Whether there was any causal connection or not, we know that the creation of effective national jurisdictions in Western Europe was followed by the commercial revolution, and in Britain ultimately by the Industrial Revolution.

In many respects, and possibly the most important ones, the creation of meaningful national governments is very different from the creation of customs unions, however effective the customs union might be. Nonetheless, in all the cases we have considered, a much wider area of relatively free trade was established, a similarly wide area of relatively free movement of factors of production was created, and the power to make at least some important decisions about economic policy was shifted to a new institution in a new location. There was in each case a considerable measure of what I shall call here *jurisdictional integration*. It would be much better if we could avoid coining a new phrase, especially such a ponderous one, but the familiar labels obscure the common features that concern us here.

Since there are several cases of jurisdictional integration followed by fairly rapid economic progress, it is now even more tempting to posit a causal connection. That would still be premature. For one thing, we should have some idea just how jurisdictional integration would bring about rapid growth, and statistical studies such as those cited above for the Common Market suggest that the gains from the freer trade are not nearly large enough to explain substantial economic growth. For another, the number of cases of jurisdictional integration is still not large enough to allow confident generalization. We must therefore look at the specific *patterns* of growth *within* jurisdictions as well as across them to see if they provide corroborating evidence. In addition, we must present a theoretical model that could explain why jurisdictional integration should have the observed effects.

III

One of the most remarkable and consistent patterns in the advancing economies of the West in the early modern period was the relative (and sometimes absolute) decline of many of what used to be the major cities. This decline of the major cities is paradoxical, for the single most important development moving the West ahead was surely the Industrial Revolution, and Western society today is probably more urbanized than any society in history. The commercial and industrial revolutions created new cities, or made great cities out of mere villages, instead of building upon the base of the larger existing medieval and early modern cities. Major capitals like London and Paris grew, of course, as administrative centers and as consumers of part of the new wealth, but they were by no means the sources of the growth. As the French economic historian Fernand Braudel pointed out, ''The towns were an example of deep-seated disequilibrium, asymmetrical growth, and irrational and unproductive investment on a nationwide scale. . . . These enormous urban formations are more linked to the past, to accomplished evolutions, faults and weaknesses of the societies and economies of the *Ancien Regime,* than to preparations for the future. . . . The obvious fact was that the capital cities would be present at the forthcoming industrial revolution in the role of spectators. Not London, but Manchester, Leeds, Glasgow, and innumerable small proletarian towns launched the new era."[3]

M. J. Daunton shows that, at least for Great Britain during the Industrial Revolution, Braudel was right. Of the six cities deemed to have been the largest in England in 1600, only Bristol, a port that profited from the economic growth, and London were among the top six in 1801. Manchester, Liverpool, Birmingham, and Leeds completed the list in 1801. York, the third largest city in 1600, was the seventeenth in 1801; Newcastle, the fifth largest city in 1600, was the fourteenth in 1801, as indicated by table 5.1.[4]

Even before 1601 there was concern about the "desolation of cytes and tounes." Charles Pythian-Adams's essay on "Urban Decay in Late Medieval England" argues from a mass of detailed, if scattered, figures and contemporary comments that the population and income of many English cities had begun to decline before the Black Death. Though Pythian-Adams finds that the decline of certain cities may be offset by the expansion of others, we are left wondering why so many towns declined while others grew. During the late fifteenth and early sixteenth centuries, and especially between 1520 and 1570, Pythian-Adams finds that most of the more important towns were "under pressure," if not in an "acute urban crisis," often involving significant loss of economic activity and population.[5]

On the Continent, towns were not so likely to be substantially autonomous institutions operating within relatively stable national boundaries. Partly because of this, and partly because the Continent did not experience the rapid changes of the Industrial Revolution until later, the situation there is not so striking. Nonetheless, there were many similar replacements of older urban centers with newer towns or rural industry. One example is the partial shift of the medieval woolen industry from the cities of Flanders to nearby Brabant and the decline of Flemish woolen production generally in relation to that of the North Italian cities, which in their turn declined as well. Another is the decline

Table 5.1. English Cities Ranked by Size

1600		1801	
Rank	Population	Rank	Population
1. London	250,000	1. London	960,000
2. Norwich	15,000	2. Manchester	84,000
3. York	12,000	3. Liverpool	78,000
4. Bristol	12,000	4. Birmingham	74,000
5. Newcastle	10,000	5. Bristol	64,000
6. Exeter	9,000	6. Leeds	53,000
		8. Norwich	37,000
		14. Newcastle	28,000
		17. York	16,000

of Naples, on the eve of the French Revolution probably Europe's fourth largest city. Domenico Sella concludes that "throughout Europe, none of the old centers of early capitalism (whether Antwerp or Venice, Amsterdam or Genoa, Bordeaux or Florence) played a leading role in the advent of modern industrialization." In seventeenth-century Spanish Lombardy, whose economy Sella studied in great detail, he finds that the cities "had few of the traits that we associate with modern industrialization and in fact some that were diametrically opposed to it. . . . The cities were thus clearly ill-suited to serve as the cradle of large-scale industrialization; far from being the vanguard of the modern economy, they must be viewed as anachronistic relics of a rapidly fading past. To find the harbingers of the modern economy, it is to the countryside that we must turn."[6] It was also commonplace that suburbs should grow at the expense of central cities.[7] A classic case is the decline of the central city of Aachen, which Herbert Kisch has chronicled in detail.[8]

IV

Medieval towns and cities were small by modern standards. Their boundaries usually were precisely defined by city walls and they often had a substantial degree of autonomy (and in some cases were independent of any larger government). Within these small jurisdictions there would be only a few merchants in any one line of commerce and only a limited number of skilled craftsmen in any one specialized craft, even if the population of the town was in the thousands. The primitive methods of transportation and the absence of safe and passable national road systems also tended to segment markets; a handful of merchants or skilled craftsmen could more easily secure a monopoly if they could cartelize local production. When the merchants in a given line of commerce had more wealth than the townspeople generally, it seems likely that they would have interacted with one another more often than with those of lesser means. To some extent, this also would have been true of skilled craftsmen.

The logic set out in chapter 2 implies that small groups have far greater opportunities to organize for collective action than large ones and suggests that, if other things are equal, there will be relatively more organization in small jurisdictions than in large ones. The logic also implies that small and homogeneous groups that interact socially also have the further advantage that social selective incentives will help them to organize for collective action. These considerations entailed Implication 3, that small groups are better and sooner organized than large ones. If the logic set out earlier was correct, it follows that the merchants in a given line of commerce and practitioners of particular skilled crafts in a medieval city would be especially well placed to organize collective action. If the city contained even a few thousand people, it is unlikely that the population as a whole could organize to counter such combinations, although in tiny villages the population would be small enough for this to occur.

V

The result of these favorable conditions for collective cartelistic action was, of course, the guilds. The guilds naturally endeavored to augment the advantages of their small numbers and social homogeneity with coercive civic power as well, and many of them did indeed influence, if not control, the towns in which they operated. This outcome was particularly likely in medieval England, where the national monarchies found it expedient to grant towns a substantial degree of autonomy. In what is now Germany, guilds would more often confront small principalities more jealous of their power and would need to work out symbiotic relationships with territorial rulers and the nobility. In France, especially, guilds would often be given monopoly privileges in return for special tax payments, in part because of the cost of wars and the limits on tax collections due to the administrative shortcomings of government. The city-states of North Italy extended well beyond the walls of the town, and in such cases the guilds would have a wider sphere of control if they shared power, but at the same time they were thereby exposed to instabilities in the North Italian environment that must sometimes have interrupted their development or curtailed their powers. In spite of all the variation from region to region, guilds of merchants and master craftsmen, and occasionally journeymen, became commonplace from Byzantium in the East to Britain in the West, and from the Hanseatic cities in the North to Italy in the South.

Although they provided insurance and social benefits for their members, the guilds were, above all, distributional coalitions that used monopoly power and often political power to serve their interests. As Implications 4 and 7 predicted, they also reduced economic efficiency and delayed technological innovation. The use of apprenticeship to control entry is demonstrated conclusively by the requirement in some guilds that a journeyman could become a master only upon the payment of a fee, by the rule in some guilds that apprentices and journeymen could not marry, and by the stipulation in other guilds that the son of a master need *not* serve the apprenticeship that was normally required. The myriad rules intended to keep one master from advancing significantly at the expense of others undoubtedly limited innovation. (Since masters owned capital and employed journeymen and apprentices, it is important not to confuse guilds of masters, or those of merchants, with labor unions—they usually are better regarded as business cartels.)

VI

What should be expected when there is jurisdictional integration in an environment of relatively autonomous cities with a dense network of guilds? Implication 2 indicated that the accumulation of special-interest organization occurs gradually in stable societies with *unchanged* borders. If the area over which trade can occur without tolls or restrictions is made much larger, a guild or any similar cartel will find that it controls only a small part of the total market. A monopoly of a small part of an integrated market is, of course, not a monopoly at all: people will not pay a monopoly price to a guild member if they can buy at a lower price from those outside the cartel. There is free movement of the factors of production within the integrated jurisdiction, providing an incentive for sellers to move into any community in the jurisdiction in which cartelization has brought higher prices. Jurisdictional integration also means that the political decisions are now made by different people in a different institutional setting at a location probably quite some distance away. In addition, the amount of political influence required to change the policy of the integrated jurisdiction will be vastly larger than the amount that was needed in the previous, relatively parochial jurisdictions. Sometimes the gains from jurisdictional integration were partly offset when financially pressed monarchs sold monopoly rights to guilds in return for special taxes, but in general the guilds lost both monopoly power and political influence when economically integrated, nationwide jurisdictions replaced local jurisdictions.

The level of transportation costs is also significant. If transportation costs are too high to make it worthwhile to transport a given product from one town to another, the jurisdictional integration should be less significant, even though there would still be a tendency for competing sellers to migrate to the cartelized locations in the integrated jurisdiction. The time of the commercial revolution was also a time of improved transportation, especially over water, which led to the development of new routes to Asia and the discovery of the New World. The growth in the power of central government also reduced the danger of travel from community to community by gradually eliminating the anarchic conflict among feudal lords and the extent of lawlessness in rural areas, and it brought road building and eventually the construction of canals. If the countryside is relatively safe from violence, not only is transportation cheaper but production may also take place wherever costs are lowest.

When jurisdictional integration occurs, new special-interest groups matching the scale of the larger jurisdiction will not immediately spring up, because, as we know from Implication 2, such coalitions emerge only gradually in stable situations. It will not, however, take small groups as long to organize as large ones (Implication 3). The great merchants involved in larger-scale trade, often over longer distances, were among the first groups to organize or collude on a national scale. They were often extremely successful; as Adam Smith pointed out, the influence of the "merchants" gave the great governments of Europe the policy of "mercantilism," which favored influential merchants and their allies at the expense of the rest of the nation. Often this involved severely protectionist policies that protected the influential merchants from foreign competitors—mercantilism is, to this day, nearly synonymous with protectionism.

It might seem, then, that the gains from jurisdictional integration in early modern Europe were brief and unimportant, since the mercantilist policies followed close on the heels of the decaying guilds in the towns. Not so. The reason is that tariffs and restrictions around a sizable nation are incomparably less serious than tariffs and restrictions around each town or fiefdom. Much of the trade will be *intra*national, whether the nation has tariffs at its borders or not, because of transport costs and the natural diversity of any large country. Restrictions at national borders do not have any direct effect on this trade, whereas trade restrictions around each town and fiefdom reduce or eliminate most of it. Moreover, as Adam Smith pointed out, "the division of labor is limited by the extent of the market," and thus the widening markets of the period of jurisdictional integration also made it possible to take advantage of economies of scale and specialization. Another way of thinking of the matter emerges when we realize that the shift of trade restrictions from a community level to a national level reduces the length of tariff barriers by a vast multiple. I believe the greatest reductions of trade restrictions in history have come from reducing the mileage rather than the height of trade restrictions.

VII

Since the commercial and the industrial revolutions took place during and after the extraordinary reduction in trade barriers and other guild restrictions and occurred overwhelmingly in new cities and suburbs relatively free of guilds, there appears to have been a causal connection. Yet both the timing of growth and the fact that guilds were regularly at the locations where the growth was obstructed could conceivably have been coincidences. Happily, there are additional aspects of the pattern of growth which suggest that this was not the case.

One of these is the "putting out system" in the textile industry, which was then the most important manufacturing industry. Under this remarkable system, merchants would travel all over the countryside to "put out" to individual families material that was to be spun or woven and then return at a later time to pick up the yarn or cloth. Clearly such a system required a lot of time, travel, and transaction costs. There were uncertainties about how much material had been left with each family and how much yarn or cloth could be made from it, and these uncertainties provoked haggling and disputes. The merchant also had the risk that the material he had put out would be stolen. Given the obvious disadvantages, we must ask why this system was used. The answer from any number of accounts is that this system, despite its disadvantages, was cheaper than production in towns controlled by guilds. There may have been some advantages of production scattered throughout the countryside, such as cheaper food for the workers, but this could not explain the tendency at the same time for production to expand in suburbs around the towns controlled by guilds. (Adam Smith said that "if you would have your work tolerably executed, it must be done in the suburbs, where the workmen have no exclusive privilege, having nothing but their character to depend upon, and you must then smuggle it into town as well as you can.")[9] Neither can any possible inherent advantages of manufacturing in scattered rural sites explain the objections of guilds to the production in the countryside; Flemish guilds, for example, even sent expeditions into the countryside to destroy the equipment of those to whom materials had been put out.

By and large there was more economic growth in the areas of early modern Europe with jurisdictional integration than in the areas with parochial restrictions, and the greatest growth in the areas that had experienced political upheaval as well as jurisdictional integration. Centralized government came early to England; it was the first nation to succeed in establishing a nationwide market relatively free of local trade restrictions. Though comprehensive quantitative evidence is lacking, the commercial revolution was by most accounts stronger in that country than in any other country except the Dutch Republic. In the seventeenth century, and even to an extent in the early eighteenth century, Britain suffered from civil war and political instability.[10] Undoubtedly the instability brought some destruction and waste and, in addition, discouraged long-run investment. But within a few decades after it became clear that stable and nationwide government had been re-established in Britain, the Industrial Revolution was under way. It is also generally accepted that there was much less restriction of enterprise of trade in mid-eighteenth century Britain than on most of the Continent, and for the most part probably better transportation as well.

Similarly, the Dutch economy enjoyed its Golden Age, and reached much the highest levels of development in seventeenth-century Europe, just after the United Provinces of the Netherlands succeeded in their struggle for independence from Spain. At least some guilds that had been strong in the Spanish period were emasculated, and guilds were not strong in most of the activities that were important to Dutch international trade.[11] As a lowland coastal nation with many canals and rivers, the Dutch enjoyed unusually easy transportation.

France apparently enjoyed very much less economic unification than did Great Britain; it did not eliminate many of its medieval trade restrictions until the French Revolution. Yet France did enjoy some jurisdictional integration well before the Revolution. Most notably under Louis XIV and Colbert, there was some economic unification and improvement of transportation. At the same time, Louis XIV, short of money for wars and other dissipations, often gave monopoly rights to guilds in return for special taxes, and a powerful special-interest group, the nobility, was generally able to avoid being taxed. Notwithstanding Colbert's tariff reforms, goods from some provinces of France were treated as though they came from foreign countries. Still, within the *cinq grosses fermes,* or five large tax farms, at least, there was a measure of unification; this area had a population as large as or larger than that of England. Thus France probably did not have as much parochial restriction of trade as the totally Balkanized German-speaking and Italian-speaking areas of Europe, and its economic performance also appears to have been better than that in those areas, however far short it fell of the Dutch and British achievement.[12] It was not until the second half of the nineteenth century that the German-speaking and Italian-speaking areas enjoyed much jurisdictional integration, and when that occurred these areas, and particularly Germany, also enjoyed substantial economic growth.

Of course, thousands of other factors were important in explaining the varying fortunes of the different parts of Europe, so it would be preposterous to offer the present argument as a monocausal explanation. It is, nonetheless, remarkable how well the theory fits the pattern of growth across different nations as well as the pattern of growth within countries.

In the United States, there was not only the constitutional provision mentioned earlier that prohibited separate states from imposing barriers to trade and factor mobility, but also more than a century of westward expansion. Any cartel or lobby in the United States before the present century had to face the fact that substantial new areas were regularly being added to the country. Competition could always come from these new areas, notwithstanding the high tariffs at the national level, and the new areas also increased the size of the polity, so that ever-larger coalitions would be needed either for cartelization or lobbying. Vast immigration also worked against cartelization of the labor market. In addition, the United States, like all frontier areas, could begin without a legacy of distributional coalitions and rigid social classes. In view of all these factors, the extraordinary achievement of the U.S. economy for a century and more after the adoption of the Constitution is not surprising.

VIII

The case with which we began, the rapid growth in the 1960s of the six nations that created the Common Market, also fits the pattern. The three largest of these countries—France, Germany, and Italy—had suffered a great deal of instability and invasion. This implied that they had relatively fewer special-interest organizations than they would otherwise have had, and often also more encompassing organizations. In France and Italy the labor unions did not have the resources or strength for sustained industrial action; in Germany the union structure growing out of the occupation was highly encompassing.

As Implication 3 tells us, small groups can organize more quickly and thoroughly than large groups, so even in the countries that had suffered the most turbulence those industries that had small numbers of large firms were likely to be organized. In Italy the Allied occupation had not been as thorough as it was elsewhere, and some industries remained organized from fascist times. In all the countries, organizations of substantial firms, which were often manufacturing firms, would frequently have an incentive to seek protection through tariffs, quotas, or other controls for their industry, and in at least some of these countries they were very likely to get it. Once imports could be excluded, the home market could also be profitably cartelized; as an old American adage tells us, "The tariff is the Mother of the Trust."[13] If foreign firms should seek to enter the country to compete with the domestic firms, the latter could play upon nationalistic sentiments to obtain exclusionary or discriminatory legislation against the multinationals. Sometimes, in some countries such as postwar Germany at the time of

Ludwig Erhard, there would, because of economic ideology or the interests of exporters, be some determined resistance to protectionist pressures, but in other countries like France and Italy in the years just before the creation of the Common Market the capacity or the inclination to resist these pressures was lacking.

In France and Italy and to some extent in most of the other countries, the coalitional structure and government policy insured that tariffs, quotas, exchange controls, and restrictions on foreign firms were the principal threat to economic efficiency. In France, for example, as Jean-François Hennart argues in ''The Political Economy of Comparative Growth Rates: The Case of France,''[14] exchange controls, quotas, and licenses had nearly closed off the French market from foreign competition; raw materials were often allocated by trade associations, and trade and professional associations fixed prices and allocated production in many important sectors. In such situations the losses from protectionism and the cartelization it facilitates could hardly have been small. If a Common Market could put the power to determine the level of protection and to set the rules about factor mobility and entry of foreign firms out of the reach of each nation's colluding firms, the economies in question could be relatively efficient. The smaller nations among the Six were different in several respects, but they would also gain greatly from freer trade, in part because their small size made protectionist policies more costly for them. Most of the founding members of the European Economic Community (EEC), then, were countries with coalitional structures, protectionist policies, or small sizes that made the Common Market especially useful to them. This would not so clearly have been the case if the Common Market had chosen very high tariff levels against the outside world, but the important Kennedy Round of tariff cuts insured that that did not happen.

It does not follow that every country that joins any institution called a common market will enjoy gains comparable to those obtained by most of the Six. Whether a nation gains from a customs union depends on many factors, including its prior levels of protection and (to a lesser extent) those of the customs union it joins. In the case of France and Italy, for example, the Common Market almost certainly meant more liberal policies for trade and factor mobility than these countries otherwise would have had. In the case of Great Britain, where the interests of organized exporters and the international financial community in the City of London have long been significant, the level of protection was perhaps not so high, and it is not obvious that joining the Common Market on balance liberalized British trade. When many high-tariff jurisdictions merge there is normally a great reduction in tariff barriers, even if the integrated jurisdiction has equally high tariffs, but a country with low tariffs already is getting most of the attainable gains from trade.

The coalitional structure of a society also makes a difference. In Britain the professions, government employees, and many firms (such as "High Street" or downtown retail merchants) that would have no foreign competition in any case are well-organized; joining the Common Market could not significantly undermine their organizations through freer trade, although a shift of decision-making to a larger jurisdiction could reduce their lobbying power. More foreign competition for manufacturing firms can reduce the power of unions, since manufacturers whose labor costs are far out of line must either cut back production or hold out for lower labor costs, but even here the influence is indirect and presumably not as significant as when imports directly undermine a cartel of manufacturing firms.

Common markets have even been tried in or proposed for developing countries with comparative advantage in the same goods and thus little reason to trade with one another, but this cannot promote growth. For these and other reasons, it is not possible to say whether a customs union will be good for a country's growth. One has to look at the prior level of protectionism, the coalitional structure, the potential gains from trade among the members, and still other factors in each individual case.

IX

The growth rates of Australia and New Zealand, we recall, were not greatly different from those of Britain. In spite of the exceptional endowments of natural resources in relation to population that these two countries possess, their levels of per capita income lately have fallen behind those of many crowded and resource-poor countries in Western Europe. If we examine the tariff levels of Australia and New Zealand in the spirit of the foregoing analysis of jurisdictional integration, and remember that these countries have also had relatively long histories of political stability and immunity from invasion, we obtain a new explanation of their poor growth performance.

There are problems in calculating average tariff levels for different countries. Tariffs on important commodities should receive greater weight than tariffs on minor commodities, but the importance of each commodity for a country cannot be determined by the amount of its imports, since the country would not import much of any commodity, however important, if its tariff against that commodity were sufficiently high. Fortunately, there have been some calculations of average tariff levels that determine the weight to be attributed to the tariff on each commodity by the magnitude of the trade in this commodity among all countries that are important in world trade. The latest such calculations that I have been able to find were prepared by the Office of the United States Trade Representative. These calculations have not previously been published; they are shown in the columns labeled "World Weights" in table 5.2. Unfortunately, the average tariff levels given in the table probably underestimate the true level of protection, for they take no account of quotas and other nontariff barriers and are based on what international trade theorists call the *nominal* rather than the *effective* rate of protection. The table is nonetheless an approximate guide to relative levels of protection on industrial products in the different countries. One reason is that nontariff barriers are generated by the same organizational and political forces as tariffs and in the developed nations, at least, seem to vary across countries in similar ways. It is probably also significant that the different types of calculations listed in different columns of table 5.2 show broadly similar results, as do earlier calculations by other institutions.

Table 5.2 shows that Australia and New Zealand—especially New Zealand—have far higher tariffs than any of the other countries described. Their levels of protection are two to three times the level in the EEC and the United States and four to five times as high as those of Sweden and Switzerland. As might be expected from the level of its tariffs, quotas on imports are also unusually important in New Zealand. The impact of protection levels that are uniquely high by the standards of the developed democracies is made even greater by the small size of Austrialian and New Zealand economies; larger economies such as those of the United States or Japan would not lose nearly as much per capita from the same level of protection as Australia and New Zealand do.

The theory offered in this book suggests that manufacturing firms and urban interests in Australia and New Zealand would have organized to seek protection. When this protection was attained, they would some-

Table 5.2. Average Industrial Tariff Levels

	No trade weighting:[a] simple average		Own country import weighting:[b]		"World" Weights[c]			
					Import weights on BTN aggregates[d]		Import weights on each BTN commodity[e]	
	1976 Ave.	Final[f] Ave.	1976 Ave.	Final Ave.	1976 Ave.	Final Ave.	1976 Ave.	Final Ave.
Australia								
Dutiable[g]	28.8	28.0	29.1	28.1	27.8	26.7	26.4	25.2
Total[h]	16.9	16.5	15.4	15.1	13.3	12.8	13.0	12.6
New Zealand								
Dutiable	31.4	28.3	28.6	25.5	33.0	30.4	30.2	27.5
Total	24.3	21.9	19.7	17.6	20.5	18.7	18.0	16.3
EEC								
Dutiable	8.8	6.0	9.8	7.2	9.5	7.0	9.6	7.1
Total	8.0	5.5	6.3	4.6	7.0	5.2	6.9	5.1
United States								
Dutiable	15.6	9.2	8.3	5.7	9.2	5.5	7.6	4.8
Total	14.8	8.8	6.2	4.3	7.1	4.1	5.6	3.5
Japan[i]								
Dutiable	8.1	6.2	6.9	4.9	8.0	5.7	7.9	5.5
Total	7.3	5.6	3.2	2.3	6.1	4.4	5.8	4.1
Canada								
Dutiable	13.7	7.8	13.1	8.9	12.0	7.3	12.9	8.3
Total	12.0	6.8	10.1	6.8	8.9	5.5	9.4	6.1
Austria								
Dutiable	14.2	9.8	18.8	14.5	15.9	12.0	17.0	13.3
Total	11.6	8.1	14.5	11.2	10.5	7.9	10.9	8.5
Finland								
Dutiable	17.0	14.6	11.6	9.2	11.2	9.0	11.5	9.1
Total	14.3	12.3	8.2	6.5	6.7	5.3	6.7	5.3
Norway								
Dutiable	11.1	8.2	10.5	8.0	10.2	7.4	10.0	7.5
Total	8.5	6.3	6.4	4.9	5.8	4.3	5.8	4.4
Sweden								
Dutiable	7.8	6.1	7.7	5.9	7.4	5.3	7.1	5.2
Total	6.2	4.9	6.3	4.8	4.6	3.3	4.5	3.3
Switzerland								
Dutiable	3.7	2.7	4.1	3.3	4.2	3.1	4.0	3.1
Total	3.7	2.7	4.0	3.2	3.3	2.4	3.2	2.4

times have been able to engage in oligopolistic or cartelistic practices that would not have been feasible with free trade. With high tariffs and limitations on domestic competition, firms could survive even if they paid more than competitive wages, so there was more scope for labor unions and greater gains from monopolizing labor than otherwise. Restrictions on Asian immigration would further facilitate cartelization of labor. Stability and immunity from invasion would ensure that few special-interest organizations would be eliminated, but more would be organized as time went on (Implication 2). The result would be that frontiers initially free of cartels and lobbies would eventually become highly organized, and economies that initially had exceptionally high per capita incomes would eventually fall behind the income levels of European countries with incomparably lower ratios of natural resources to population.

There is a need for detailed studies of the histories of Australia and New Zealand from this theoretical perspective. The histories of these countries, like any others, are undoubtedly complicated and no mono-causal explanation will do. Final judgment should wait for the specialized research. But preliminary investigation into Australia and New Zealand suggests that the theory fits these countries like a pair of gloves.

A comparison with Australia and New Zealand puts the British

Table 5.2. (*Continued*)

SOURCE: Dr. Harvey Bale, Office of the United States Trade Representative.

a. An average of tariff levels on the assumption that all commodities are of equal significance.

b. The relative weight attributed to each tariff is given by the imports of that commodity by that country.

c. The significance of each tariff determined by world imports of the commodity, or aggregate of commodities, to which the tariff applies. World imports are the imports of the countries listed and the EEC.

d. "BTN" means Brussels Tariff Nomenclature. The weight attributed to each tariff is given by the world imports of the BTN class of commodities in which it falls.

e. Each tariff weighted by world imports of that particular commodity—the maximum attainable disaggregation.

f. "Final" means after the Tokyo Round of tariff reductions.

g. Average tariff rates considering only those commodities on which tariffs are levied.

h. Average tariff levels of duty-free commodities as well as those to which duties apply.

i. Some anecdotal evidence, as well as casual impressions of the relatively high costs that Japanese consumers must pay for many imported goods, and the fact that agriculture tariffs are not included raise the question whether these figures may give the impression that the level of protection is lower than it actually is. This is a matter in need of further research.

economy in a more favorable light. The less restrictive trade policies that Great Britain has followed, presumably because of the importance of the organized power of industrial exporters and its free trade inheritance from the nineteenth century, probably mean that parts of its economy are open to more competition than corresponding sectors in Australia or New Zealand, notwithstanding Britain's still longer history of stability. Australia, like Britain, is an industrialized country with the overwhelming proportion of its work force in cities. But how many readers in competitive markets outside Australia and its environs have ever purchased an Australian manufactured product? Transport costs from Australia to the United States and Europe are high, but so are they high from Japan. Australia probably does not have comparative advantage in many kinds of manufactures, so we might not see many Australian manufactured goods even if Australia had different trade policies. Nonetheless, with a large part of Australia's healthy and well-educated population devoted to the production of a wide range of manufactured products, the paucity of sales of manufactures abroad is evidence of a serious misallocation of resources. British manufacturing exports, by contrast, are fairly common, although of diminishing relative significance. Social manifestations of distributional coalitions, on the other hand, are more serious in Britain, with its inheritance from feudal times, than in Australia or New Zealand.

The present argument also casts additional light on some other variations in economic performance. Consider Sweden and Switzerland, which have enjoyed somewhat higher per capita incomes than most European countries. As table 5.2 reveals, Sweden and Switzerland, and especially the latter, have had unusually low levels of protection. Note also that the Japanese economy grew more rapidly in the 1960s than in the 1950s, despite the fact that Japan could gain more from catching up by borrowing foreign technology in the earlier decade than the later. As Alfred Ho emphasizes in *Japan's Trade Liberalization in the 1960's*,[15] between 1960 and 1965 the Organization for Economic Cooperation and Development (OECD) "liberalization rate" measure for Japan improved from 41 percent to 93 percent. Finally, note that Germany, which considerably liberalized its economic policies before entering the Common Market, grew more rapidly in the 1950s than in the 1960s, in contrast to EEC partners like Belgium, France, and the Netherlands. Although again I want to emphasize that many different causes are normally involved, it is certainly not difficult to find instances in which freer trade is associated with growth and prosperity.

X

The paradox arising from the frequent association of freer trade (whether obtained through jurisdictional integration or by cutting tariff levels) and faster growth, and the skillful calculations suggesting that the gains from trade creation are relatively small, remains. Indeed, since we now have a wider array of cases where freer trade is associated with more rapid growth and several aspects of the patterns of growth suggest that the freer trade is connected with the growth, the paradox is heightened. If freer trade leads to more rapid growth, why does it not show up in the measures of the gains from the transactions that the trade liberalization allows to take place?

The reason is that there is a further advantage of freer trade that escapes the usual comparative-static measurements. It escapes these measurements because the gains are *not* direct gains of those who take part in the international transactions that the liberalization permitted, but *other* gains from increases in efficiency in the importing country— increases that are distinct from and additional to any that arise because of comparative advantage.

In the interest of readers who are not economists, it may be helpful to point out that the conventional case for freeing trade rests on the theory of comparative advantage. This theory goes back at least to David Ricardo, one of the giants on whose shoulders the economist is fortunate to stand. The theory of comparative advantage is lucidly and rigorously stated in many excellent textbooks, so there is no need here to go into it, or into certain exceptional circumstances that could make tariffs possibly advantageous. The literature on comparative advantage is so valuable and fascinating that it ought to be part of everyone's education. Only one point in that rich literature, however, is indispensable to what follows. This is the point that *differences in costs of production* drive the case for free trade because of comparative advantage. These differences are conventionally assumed to be due to differences in endowments of natural resources among countries, to the different proportions of other productive factors such as labor and capital in different economies, or to the economies of scale that sometimes result when different economies specialize in producing different products. If there is free trade among economies and transport costs are neglected, producers in each country will not produce a product if other countries with their different endowments of resources can produce it at lower cost. If each country produces only those goods it can produce at costs as low as or lower than those of other countries, there will be more production from the world's resources. A country that protects domestic producers from the competition of imports gives its consumers an incentive to buy from more costly domestic producers, and more resources are consumed by these producers. These resources would, in general, yield more valued output for the country if they were devoted to activities in which the country has a comparative advantage and the proceeds were used to buy imports; normally with freer trade a country could have more of all goods, or at least more of some without less of any others.

The argument offered here is different from the conventional argument for comparative advantage, although resonant with that argument. To demonstrate that there are gains from freer trade that do not rest on comparative advantage or differences in cost of production, let us look first at the case of a country that has comparative advantage in the production of a good and exports that good, but that also is subject to the accumulation of distributional coalitions described in Implication 2. Suppose that the exporters who produce the good in question succeed in creating an organization with the power to lobby and to cartelize. It might seem that the exporters would have no interest in getting a tariff on the commodity they export, since their comparative advantage ensures that there will not be lower-cost imports from abroad in any case. In fact, exporters often do not seek tariffs. To illuminate the logic of the matter, and also to cover an important, if untypical, class of cases, we must note that they might gain from a tariff. With a tariff they may be able to sell what they sell on the home market at a higher price by shifting more of their output to the world market (where the elasticity of demand is usually greater), because they do not affect the world price that much (in other words, the organized exporters engage in price discrimination and thereby obtain more revenue than before). Even though the country had, and by assumption continues to have, comparative advantage in producing the good in question, eliminating the tariff will still increase efficiency. The reason is that the tariff is necessary to the socially inefficient two-price system that the organized exporters have arranged. This example is sufficient to show gains from freer trade that do not flow from the theory of comparative advantage or differences in costs across countries, but rather from the constraints that free trade and factor mobility impose on special-interest groups.

To explore a far more important aspect of this matter, assume that a number of countries have comparative advantage in the same types of production. Their natural resources and relative factor endowments are by stipulation *exactly* the same, and there are by assumption no economies of scale. Suppose that these countries for any reason have high levels of protection and that they have been stable for a long while. Then, by Implication 2, they would each have accumulated a dense network of coalitions. These coalitions would, by Implication 4, have an incentive to try to redistribute income to their clients rather than to increase the efficiency of the society. Because of Implications 6, 7, 8, and 9, they will entail slower decision-making, less mobility of resources, higher social barriers, more regulation, and slower growth for their societies.

Now suppose the tariffs between these identical countries are eliminated. Let us assume, in order to insure that we can handle the toughest conceivable case, that even the extent of distributional coalitions is identical in each of these countries, so there is no case for trade even on grounds of what I might call "institutional comparative advantage." Even on these most difficult assumptions, however, the freeing of trade can make a vast contribution. We know from *The Logic of Collective Action* and from Implication 3 that it is more difficult to organize large groups than small ones. When there are no tariffs any cartel, to be effective, would have to include all the firms in all the countries in which production could take place (unless transport costs provide natural tariffs). So more firms or workers are needed to have an effective cartel. Differences of language and culture may also make international cartels more difficult to establish. With free trade among independent countries there is no way the coercive power of governments can be used to enforce the output restriction that cartels require. There is also no way to obtain special-interest legislation over the whole set of countries because there is no common government. Individual governments may still pass inefficient legislation for particular countries, but even this will be constrained if there is free movement of population and resources as well as free trade, since capital and labor will eventually move to jurisdictions with greater efficiency and higher incomes.

Given the difficulties of international cartelization, then, there will be for some time after the freeing of trade an opportunity for firms in each country to make a profit by selling in *other* countries at the high cartelized prices prevailing there. As firms—even if they continue to follow the cartel rules in their own country—undercut foreign cartels, all cartels fall. With the elimination of cartelization, the problems growing out of Implications 4, 6, 7, 8, and 9 diminish, efficiency improves, and the growth rate increases.

Economic theory, I have argued earlier, has been more like Newton's mechanics than Darwin's biology, and there is a need to add an evolutionary and historical approach. This also has been true of that part of economic theory called the theory of international trade. The traditional expositions of the theory of international trade that focus on the theory of comparative advantage are profound and valuable. The world would be a better place if they were more widely read. They also must be supplemented by theories of change over time of the kind that grew out of the analysis in chapter 3. The failure of the comparative-static calculations inspired by conventional theory to capture the increases in growth associated with freer trade is evidence that this is so.

XI

In the last chapter the question arose of what the policy implications of the present argument might be. Some commentators on early drafts of the argument had suggested that its main policy implication was that there should be revolution or other forms of instability. Concerned that ideological preconceptions, both left-wing and right-wing, would distort our reading of the facts and the logic, I belittled that conclusion and promised readers who thought it was the main policy implication of my argument that they were in for some surprises. Now that a gentler and more conventional policy prescription is close at hand, it may not frighten most readers away from the rest of the book to say that, yes, if one happens to be delicately balancing the arguments for and against revolution, the theory here does shift the balance marginally in the revolutionary direction.

Consider the French Revolution. It brought about an appalling amount of bloodshed and destruction and introduced or exacerbated divisions in French political life that weakened and troubled France for many generations, perhaps even to the present day. At the same time, if the theory offered here is correct, the Revolution undoubtedly destroyed some outdated feudal restrictions, coalitions, and classes that made France less efficient. To say that the present theory adds marginally to the case for revolution, however, is for many readers in many societies similar to saying that an advantage of a dangerous sport like hang gliding is that it reduces the probability that one will die of a lingering and painful disease like cancer; the argument is true, but far from sufficient to change the choice of people who are in their right minds.

Now that we are all, I hope, reminded of the overwhelming importance of other considerations in most cases, it should not be misleading to point out that this "revolutionary" implication of the present argument is not *always* of minor importance. We can now see more clearly that the contention of *some* conservatives that if social institutions have survived for a long time, they must necessarily be useful to the society, is wrong. We can also appreciate anew Thomas Jefferson's observation that "the tree of liberty must be refreshed from time to time with the blood of patriots and tyrants."[16] Let us now put this unduly dramatic matter aside and turn to a policy implication of vastly wider applicability.

The policy prescription is not in any way novel or revolutionary. Indeed, in keeping with my general emphasis on the contributions of my predecessors and professional colleagues, I would say that this policy recommendation has been shared by nearly every scholar of stature who has given the matter specialized thought. The recommendation unfortunately has far more often than not been ignored, and when it has been taken into account it almost always has been followed only to a limited degree. The policy implication, as readers of this chapter have long foreseen, is that there should be freer trade and fewer impediments to the free movement of factors of production and of firms.

Any readers who doubt that this policy recommendation has more often than not been ignored should note that most of the great examples of the freeing of trade and factor mobility have come about not because the recommendations of economists were followed, but wholly or largely as an incidental consequence of policies with other objectives. I have attempted to show in this chapter that the most notable reductions in barriers to the flow of products and productive factors have been reductions in the length rather than in the height of barriers—that they have resulted from jurisdictional integration. The jurisdictional integration brought about by the centralizing monarchs of early modern Europe was not inspired by liberal teaching, but by the monarchs' lusts for power and pelf. The jurisdictional integration of the United States and Germany owed more to nationalistic, political, and military considerations than to economic understanding; the mainly inadvertent character of the massive liberalization these two countries brought about is proven by the tariffs, trusts, and cartels they accepted at a national level. Even the creation of the Common Market owed more to fears of Soviet imperialism, to a desire to insure that there would not be yet another Franco-German war, and to imitation of and uneasiness about the United States, than it did to a rigorous analysis of the gains from freer trade and factor mobility. Specialists have long known that a country could get most or all of the gains from freer trade without joining a customs union simply by reducing its own barriers unilaterally, and would indeed often gain much more from this than from joining a customs union. Unilateral tariff reductions are nonetheless rare.

Although the textbooks explain the other reasons for liberal or internationalist policies, such policies can draw additional support from the theory offered here, because free trade and factor movement evade and undercut distributional coalitions. If there is free international trade, there are international markets out of the control of any lobbies. The way in which free trade undermines cartelization of firms, and indirectly also reduces monopoly power in the labor market, has already been discussed. Free movement of productive factors and firms is no less subversive of distributional coalitions. If local entrepreneurs are free to sell equities without constraint to foreigners as well as to borrow abroad, those with less wealth or inferior connections at home will be better able to get the capital needed for competition with established firms, and may even be able to marshall enough resources to break into collusive oligopolies of large firms in industries where there are substantial economies of scale. If foreign or multinational firms are welcome to enter a country to produce and compete on an equal basis with local firms, they will not only often bring new ideas with them but also make the local market more competitive and perhaps destroy a cartel as well. That is one reason why they are usually so unpopular—the consumers who freely choose to buy their goods and the workers who choose to accept the new jobs they offer do not lose from the entry of the multinationals, but these consumers and workers may be persuaded that this foreign entry is undesirable by the propaganda of those who do.

The resistance to labor mobility across national borders has a similar inspiration. Whereas rapid and massive immigration obviously can generate social tensions and other costs, these costs are not the only reason for the barriers against foreign labor. The restrictions on immigration and guest workers in many countries and communities are promoted mainly by special-interest organizations representing the groups of workers who have to compete with the in-migrants; labor unions obtain limitations on the inflow of manual workers, medical societies impose stricter qualifying examinations for foreign-trained physicians, and so on. The separate states of the United States, for example, not only control admission into most professions, but often also into such diverse occupations as cosmetology, barbering, acupuncture, and light-ning-rod salesmen. These controls are frequently used to keep out practitioners from other states. The nations of Western Europe also vary greatly in the proportion of migrants and guest workers they have admitted. Many other factors are involved, but the initial impression is that countries with weaker labor unions have accepted relatively larger inflows of labor.

The law of diminishing returns suggests that the growth of income per capita or per worker would be reduced when an already densely populated country imports more labor. However, as Charles Kindleberger has argued,[17] the developed industrial economies in which per capita income has grown most rapidly are often those which have absorbed the most new labor. Kindleberger explains this in terms of Arthur Lewis's famous model of growth with "unlimited supplies of labor," and this hypothesis deserves careful study.

Another part of the explanation is that the size of the inflow of labor affects the strength of special-interest groups of workers. If a large pool of less expensive foreign labor may easily be tapped, and unions have significantly raised labor costs for domestic firms, then it will be profitable to set up new firms or establishments employing the outside labor. The competition of these new undertakings will in turn reduce the gains from monopoly over the labor force in the old establishments. Union co-optation of the outside workers will be at least delayed by cultural and linguistic differences or by the temporary status of guest workers. Similar freedom of entry for foreign professionals, of course, will undermine the cartelization that is characteristic of professions.

We are finally in a position to assess the ad hoc argument that Britain's economic plight is due to its trade unions. This argument is in part profoundly wrong, and in part right and important. It is profoundly wrong because combinations of firms (being fewer in number) can and often do collude in their common interest more than larger numbers of employees can. The ad hoc anti-union argument also overlooks the professions, whose cartelization is generally older, and probably more costly to British society per person involved, than the average union. It also neglects the class structure and the anti-entrepreneurial and anti-business attitudes which grow in large part out of the same logic and history that underlie the British pattern of trade unions.

Despite its shortcomings, the blame-it-on-the-unions argument does have one important merit (if the professional associations are counted as unions). That arises because the net migration of labor into the United Kingdom has been relatively modest and was quickly restricted when it promised to become great (as was the case with Commonwealth immigrants from South Asia and the Caribbean). If we take a long-run or historical view, we can probably conclude that, relative to many other countries, Britain has not had especially high levels of protection or unusually restrictive legislation against foreign capital or multinational firms. Postwar multilateral tariff-cutting agreements, the Common Market, and falling transport costs have brought about a substantial increase in international trade. Thus many firms that export or that compete with importers are denied most of the gains from collusion, except in those cases where they have been able to form international cartels. The firms that provide international financial and insurance services in the City, for example, must be roughly as efficient as the foreigners with which they compete. This suggests that the British disease is most serious for goods and services and factors of production that do not face foreign competition and are at the same time in a situation where they are susceptible to organization for collective action. Those major "High Street" merchants who resist suburban shopping centers and hyper-markets, for example, can lobby and collude without any real fear that their customers will go overseas to shop. Thus relatively parochial industries and services, construction, government, the professions, and (as the ad hoc argument states) the unions probably account for a large share of the inefficiencies in the British economy. Since wages absorb most of the national income and much of British labor is organized, the unions also have great quantitative significance.

Unfortunately, as British experience in the late nineteenth and early twentieth centuries shows, free trade alone is not enough. Even in combination with free factor mobility it would not come close to being a panacea or complete solution. Freedom of trade and of factor mobility have to be used in combination with other policies to reduce or countervail cartelization and lobbying. But even with other policies, there are no total or permanent cures. This is because the distributional coalitions have the incentive and often also the power to prevent changes that would deprive them of their enlarged share of the social output. To borrow an evocative phrase from Marx, there is an "internal contradiction" in the development of stable societies. This is not the contradiction[18] that Marx claimed to have found, but rather an inherent conflict between the colossal economic and political advantages of peace and stability and the longer-term losses that come from the accumulating networks of distributional coalitions that can survive only in stable environments.

6

Inequality, Discrimination, and Development

When testing any theory, it is by no means enough to find a few cases that seem to support it. If the predictions of the theory apply to a large number of cases and only a small number of those cases are discussed, then there is always the possibility that only those cases that happen to be consistent with the theory have been considered and that a thorough analysis of the available evidence would indicate that the theory was false. Unfortunately, the present theory has implications for such an incredibly wide array of phenomena in different countries and historical periods that a thorough and meticulous testing is out of the question here. It would not only make this book impossibly long, but it would also require vastly more knowledge than I have or could hope to acquire. There is, however, protection against the possibility that I have considered only unrepresentative cases in the fact that we have looked at the growth rates of *all* of the developed democracies in the years since regular estimates of national income were first prepared, shortly after World War II (see table 1.1, p. 6 above). Thus, so far as the postwar developed democracies are concerned, there is no possibility that only those cases that happen to fit the theory have been considered. It may be a matter of dispute whether the theory is consistent with all of the major variations in growth rates in this subset or just with most of them, but since the importance of other causal factors is emphasized, there is *some* support for the theory in the postwar experience of the developed democracies on even the most skeptical reading of this evidence.

It is, on the other hand, still possible that the developed democracies since the war are unrepresentative in ways that are crucial to deciding what claim to credence, if any, the theory has. One real possibility is that the data on these countries fit the argument purely by chance, although the collateral evidence on industry comparisons and temporal patterns of growth and the mass of corroborative data on the forty-eight states make this extraordinarily unlikely. Another possibility is that there is some altogether different causal mechanism operating that has much the same results as the theory here predicts. A third possibility is that the theory is true or largely true for these countries but does not apply to other types of societies, such as the developing nations or the communist countries.

There is some protection against all these possibilities in the way the theory appears to fit the experience of Britain, Holland, and France in the early modern period, the patterns of growth within European countries in that period, and the growth of the United States and Germany in the nineteenth century. Indeed, as we shall see in the last chapter, the theory is consistent with some dramatic features of the interwar period also, so the claim that it fits the most striking departures from normal economic experience among the nations of the West since the late Middle Ages has some basis.

No matter how much additional evidence might substantiate the findings on the developed democracies and on the modern economic history of the West, it still would not support compelling conclusions about non-Western societies (except perhaps Japan). Possibly different causal processes are operating in non-Western areas. Erudite scholars like Max Weber have argued that certain features of Western European christendom, and especially of puritanism, were uniquely favorable to capitalism and economic progress. Although the historical support for Weber's fascinating argument is at best mixed, we must ask whether the coalitional processes described in this book are dependent on certain cultural or religious attitudes and confined more or less to Western civilization. We should not conclude that the same tendencies are at work in other civilizations unless there is evidence of similar coalitional processes in several other cultural traditions.

II

There is, in fact, massive evidence of coalitional processes in a variety of non-Western societies. There have been guilds, for example, in Moslem countries (and even in Mecca),[1] in Byzantium, in China, in Hellenistic times, and even in Babylonia.[2] These guilds, moreover, bear the same dead-giveaway signs of cartelistic purposes: restrictive membership, price-fixing, long apprenticeships from which the sons or relatives of members are often exempt, and rules limiting output and innovation. As might be expected from the many modern studies finding similar motivations and responses to prices and profit opportunities in developed and developing nations,[3] the eager acceptance of the gains from cartelization and political power seems much the same in very different cultural and religious traditions. Whereas those parts of the world that have never developed very far cannot show us quite the contrasts that European economic history offers, it is still clear that guilds and other distributional coalitions have normally had the same harmful effects on economic efficiency and growth, whatever the culture.

The Chinese economy in the latter part of the nineteenth century offers a good example. Even though some guilds had been destroyed in the instability associated with the Taiping rebellion in the mid-nineteenth century, guilds were powerful, especially in the latter part of the century. Hosea Ballou Morse, a leading scholar on China (and Commissioner of Chinese Maritime Customs for a time during the "treaty ports" period), wrote in *The Guilds of China* (1909) that "all Chinese trade guilds are alike in interfering with every detail of business and demanding complete solidarity of interest of their members, and they are alike also in that their rules are not a dead letter, but are actually enforced. The result is tyranny of the many over the individual, and a system of control which must by its nature hinder freedom of enterprise and independence of individual initiative."[4]

Some economists argue that there cannot be much monopoly or cartelistic power unless the coercive power of government is brought into play, but Chinese guilds provide unusually clear evidence that this view is wrong. There were, to be sure, symbiotic relations between guilds and government officials in which the coercive power of government was brought to bear in the common interests of the guild and the officials. Nonetheless, as Morse stated it, "The trade guilds have grown up apart from and independent of the government; they . . . devised their own regulations, and enforced them in their own way and by their own methods."[5] He argued that Chinese guilds could enforce their regulations.

> Partly because of the enormous impulsive power of a mediaeval form of public opinion and the development of the boycott by

centuries of practical use, the guilds have in fact obtained an enormous and almost unrestrained control over their respective
trades. . . . Their jurisdiction over their members is absolute, not
by reason of any charter or delegated power, but by virtue of the
faculty of combination by the community and of coercion on the
individual. . . . The craftsman who is not a guild member is as one
exposed to the wintry blast without a cloak.[6]

Even individual appeals to the government on matters of interest to the
guild were excluded, unless the guild had first considered the matter.
Another observer, Daniel J. Macgowan, cites guild rules specifying that
if a "complainant have recourse to the [government] official direct,
without first referring to the guild, he shall be subject to a public
reprimand, and any future case he may present for the opinion of the
guild will be dismissed without a hearing."[7]

Guild power could be used even *against* the government. There is
a ghastly illustration of this in Macgowan's reports of the gold beaters
guild, which provided gold leaf that the emperor purchased in large
quantities. The rule of the trade was that no employer could have more
than one apprentice at a time, but one member of the craft represented to
the magistrate that, if he were allowed to take on a number of apprentices, the work would be expedited. He received permission to do so
and engaged a great many apprentices. This output-increasing, price-
reducing conduct infuriated the craft. The word was passed around that
"biting to death is not a capital offence," apparently on the gruesome
theory that no one of the morsels taken is fatal, and the cartel-buster was
soon dead from the fiendish efforts of 123 of his fellows.[8] None of the
guild members was allowed to leave the shop until his teeth and gums
attested to what, in more delicate settings, might be called his "professional ethics." Although the man who took the first bite was, it turns
out, discovered and executed, one can well imagine that the squeamish,
at least, must have been made apprehensive about increasing output or
cutting prices, even when the emperor was the buyer.

The effect of guilds was no doubt increased by the fact that China,
ostensibly a unified nation, had tariffs or transit taxes on trade within
the country.[9] In addition, there was effectively a prohibition against
foreign trade (because all imports had to go through a single guild in
Canton), until the Western powers imposed treaties on the Chinese that
opened certain ports and commercial opportunities to foreigners. After
these treaties there were many efforts to introduce various types of

production with modern Western technology, many of which were defeated by boycotts or governmental discouragements organized by guilds of competitors. Guilds blocked or delayed the use of modern technologies in silk reeling, coal mining, soybean-oil pressing, steamboat transportation, and railways, for example. Chinese as well as foreign businessmen were discouraged from investing in new technologies, and the most successful Chinese businessmen were concentrated in the treaty port cities under European jurisdiction.[10]

China, though possessed of an extraordinarily ancient and rich culture, did not of course industrialize. Only a few decades ago it was often taken for granted, even by the most erudite and sympathetic observers, that something in the Chinese spirit or culture was inherently unsuited to modern economic life.[11] This is nearly the opposite of the conventional wisdom now. In the last three decades the most rapidly growing areas in the world have been Chinese or profoundly influenced by Chinese culture. Consider the communities that I. M. D. Little has called the "gang of four": Hong Kong, Korea, Taiwan, and Singapore. All four, it is worth noting, have recent histories that have been inimical to the development of distributional coalitions and have had relatively liberal trade policies as well. Korea and Taiwan did not have the freedom to develop independent interest groups while they were colonies of Japan, Singapore had little to gain from lobbies when it was run by Britain, and Hong Kong is still a colony run along nineteenth-century British free-trade lines.[12]

III

Western observers usually greatly underestimate the differences between Chinese and Japanese cultures, but Japan can nonetheless also be considered an area that has been profoundly influenced by Chinese culture. The rapid growth of Japan since World War II has already been analyzed, but there is also the exceptional growth Japan enjoyed for a couple of generations after the Meiji restoration in 1867–68. This earlier phase of Japanese growth also stands in sharp contrast to what occurred in China, and for that matter to what happened at that time in all other non-Western areas of the world.

Many accounts of Japanese growth attribute it mainly to special characteristics of the Japanese culture or people. The Japanese were not, however, always considered economic supermen. Western visitors in the mid-nineteenth century were often struck with the utter poverty of the people and even with the number of families that were reduced to infanticide. Although the rate of literacy was quite high by the standards of poor societies at that time, and the society had been progressing in certain respects,[13] it was pathetically weak both technologically and militarily and subject to humiliation by even the most casual efforts of Western navies. In those days the conventional wisdom among Western observers was far different than it is today, with some alleging that Japanese character or culture was intrinsically incapable of economic development.[14]

Before Admiral Perry's gunboats appeared in 1854, the Japanese were virtually closed off from the international economy; foreign trade was largely confined to one port and trade through that port was severely limited. A central government of sorts under the shogun had maintained peace and stability for several centuries, but much of the power to determine economic policies remained in the hands of more than 200 separate *daimyo,* or feudal lords. The tolls, tariffs, regulations, and legal monopolies of these separate fiefs, with their own coinages and currencies, drastically limited trade within Japan.

As we know, the theory offered here predicts that protected markets enjoying a period of stability will become cartelized, at least if the number of enterprises in the market is small enough to allow each individual enterprise to get a significant share of the gain from collective action. This prediction fits Japan no less than other societies; there were any number of powerful *za,* or guilds, and the shogunate or the daimyo often strengthened them by selling them monopoly rights. Various guilds controlled major markets, although there were also independent enterprises in rural areas and even merchants who used the "putting-out" system. Of course, Japanese guilds fixed prices, restricted production, and controlled entry in essentially the same way as cartelistic organizations elsewhere.

The reader may be weary of seeing the same story over and over again in different settings, but since the causes of Japanese growth are shrouded by tenacious myths, it is perhaps best to be explicit. The upheaval that led to the Meiji restoration not only deposed the shogun and effectively dispossessed many of the vested interests tied to the shogunate, but soon also abolished the domains of the feudal daimyo as well and all of the restrictions on trade and enterprise that went with them. At about the same time that the Meiji government eliminated the barriers to a national market, Britain and other Western powers imposed treaties upon the Japanese that required something approaching free trade with the rest of the world. In particular, a treaty of 1866 restricted the Japanese to a revenue tariff of not more than 5 percent, which lasted until 1899. It was the military, technological, and economic weakness of the Japanese that forced them to accept the provisions of this and similar agreements, which the Japanese are accustomed to describing as "humiliating."

Lo and behold, the Japanese were humiliated all the way to the bank. Trade immediately expanded and economic growth apparently picked up speed, particularly in the 1880s and 1890s, and just after the turn of the century a new Japan was able to triumph in the Russo-Japanese War. Once again, multiple causation must be emphasized. For example, the government subsidized industries that were deemed important for military purposes and also promoted education effectively. Quantitatively speaking, however, the overwhelmingly important source of Japanese growth in the nineteenth century was the progress of small-scale private industry and agriculture, such as exports of silk and tea. Interestingly, most of the important Japanese entrepreneurs in this period do not trace their origins to the merchant houses belonging to the guilds of the pre-Meiji period; but rather, they came disproportionately from the ranks of impoverished lesser samurai (who, by the precepts of traditional Japanese culture, were not supposed to engage in commerce at all) or from rising farm and trading families in rural areas that were more likely to be beyond control by guilds or officials. It is said that when markets opened up, many of the houses that had belonged to guilds were disoriented and at a loss what to do.[15]

IV

It is natural to turn from East Asia and the countries that have been most influenced by China to South Asia and particularly to India. Like China, India has an unusually ancient history, a rich culture, and a huge impoverished population. Yet there are also colossal and oft-neglected differences between these two countries. China was among the earliest, if not the earliest, of the nation-states, and, in spite of the several occasions when its empires have collapsed, it has an extremely long history as (more or less) a single country. India, of course, did not have a single government over the whole of the subcontinent, or over all of what is now India, until it fell under British control. The Indian subcontinent is also geographically divided, by deserts, jungles, and mountains, to a greater extent than the populous parts of China are. The conquest of formative areas of Indian civilization by Aryan-speaking peoples about 1500 B.C. also introduced a further disparity into Indian life that has no counterpart in Chinese history—the Mongol conquerors of China did not impose their religion, for example, on Chinese society but were instead thoroughly assimilated by it. For these and no doubt other reasons, India is in several important respects more diverse than China. It does not have a single language common to its many peoples, whereas China (despite the vast differences in its dialects) has at least a common written language. Even a glance at the physical appearances of people from the two nations suggests much less diversity among the Chinese than among the Indians. This great diversity suggests that it is wise to be skeptical about any generalizations concerning India, including those that will be offered here.

The mosaic of jurisdictions that covered the Indian subcontinent in the pre-British era changed many times. Thus there was often a good deal of instability and war, as some warlords or dynasties expanded and others retreated or were defeated. In many periods of Indian history, however, there was what the British called "indirect rule." The British in India and throughout their empire usually did not seek to impose their government down to a local level, much less require every community or tribe to follow uniform rules. They would often rule indirectly by letting traditional authorities, decision-making arrangements, and customs prevail, provided there was no insurrection or outrage against British sensibilities or interests. As time went on or conditions changed, there might be somewhat more obtrusive government, but the British never attempted to eliminate the traditional religion or social structure of India or to remake all of Indian society along British lines; they deliberately kept out all missionaries, for example, until 1813.[16] Indirect rule was also characteristic of the Moghuls who earlier ruled the more northerly parts of India, although some of these rulers did encourage or require conversions to Islam. The Moghuls did not have bureaucracies akin to those of modern governments, or even to those of the Chinese emperors, and could not impose detailed or uniform government at a village level. Often supporters were given a *jagir* (a right to tax a collection of villages), but they would not normally own land or manage the daily life in these villages. Sometimes Hindu nobles, or *zamindars,* retained hereditary control of village revenues, and some Hindu princes continued to rule and collect taxes in autonomous states within the Moghul empire.[17] The diverse rulers of the various parts of India before the Moslems did not appear to have the bureaucracy and efficiency needed to administer vast areas in a uniform way and also appear to have taxed villages as units rather than separately taxing the individuals in the village. In general, traditional India did not have individual ownership of land, and both the different groups in the village and the rulers would share in the output resulting from the cooperative effort and division of labor in the village. At local and especially village levels, then, life could often continue without great change or instability even when new rulers came to exact taxes and tribute.

V

My thoughts about how the theory offered in this book relates to India occurred when, quite by chance, I was reading Jawaharlal Nehru's *The Discovery of India.* This remarkable book was written in only five months in 1944, while Nehru was confined by the British to Ahmadnagar Fort prison. Even though I had previously read accounts of how profoundly Nehru had been influenced by his English education and experience, I nonetheless expected that Nehru—who was after all a political figure who already may have hoped to become the leader of an independent India—would celebrate the glories of India's ancient civilization and place almost all of the blame for the country's problems on the British. Nehru naturally did point with pride to many of the great achievements of India and Indians, but what was most notable was that his praise was confined almost exclusively to certain periods of Indian history, whereas Indian society and institutions in other periods were criticized if anything more seriously than he criticized the rule of his British jailers.

Nehru was impressed, as everyone must be, by the precocious civilization in the Indus valley, one of the world's earliest societies with settled agriculture and what can fairly be called civilization. He cites, for example, the impressive houses, baths, and drainage systems evident in the excavations of the ancient city of Mohenjo-daro and quotes Western authorities who compare aspects of this Indus valley civilization favorably with contemporary civilizations in Egypt and Mesopotamia. He also points out that what the West calls "Arabic" numerals came originally from early India and that the discoveries of the concept of zero in a number system and of symbolic, algebraic notation were further examples of the creativity of early Indian civilization. Western Europe in the Dark Ages, he argues, was backward by the standards of Asia at that time.

He offered a very different view of Indian civilization at the coming of the Moslems and at the conquest of India by the Europeans. India in this epoch was "drying up and losing her creative genius and vitality"; it was the "afternoon of a civilization." This "stagnation and decay" was pervasive: "There was decline all along the line—intellectual, philosophical, political, in technique and methods of warfare, in knowledge of and contacts with the outside world, in shrinking economy." It was true, Nehru conceded, "that the loss of political freedom leads inevitably to cultural decay. But why should political freedom be lost unless some kind of decay has preceded it? A small country might easily be overwhelmed by superior power, but a huge, well-developed and highly civilized country like India cannot succumb to external attack unless there is internal decay, or the invader possesses a higher technique of warfare. That internal decay is clearly evident in India." Most of the above quotations from *The Discovery of India* relate to India at the time much of it was conquered by the Moslems, but he is clear that the same stagnation was evident when the Europeans conquered India a few centuries later and points out that they were able to capture the subcontinent "with remarkably little effort"; there was "a certain inevitability in what happened."

Nehru attributed the decay to "the static nature of Indian society which refused to change in a changing world, for every civilization which resists change declines." He reasoned that "probably this was the inevitable result of the growing rigidity and exclusiveness of the Indian social system as represented chiefly by the caste system." The caste system, he wrote, was a "petrification of classes" that "brought degradation" and is "still a burden and a curse."[18] Nehru did not claim any originality for this diagnosis and it is fairly common. There are also limits to the reliance that can be placed upon the hurried writings of a jailed political leader without the best access to sources and specialists. Nonetheless, I think that the account must have resonated with the experience and observations of many educated Indians, for the book as well as the author have been widely celebrated in India as elsewhere.

Quite apart from its effects on efficiency, the caste system is also a source of profound inequality, both in opportunities and in results. In India today there have been changes, but one must remember that in the traditional caste system groups in the population were condemned for life, and their descendants in perpetuity after them, to such tasks as the cleaning of latrines and the removal of dead carcasses. Their very touch, and in some cases even their nearness, was deemed to be polluting, their presence in temples defiling. Apart from slavery, it is hard to think of a system with greater inequality of opportunity, and the results are also most unequal. This inequality was, of course, also of great concern to Nehru.

VI

It is not sufficient to explain the decline of India by the era of the Moslem and European invasions in terms of the caste system. That, too, is an untestable ad hoc explanation; Indian history is unique in countless ways, and there is no way to determine whether a given unique trait was in fact the source of the decline Nehru noted. We have not reached home until we have explained *why* India acquired the caste system when it did and have comprehended the caste system in a theory that is testable against the experience of many countries.

The sources for the distant past of India are scanty and so little is known that agnosticism is very much in order. There is general agreement that India did not always have the caste system. It is not normally thought to have been part of the civilization in the Indus valley that preceded the Aryan conquests. Neither do the Vedas of the Aryan invaders speak of the ritual purity and pollution or the prohibitions against intermarriage or change in rank that characterized the caste system. How then did the caste system emerge?

One of the most common hypotheses is that the castes emerged out of guilds or similar organizations; most castes bear the names of occupations and there is evidence of guilds in earlier Indian history. Another common hypothesis is that visible racial differences among the indigenous peoples of India and between these peoples and the Aryan-speaking invaders were the source of the caste system; there are visible differences among some caste groups to this day, and the English word *caste* stems from the Portuguese *casta,* meaning race. Yet another familiar explanation ascribes the castes to common descent; a crucial feature of the caste system is endogamy or the prohibition against marriage outside the basic unit of caste grouping, the *jati,* and many tribes have been incorporated into the caste system. It might seem that the theory here would focus exclusively on the hypothesis that the castes grew out of guilds, but the other two hypotheses are also important, if the theory offered here is right, and we shall return to them shortly.

Castes traditionally have behaved like guilds and other distributional coalitions. With modernization many new occupations have emerged and the caste system has changed for other reasons as well, so the caste need not be primarily an occupational or guild-type classification for the educated Indian today. Traditionally, however, caste groups were not only mainly occupational, but also exhibited all the features of cartels and other special-interest organizations. They controlled entry into occupations and lines of business, kept craft mysteries or secrets, set prices monopolistically, used boycotts and strikes, and often bargained on a group rather than an individual basis.

The caste system also had several features that would be expected of distributional coalitions. One of these is that often groups rather than individuals change status. A caste group that enjoys prosperity will rise gradually to a higher status and also may decide collectively to adopt more restrictive ritualistic rules, thereby rising even in terms of the religious concepts of purity and pollution. Another feature is that Hinduism emphasizes the concept of *dharma,* the duties appropriate to the caste or group. Morality, in other words, is defined not in a universalistic way, but in terms of obedience to the rules of one's caste or station, so it is similar to professional ethics that rule out competition in a profession. Even the murderous thugs or other criminal castes were behaving consistently with their dharma when they carried on their caste's activities. A reward for fidelity to the rules of the caste or group into which one is born is a favorable reincarnation. Finally, the one way in which those born into humbler castes can rise in religious status during one lifetime is by leaving the system of group competition and forgoing material satisfactions and affiliations; higher religious status, such as that of Brahmins, is associated with privilege, and any rise in religious status that does not involve renunciation threatens other groups.

VII

None of the preceding, however, is an explanation of the prohibition against marriage out of the group that is such a basic feature of the caste system, nor does it explain any correlation of caste with racial or ethnic differences. For that we must turn to Implication 8, which is that distributional coalitions are characteristically exclusive and seek to limit the diversity of their memberships. We must ask how that implication would apply over a multigenerational time span.

Consider the situation of an older member of a profitable guild. As one of the co-owners of an advantageous coalition, the older member would have an interest in how he or his descendants might share in the future returns. One logical possibility is that he could upon his death or retirement bequeath his share of the future returns of the coalition to his children; his son, for example, could take his place in the craft. But some of the members of the coalition will have daughters and some only daughters. Suppose that the coalition is a guild with only male workers, and that the members with daughters then offer access to the profitable cartel as part of a marriage bargain with sons-in-law. That will offer the old member a way of getting something for his share of his coalition's worth, but we must ask what will happen if both sons and sons-in-law enter the trade. Even with a steady-state population *the number in the craft will double if both sons and sons-in-law are allowed to enter, and normally a doubling of the craft's membership would eliminate the gains of the cartelistic output restriction that gave the guild its value in the first place.* The same problem will occur if both sons and daughters practice a craft that was previously restricted to one sex. The multigenerational guild can be successful only if it can keep its membership from increasing faster than can be justified by any expansion in its market, which will depend on such things as the growth of population and income in the areas in which it is located. Unless some sons are left out, the *only* way those members who have only or mainly daughters can gain their share of the value of the cartel, without making the cartel valueless, is to restrict the sons allowed to enter the trade to marriages with daughters of members of the trade.

The same is true of a coalition that has, say, disproportionate rights to the village harvest. The greatest distributional gains come from a minimum winning coalition. Thus if the favorable share of the harvest is divided up among more families, there is less for each family. But if each family has on average two surviving children who marry, then there will be two families in the next generation for every family in the first generation, and in a few generations even the grandest entitlement will provide very little per family. The only way the distributional coalition can retain its value over several generations is by restricting the children of members to marriages with one another or by disinheriting a large portion of the children. I hypothesize that the Indian castes mainly used the first method. The English nobility used this method to a great degree and combined it with primogeniture as well (thus it is not astonishing that some great fortunes were passed on for several generations in the English aristocracy).

This reference to the British nobility brings us back to the discussion of Implication 8 in chapter 3, where the nobility and royalty of Europe were used to illustrate the exclusiveness of marriages (or bequests) that is essential to any successful multigenerational special-interest group. Those who have a chauvinistic turn of mind or who are convinced that fundamentally different processes must operate at different levels of wealth or status no doubt will be surprised by this alleged similarity of motivation in groups as different in wealth and background as the European nobility and the Indian castes. Those who have done a lot of empirical and historical research in economics would, I think, be surprised by anything else. Those who have studied barriers to intergenerational mobility across social classes in any societies with significant class barriers will also, I conjecture, find incipient castes.

Just as the origin of the caste system is often ascribed to guilds, so is it often related to the racial diversity of India at the time of the Aryan migrations and also to descent groups. Given the repeated emphasis on multicausality and the complexity of reality in this book, we should examine these hypotheses sympathetically. They are, as it turns out, also very much in keeping with the logic behind Implication 8. If a racially distinct distributive coalition is formed by alien conquerors, it will be able to preserve itself over many generations only by arbitrary rules of bequest such as primogeniture or through endogamy. If it is largely endogamous the differences in appearance will be preserved.

Indeed, it will be far easier for a racially, linguistically, and culturally distinctive group to maintain a multigenerational coalition. The linguistic and cultural similarities will reduce differences in values and facilitate social interaction, and, as chapters 2 and 3 show, this reduces conflict and makes it easier to generate social selective incentives. Moreover, any special-interest group that uses endogamy to preserve its benefits over a multigenerational period must be large enough to avoid inbreeding. As the endogamous group gets larger, however, the difficulty of enforcing endogamy rises. How is this or that son to be restrained from marrying some especially appealing girl outside the group, or how are his parents to be prevented from making an especially advantageous marriage contract for him with relatively wealthy or powerful people outside the group? How can the astute outsider be kept from marrying into the coalition? If exogamy is not prevented, at least some of the families must lose their share of the coalition's future gains. If there are visible differences, it will be easier to determine who is in the group and who is not and to enforce the endogamy rule. Differences in speech, culture, and lifestyle are also shibboleths that make it harder for the outsider to blend in. Unfortunately, *the promotion of prejudices about race, ethnicity, culture, and intergroup differences in lifestyle will also make the coalition work better.* The inculcation of these prejudices will increase the probability that the members will follow the rule of endogamy and strengthen selective incentives by interacting socially only with their own group, of their own accord.

Though multigenerational distributional coalitions foster inefficiency, inequality, and group prejudice, it is nonetheless important to realize that some individuals and groups outside the society containing these coalitions may improve their positions by joining that society, even if they enter at the bottom. Tribes without settled agriculture, for example, might in some circumstances have found that they would be better off joining Indian society than by staying out of it, even though they were accorded the lowest status and were victims of special-interest groups to boot. There have been many observations of such assimilation of tribal groups into India's caste system, and they must help to account for its great diversity.

This diversity, once again, reminds us of the complexity of the matter. Because of this complexity and the limited sources on the early years of the caste system, we must not jump to any conclusions. The hypotheses that emerge from the theory here should be considered primarily a stimulus to further research. There has been no theoretical consensus on caste and class: a fresh perspective could provide some help. It is, I submit, worth doing serious research on whether multigenerational processes of the sort the theory suggests have in fact emerged over the millennia of Indian history. This exceptionally long history of settled agriculture and civilized life was combined for the most part with indirect or parochial rulers who could not or did not challenge the power or usurp all the gains of the distributional coalitions. It was combined also with racial diversity and geographical segmentation of markets favorable to the coalition formation by small groups. If the processes of the kind described above did not occur, then how do we explain what happened?

VIII

In keeping with the scientific principle that the theory that explains the most with the least is most likely to be true, any alternative explanation of the Indian caste system should also be capable of explaining some developments outside India, as the present theory does, or at least parsimoniously explain a good deal more about the caste system. By the same token, the explanation offered here of the Indian caste system will be stronger if the theory in the book explains not only diverse developments outside India, but also developments outside India that are similar to the Indian developments. To some extent the previous analysis of class rigidities was in that category, but there is still the problem that the Indian caste system is unique, so that developments in other countries do not provide the close parallelism we seek. In particular, in most other countries any class rigidities usually do not involve rigid requirements of endogamous marriage and group or race prejudice. Since the theory here implies that over a sufficiently long run distributional coalitions will stimulate group prejudice and promote endogamous marriage, it is wise to look for countries other than India where this is occurring. Other societies will not have the extraordinary antiquity and cultural richness of India, but perhaps some of them will in certain respects resemble India in the era when the caste system emerged. We should particularly look for societies with racial and cultural differences.

The extraordinary system of apartheid in South Africa is a relatively recent development. The more severe forms of racial segregation and discrimination do not go back to the early days of the Boers in South Africa. On the contrary, there was more than a small amount of interbreeding between the Boers or other Europeans and the Africans. There is, after all, a large population of "Coloured" or mixed-race people in South Africa today; the South African government treats them as a separate category and segregates them from Africans and Asians as well as from Europeans.

A distinguished South African economist, W. H. Hutt, in *The Economics of the Colour Bar*,[19] has written a startling history of the evolution of progressively tighter systems of racial segregation and discrimination in South Africa. Although Hutt is perhaps insufficiently detached about his classical liberal ideology and may offend some readers of other persuasions, my checks with other specialists on South Africa suggest that even those who do not share his interpretation are generally in agreement on his rendition of the historical facts.

Hutt's account focuses closely on the mining industry in South Africa early in the present century. The mine owners and management needed labor and naturally preferred to secure it at low wages rather than high wages. Since Africans had few other opportunities outside the traditional sector of African society, they were often available at low wages. The mine owners also drew upon the huge pool of low-wage labor in Asia and for a time used indentured Chinese labor. European workers were employed in the mines mainly as foremen and skilled and semi-skilled laborers. It was clear that that the far-cheaper African laborers could at very little cost soon be taught the semi-skilled jobs and the employers naturally coveted the savings in labor cost that this would bring.

The competition of cheaper African and Asian labor did not appeal to the higher-paid workers of European stock or their recently formed unions. There were strikes. In part because of these strikes there were changes in labor policy in South Africa. The Mines and Works Act of 1911, also called the "Colour Bar Act," was passed. On a superficial reading relatively innocuous, as administered it constrained employers in their use of African labor in semi-skilled and skilled jobs. The regulations promulgated under the act prevented Africans in the Transvaal and the Orange Free State from entering a wide variety of mining occupations. They even specified *ratios* between foremen (whites) and mining laborers (Africans).[20]

Disagreement about the ratios emerged. After World War I, the mine employers asked for a ratio of 10.5 Africans per white worker, whereas the labor union demanded 3.5 to 1. A general strike in the Rand followed in 1922. This strike and the agitation that followed became a common cause of conservative Afrikaaners and communist and socialist leaders, with all of them supporting the efforts to deny opportunities to the poorer Africans who were competing with white labor. The South African Labour Party, modeled more or less after its British counterpart, prospered in the wake of the strike and joined with the mainly Afrikaaner, white supremacist Nationalist Party in a coalition government. The Nationalist-Labour "Pact" government soon introduced the second "Colour Bar Act," the Mines and Works Act of 1926. Hutt calls this "probably . . . the most drastic piece of colour bar legislation which the world has ever experienced."[21] It was accompanied by a "civilized labour policy," which limited opportunities for Africans still further. One of the devices used to keep African laborers out of jobs where they would compete with whites was the requirement of "the rate for the job." If the wage for a given job is fixed at a level attractive to Europeans, the employer has no incentive to seek African workers who would work for less. Apprenticeship rules under the "civilized labour policy" also had the effect of excluding Africans.

These and similar policies drastically limited opportunities for African workers. The denial of various skilled and semi-skilled jobs to Africans not only raised the wages of the European (and sometimes Coloured and Asian) workers, but it also crowded more labor into the areas that remained open to Africans, making the wages there lower than they would otherwise be. It is important to remember, though, that there was a continuing demand of Africans from farther north to enter, notwithstanding the policies against them. They came in at the bottom and were victimized by the rules, but it was still better than the alternatives some of them had in the traditional sector. The analogy with the tribes that have been assimilated into the bottom of the Indian caste system is striking.

Since firms that could hire unusually inexpensive African labor had an advantage over foreign or domestic competitors without such opportunities, they would often be profitable even if they were forced to pay more for certain skills because only whites could be employed, to hire more foremen than needed, and so on. There were efforts of firms to move to areas where restrictions on the use of African workers were fewer, but this too was curtailed, as were some African entrepreneurs. Thus the system, while it forced employers to adopt less profitable and more discriminatory policies than they preferred, brought substantial gains to organized white (and sometimes Coloured and Asian) workers.

The theory offered in this book suggests that the employers would have been just as interested in excluding competitors as the workers were, and would as small groups have been better able to organize to do so than the workers. But the competitors of the employers were other firms or capitalists, often in other lands; the employers were not competing against African laborers, as the white workers were, so the employers were not a principal source of the racial exclusion and discrimination that the Africans suffered. South African consumers of all races paid higher prices because of the higher costs growing out of the discriminatory policy, but, as in other countries, they were not organized.

Let us now ask what necessary conditions must be met if the South African system, and the cartelistic gains it provides for many, are to be preserved over the long run. There is a need for police and military power, but this is widely understood and discussed, so it need not be considered here. The system could not possibly survive for many generations unless the demarcation between the races was preserved. If less-favored groups could enter the more-favored groups, as they would have massive incentives to do, wage differentials could not be maintained. A continuation of the processes that generated the Coloured population would make the system untenable in the long run, and even in what (by the standards of Indian history) would be the medium run.

That is not only an implication of the present theory but evidently the conclusion of the South African government as well. Just as the restrictions on the use of African labor in skilled and semi-skilled jobs increased over time, so did the rules separating the population into rigid racial categories and forbidding sexual relations, in marriage or otherwise, between them.

Undoubtedly any number of other causal factors have been at work in South Africa, and any account as brief and monocausal as this must be in many respects misleading. The purpose, however, is not to give a complete account, but to induce reflection on the sources of racial and other forms of discrimination. As others have argued before, the individual as a consumer, employer, or worker finds it costly to discriminate. The consumer who discriminates against stores owned by groups he finds offensive has to pay higher prices or suffer a lesser selection by shopping elsewhere. The employer who discriminates against workers of a despised group has higher labor costs, and his business may even bankrupt itself competing against other firms that do not let prejudice stand in the way of profit. Similarly, the worker who does not accept the best job irrespective of the group affiliation of the employer essentially is taking a cut in pay. A similar logic applies to individual social interactions of other kinds. The fact that *individuals* find discrimination costly means that, if individuals are free to undertake whatever transactions they prefer, there will be a constraint on the extent of discrimination.

Distributional coalitions of individuals, on the other hand, can sometimes gain enormously from discrimination. Any group difference that facilitates exclusion, by Implication 8, will be advantageous. For periods of only a generation or two in length, the group differences can usually be considered as given, but over the centuries and certainly the millennia they cannot. In the long run, then, multigenerational special-interest groups must tend toward endogamy. This is equally true of the South African whites, the Indian castes, and the European nobility.

IX

This book has not even touched upon societies of the soviet type. The declines in the growth rates of these societies over the stable postwar years are quite as notable as in other countries. Unfortunately, the way the present theory applies to societies of this type cannot be set out briefly; the theory of collective action by small groups needs to be elaborated and the limited role of markets in these societies analyzed. It would be digressive to go into these issues now, and so an account of how the present theory applies to these societies must be left for another publication.

The other class of contemporary societies that has so far been ignored is the characteristically unstable countries. Instability in France and on the Continent were discussed earlier, but nothing has been said about the depressingly large number of less developed countries, in Latin America, Africa, and elsewhere, that have been persistently unstable.

The dense network of distributional coalitions that eventually emerges in stable societies is harmful to economic efficiency and growth, but so is instability. There is no inconsistency in this; just as special-interest groups lead to misallocations of resources and divert attention from production to distributional struggle, so instability diverts resources that would otherwise have gone into productive long-term investments into forms of wealth that are more easily protected, or even into capital flights to more stable environments. On the whole, stable countries are more prosperous than unstable ones and this is no surprise. But, other things being equal, the most rapid growth will occur in societies that have lately experienced upheaval but are expected nonetheless to be stable for the foreseeable future.

The characteristically unstable countries are usually governed part of the time by dictators or juntas; they have intervals of democratic or at least relatively pluralistic government. The policies of the dictators or the juntas obviously will depend dramatically on the interests, the ideology, and sometimes even the whims of the dictator or the leadership group. Experience and common sense tell us that dictators and juntas may be right-wing or left-wing, this or that, although they are systematically more likely to be specialists in violence than in economics. The theory here cannot tell us what policies the dictators and juntas will have. As the better historians remind us, much of what happens in history is due to chance and must remain beyond the explanatory powers of any theory.

Fortunately, something of a systematic or theoretical nature can be said about the influences and pressures that will be brought to bear on the changing governments of the unstable societies, and about their intervals of democracy or pluralism. Implication 3 states that small groups are more likely to be organized than large ones, but that (since small groups organize less slowly) the disproportionate organizational and collusive power of small groups will be greatest in lately unstable societies. The theory here predicts that the unstable society will have fewer and weaker mass organizations than stable societies, but that small groups that can collude more readily will often be able to further their common interests. The groups may be at any level, but usually those which can gain from either lobbying or cartelizing at a national level are small groups of substantial firms or wealthy and powerful individuals.

The tendency for small groups to be better organized than large ones is further accentuated in unstable societies by two other factors. One is that large groups are more likely to be a threat to a dictator or a junta than small ones. If there were an association that included most of the peasants, or a labor union that represented most of the workers, in an unstable country with a dictator, that organization could pose a threat to the dictator. The sheer numbers of the membership of the mass organization would give it some coercive power. (Actually, this point holds for undemocratic regimes whether they are unstable or not—even the stable totalitarian state does not like the threat inherent in independent mass organizations. Unobtrusive small groups accordingly also play a leading role in the application of the theory to totalitarian societies.)

The second factor is that the small group can be discreet and inconspicuous during the dictatorial periods, whereas the organized large group cannot. Dictators, juntas, and totalitarian leaders are not enthusiastic about independent organizations of any kind, but they cannot repress collusions they do not know about. The likelihood that a group will be exposed by an indiscretion of one of its members must rise with its size and becomes a virtual certainty with a large group. Thus if a small group should feel threatened in a repressive society, it can often retain its coherence by becoming invisible to the authorities and then be able to act promptly when there is relaxation or elimination of the repression. (This point, too, applies to stable despotisms as well as unstable ones.)

The most basic implication of the theory for unstable societies, then, is that their governments are systematically influenced by the interests, pleas, and pressures of the small groups that are capable of organizing fairly quickly. Admittedly, the policies of unstable countries may shift wildly, with each coup d'etat bringing new policy preferences. The economic policy of such countries is similar to a leaf blowing in the wind—a gust may blow it suddenly in any direction, but over time gravity still will pull it to the ground.

The small groups that can organize or collude in the unstable societies will have different interests in different countries at different times. In one period they might be landed oligarchs, in another manufacturing firms; in one country they might have a vested interest in exports, in another, in import substitution. Again, it is important to respect the diversity and detail of actual experience and not to push this theory, or any other general theory, farther than it can go. The only general point so far about the unstable societies is that one must look at the vested interests of the small groups capable of relatively prompt collective action to understand one systematic element in economic policies.

X

By bringing additional information to bear we can make more specific predictions. One fact is that, since almost all the unstable governments are in developing nations, they usually do not have anything like a complete modern system of transportation and communication, at least in the rural areas. This makes it more costly and difficult for those in rural areas to mobilize political power to influence the government and gives the residents of the major metropolitan areas, especially the capital city, a disproportionate influence. Before the Industrial Revolution and the railway, transportation was slow and expensive everywhere, and this presumably explains why in his time Adam Smith observed that farmers were unable to organize to gain monopoly or political influence, whereas businessmen rarely met without conspiring against the public interest. In the developing nations today the rural interests are at a similar disadvantage, and the residents of the capital city obtain an altogether disproportionate share of governmental favors.

Although this was not always true, in most developing nations the largest firms and the wealthiest individuals are involved in producing import substitutes and goods that can also be provided by foreign firms. That is, they produce goods and services that are also available at lower cost on the world market or that could be provided more economically by local branches of foreign firms. The enterprises engaged in import substitution will in some developing countries include heavy industry, but in others they may only manufacture textiles or brew beer. Sometimes the wealthiest families will own banks or insurance companies that provide services that foreign firms could also provide. Of course, nowadays these enterprises and families will also tend to be located in the great cities with the easiest access to the government.

When the most substantial firms are in the import-substitution and foreign-replacement sectors, and especially when there is poor transportation in the rural areas, a special *perverse policy syndrome* develops in the "top-heavy" society. The key to this policy syndrome is the markedly disproportionate strength of small groups in the unstable societies.

The large enterprises and wealthy families in the situations described above have an obvious interest in protection against imports and discriminatory legislation against the foreign or multinational firms with which they compete. This drives up prices for consumers, but consumers are in latent groups that cannot organize, and many of them are out in the provinces as well. The most drastic forms of protection, such as quotas and exchange controls that deny citizens foreign currency for the purchase of imports for which there are domestic substitutes, are often used. These methods of protection are not readily subject to measurement. But in many cases, the level of protection is staggeringly high and quite beyond comparison with the levels of protection in the major developed democracies.

Let us look at the effects of these protective policies on the distribution of income. The imports and foreign firms are normally a source of competition because they have lower costs. In other words, the unstable developing country and its firms do not have a comparative advantage in the types of production in question. If they did, in most cases they would not care for protection.[22] Most developing countries do not have comparative advantage in many manufactured import substitutes because these types of production involve large proportions of capital and technical expertise, which are usually scarce and therefore tend to be relatively expensive.

When the goods and services that are intensive in capital and technical expertise are protected, the price of capital and technical expertise in the developing nation rises, particularly in the favored firms and industries. Some of the gains to owners of the favored enterprises will be consumed by the efforts to secure or maintain the political favors. The employees of some of these firms also may be able to share in the gains. Nonetheless, in at least some countries, the owners of capital and technical expertise, who were probably well rewarded because of their scarcity in the first place, now get even higher rates of return. Since it was the wealthier individuals and larger firms that initially were able to organize fastest, and since the mobilization of large amounts of capital and the acquisition of rare expertise requires wealth, the protection in most cases presumably favors the wealthy.

In addition, the protection makes the country's currency more valuable than it would otherwise be; less of the national currency is supplied to buy the foreign exchange needed for imports. The higher the price of the national currency, the more expensive the country's exports and the less of them foreigners will buy. The exports are in general the goods that the country has a comparative advantage in producing. Poor developing nations naturally have a lot of poor people and thus cheap labor, and some natural resources, so they tend to have a comparative advantage in producing goods that are intensive in labor and natural resources. The owners of labor and of natural resources, and the peasantry in particular, are the victims of the loss in exports. In some African countries, especially, the rural exporters are further exploited by government marketing monopolies that give the farmers only a portion of the price at which the government sells their commodities. The plentiful factors of production earn relatively little to begin with and the loss of export earnings reduces their incomes still further. The owners of the plentiful factors—which include in every developing nation the working poor—not only are denied access to cheaper imports by the protection, but also get lower prices for the labor and the products they have to sell.

There are a host of qualifications and technical niceties that it would be interesting to explore at this point. It is also important to point out that situations are somewhat different in each country. Nonetheless, the general nature of the process is clear. The most substantial and wealthy interests are relatively better organized in the unstable society, but they often own an unrepresentative mix of the country's productive factors. They obtain policies that favor themselves and work in different ways against the interests of the larger unorganized groups in the society, thereby making the distribution of income far more unequal.

The available statistics are poor and incomplete, but it is clear that many of the unstable countries have unusually unequal distributions of income, with giant fortunes juxtaposed with mass poverty. In some of these countries it is obvious even from casual observation that, as the foregoing argument would lead us to expect, the unskilled workers are trying desperately to get out, and (when they think the chances of being nationalized are not great) the multinationals are trying to get in. A research assistant and I have compared some (very shaky) data on income distribution across countries with some (even shakier) data on the degree of instability. The weakness of the data and the multiplicity of alternative explanations of the results have forced me to conclude that the tests are not worth relating here. But for whatever little they are worth, they are consistent with the theory.

All the arguments and evidence in the preceding chapter about the losses from protection also apply to the unstable developing countries, especially the smaller ones. Thus the perverse policy syndrome described above promotes inefficiency and stagnation as well as inequality.

When the import-substituting industries in the capital and other metropolitan areas are protected and cartelized, they can survive even if they pay wages far above the competitive level. This allows greater gains from the monopolization of the labor force and promotes unions, although episodic repression and the difficulties of organizing large-scale collective action may prevent unionization. Whether unions emerge or not, the population of the capital city—even the poor—will tend to have more influence on public policy than their rural and provincial cousins because of the inadequacies of the transportation system. Popular demonstrations, strikes, and riots in the capital are a special threat to governments.

The civil and military bureaucracies, which are well placed to influence any government, will be disproportionately in the capital city.

University students, with their untypically intense interest in politics and flexible schedules, are usually important in politics and are often in the large cities. The unions, the bureaucracy, and the students frequently will have different ideological colorations than the owners of large firms, but they may be equally disposed to economic nationalism and may not in practice be much in conflict over the detailed and inconspicuous policies the separate small groups normally seek. In any case, the bureaucracy, and often also the unions and the students, will support the subsidization of life in the capital and perhaps other large cities.

The provision of extra facilities and other forms of subsidization to urban areas encourages more migration to the capital and to other cities, beyond that already spurred by the import-substitution policies. So another aspect of the perverse policy syndrome is inefficiently large capital cities and major metropolitan areas. The capital cities of most of the poorer nations today are vastly larger in relation to the population of these nations than were the capital cities in the developed nations when those nations had the levels of per capita income the poorer countries have.

The unstable countries are so diverse, and their policies influenced by so many factors, that the preceding argument should be regarded as a "researchers' parable" rather than an analysis; it should be read as a story meant to have heuristic value. Researchers and others with a specialized knowledge of particular unstable countries will, it is hoped, be stimulated to analyze the situation in a particular country, or some small set of countries, in a systematic way.

One type of inquiry that is needed is historical. Some of the countries that now have the perverse policy syndrome, or something rather like it, were probably once in a different situation. For some Latin American countries in the nineteenth century, for example, it is worth asking whether the group that could best organize to influence the government would have been a small group of landed families of great wealth. The difficulties of transportation would have made their collusion more difficult, and sometimes their power may have been exercised only locally, in a feudal fashion. If these families could collude on national policy, however, they would have had interests different from those who profit from the perverse policy syndrome. As owners of land and sometimes of labor in peonage, they would have held a mix of factors representative of the economies of which they were a part. As such they would have gained from liberal trade policies. To the extent that their poorer compatriots also owned some land and labor, they too would have profited. With revolutions and the gradual growth of cities, landed magnates lost influence or disappeared. Liberal and socialist writers in the capital cities pressed for egalitarian policies that did not appeal to the great landowners. There is a need for research to determine whether the changes have, in fact, reduced inequality. In some countries we may find that the small groups in urban areas that have influenced policy more recently have a vested interest in less efficient policies, and ones that have more inegalitarian consequences as well.

XI

Now that we have considered the unique inequality of the caste system, the racial discrimination in South Africa, and the inegalitarian policies of the top-heavy societies with the perverse policy syndrome, we can examine a modern myth that has in my judgment forced needless poverty and humiliation on millions of people. Among economists, who are about the only people who have given the matter specialized study, there is a consensus that competitive markets are efficient. Indeed, in economic theory the definition of a perfectly competitive market entails that it is perfectly efficient, with the only possible improvement being in the distribution of income that results. Even among those who are in other vocations, there is, at least in the developed countries, a fairly widespread understanding that competition encourages efficiency.

There is at the same time the standard assumption, among economists as well as the laity, that competitive markets generate a considerable degree of inequality. A soft-hearted majority holds the further view that government action—or in some versions the operation of unions, professional ethics, and so forth—is needed to reduce the inequalities generated by the market. A hard-boiled minority willingly accepts or even rejoices in the inequality or believes that governmental efforts to reduce inequality are harmful. Most of the soft-hearted and most of the hard-boiled agree in taking it for granted that markets generate considerable inequality and differ about whether this inequality is unjust. The economist often speaks of the trade-off between efficiency, obtained through competitive markets, and equity, obtained at some social cost by other means.

Perhaps the most intelligent and humane expression of the view that competitive markets are a source of considerable inequality that government and other nonmarket institutions then reduce at some social cost is Arthur Okun's widely respected book, *Equality and Efficiency: The Big Trade-Off.*[23] In this book it is taken for granted that governments are an egalitarian force that evens out the inequality resulting from the operation of markets, and that some price must be paid for this reduction in inequality because it interferes with the operation of generally efficient markets. Some other writers suppose that unions and other special-interest groups reduce the inequalities that result from competitive markets.

I submit that the orthodox assumption of both Left and Right that the market generates more inequality than the government and the other institutions that "mitigate" its effects is the opposite of the truth for many societies, and only a half-truth for the rest. In South Africa there are black workers who are paid *one-eleventh* as much as white workers doing slightly different jobs that require about the same degree of skill. In a truly competitive economy, as the textbooks lucidly explain, it is difficult indeed to see how people with the same skills and effectiveness could earn very different rates of pay in the long run. Employers could profit by hiring the low-wage victims of discrimination, and firms that refused to do so would eventually be driven out of business by their lower-cost competitors. As we should expect, employers in South Africa argue that they should be allowed to use the African workers for jobs that are now restricted to whites. If this is allowed, both efficiency and equity will improve. In India many tens of millions of people historically have been condemned, and their children after them, to lives of special poverty and humiliation by caste rules that prevent the free operation of markets; and these rules have led to inefficiency and stagnation as well as inequality. Most of the countries of this world are unstable developing nations, and in most of them the policies on international trade, foreign investment, and many other matters make these societies generate colossal inequalities as well as inefficiency. This is evidence that, as I argued in justification of Implication 9, the gang fight is no gentler than the individual duel.

Now let us turn to the developed democracies with their welfare states. Those of us who believe that we ought to make a decent provision for the least fortunate in our societies, even though it will require that we make some sacrifices ourselves, have to face up to the logic of collective action. We can help our friends, relatives, or neighbors and can see the benefits that result from our generosity, so we may make significant sacrifices on their behalf. But if we strive as individuals to reduce the poverty in the country in which we live, we find that even if we gave up all of our wealth it would not be enough to make a noticeable difference in the amount of poverty in the society. The alleviation of poverty in a society is, in other words, a public good to all those who would like to see it eliminated, and voluntary contributions will not obtain public goods for large groups. If everyone who is concerned about poverty made a contribution to its alleviation, in the aggregate that would, however, make a difference. So a majority of us in each of the developed democracies votes for raising some money by imposing compulsory taxes on ourselves, or more precisely on the whole society, and devoting these monies to the needy. Since the alleviation of poverty on a society-wide basis is a public good, efforts to redistribute income to the poor as a group require governmental action. In this respect, it is true that governments in some societies do mitigate inequalities. Since both the taxes and the transfers have adverse effects on incentives, it is also true that there are trade-offs between equality and efficiency.

The trouble is that the current orthodoxies of both Left and Right assume that almost all the redistribution of income that occurs is the redistribution inspired by egalitarian motives, and that goes from the nonpoor to the poor. In reality many, if not most, of the redistributions are inspired by entirely different motives, and most of them have arbitrary rather than egalitarian impacts on the distribution of income— more than a few redistribute income from lower to higher income people. A very large part of the activities of governments, even in the developed democracies, is of no special help to the poor and many of these activities actually harm them. In the United States there are subsidies to the owners of private airplanes and yachts, most of whom are not poor. The intervention of the professions and the government in the medical care system, as I have shown elsewhere,[24] mainly helps physicians and other providers, most of whom are well-heeled. There are innumerable tax loopholes that help the rich but are without relevance for the poor and bail-outs for corporations and protection for industries when the workers' wages are far above the average for American industry. There are minimum-wage laws and union-wage scales that keep employers and workers from making employment contracts at lower wages, with the result that progressively larger proportions of the American population are not employed. The situation in many European countries is much the same and in some cases a little worse.

The reason that government and other institutions that intervene in markets are not in general any less inegalitarian than competitive markets is evident from the discussion in chapter 3 of Implications 3 and 9. There is greater inequality, I hypothesize, in the opportunity to create distributional coalitions than there is in the inherent productive abilities of people. The recipients of welfare in the United States are not organized, nor are the poor in other societies. But in the United States, as elsewhere, almost all the major firms are represented by trade associations and the professions by professional associations. There are admittedly differences in the productive abilities of individuals, just as there are differences in height. But such measurement as we are now capable of suggests that the individual differences are normally distributed—the vast majority at least fairly close to the middle. There are a few dwarfs and a few giants, but not many. Larger differences are apparent, it is true, in the holdings of capital and some huge fortunes. Yet, if the accumulation of capital is unobstructed and policies such as those in the perverse policy syndrome are avoided, the return to capital will fall as more capital is accumulated[25] and the wages of the labor with which the capital is combined will rise; it is no accident that wages are highest in the countries that have enjoyed the greatest accumulation of capital. If economic nationalism does not keep the capital from crossing national borders, more will have an incentive to migrate to areas with the lowest wages and thus significantly raise the wages of the poorest. As the history of India tells us, even in the longest run there is no comparable tendency for inequalities to diminish over time through distributional coalitions.

XII

Another myth that generates a lot of poverty and suffering is that the economic development of the poor countries is, for fundamental economic or extra-institutional reasons, extremely difficult, and requires special promotion, planning, and effort. It is sometimes even argued that a tough dictator or totalitarian repression is required to force the sacrifices needed to bring about economic development. As I see it, in these days it takes an enormous amount of stupid policies or bad or unstable institutions to *prevent* economic development. Unfortunately, growth-retarding regimes, policies, and institutions are the rule rather than the exception, and the majority of the world's population lives in poverty.

The examples of successful growth that have been referred to in this study did not occur because of any special promotion or plans. Neither did that of Korea, Taiwan, Hong Kong, or Singapore. The former two received some aid from the United States, but they also felt compelled to spend unusually large amounts on military purposes. If the analysis in this book is right, the growth in Germany and the United States before World War I was more the result of a widening of product and factor markets than of any special promotion or plan. So it was with the growth in early modern Europe. Britain did not seek or plan to have an industrial revolution; it grew for other reasons such as those explained earlier in this book. In the many countries that have failed to grow or failed to grow as fast or as far as the leaders, there are quite enough stupidities, rigidities, and instabilities to explain the lack of success.

Some people suppose that it is more difficult for poor nations to grow now than it was in the eighteenth or nineteenth centuries, and that the explanation for this is in some sense also economic rather than institutional. This overlooks the fact that the poor nations now can borrow the technologies of more developed nations, some of which will be readily adaptable to their own environments, and improve their techniques of production very rapidly. Great Britain in the Industrial Revolution could improve its technology only through the inventions that occurred in that period. Similarly, most highly developed nations today can improve their technology only by taking advantage of current advances. The poorest of the developing nations can telescope the cumulative technological progress of centuries into a few decades. This is not only an obvious possibility but has actually occurred in places like Korea, Taiwan, Hong Kong, and Singapore. The nations of continental Europe and Japan were far behind the United States technologically at the end of World War II, but they borrowed American technology, grew far faster than the United States, and very nearly caught up with the United States in both technology and per capita income in less than twenty-five years.

In claiming that international product and factor markets unobstructed by either cartelization or governmental intervention will bring irrepressible and rapid growth to any poor country, I am *not* arguing that laissez-faire leads to perfect efficiency. As I pointed out in chapter 3, I do not assume perfect competition anywhere in this book. As it happens, most of my own writing in economics is about externalities and public goods, which normally keep a laissez-faire economy from achieving Pareto-optimality and which I believe are quite important.[26] An economy can be dynamic and rapidly growing without at the same time being optimal or perfectly efficient. An economy with free markets and no government or cartel intervention is like a teen-aged youth; it makes a lot of mistakes but nonetheless grows rapidly without special effort or encouragement.

If poor institutions that prevent or repress growth are the norm in much of the world, it may not help to say that "only" institutional problems stand in the way of rapid growth in poor countries. If poor institutions are so common, it presumably is not always easy to obtain good institutional arrangements and the rapid growth that they permit. Still, the problems are more likely to be solved if they are understood than if they are not.[27]

XIII

As might be expected from my concern about ideological preconceptions, and from the methodological discussion in chapter 1 on the standards a satisfactory answer must meet, I do not believe any of the ideological approaches are sufficient to meet our needs. In keeping with that belief, I want to underline the contrast between the argument here and the classical liberal or laissez-faire ideology. The present argument and the classical liberal ideology do share an appreciation of the value of markets. An appreciation of markets is common to nearly everyone, Right or Left, who has given the matter a decade or more of specialized study. If you stand on the shoulders of the giants, it is virtually impossible to see it any other way.

But there the similarity between the present argument and classical liberal laissez-faire ideology stops. As I read it, the ark and covenant of the laissez-faire ideology is that the government that governs least governs best; markets will solve the problem if the government only leaves them alone. There is in the most popular presentations of this ideology a monodiabolism, and the government is the devil. If this devil is kept in chains, there is an almost utopian lack of concern about other problems.

If the less optimistic theory in this book is right, there often will *not* be competitive markets even if the government does not intervene. The government is by no means the only source of coercion or social pressure in society. There will be cartelization of many markets even if the government does not help. Eliminating certain types of government intervention and freeing trade and factor mobility will weaken cartels but will not eliminate many of them. Moreover, the absence of government intervention (even if it were invariably desirable) may not be possible anyway, because of the lobbying of special-interest groups, unless we fly to the still greater evil of continuous instability.

The questions of whether laissez-faire alone is sufficient to prevent or eliminate cartelization, and whether laissez-faire is in the long run not viable because special-interest groups will accumulate and lobby it out of existence can be settled only by an appeal to the facts. Thanks to British imperialism, history has given us one experiment of remarkable aptness. Milton and Rose Friedman, in *Free to Choose*,[28] made much of a comparison between Japan after the Meiji restoration in the late 1860s and India since World War II. The point of comparison was, of course, that the Japanese after the Meiji restoration had relatively free enterprise, along with very low tariffs, whereas independent India has had dramatically interventionist and protectionist policies. As the Friedmans correctly point out, the policies the Japanese chose produced great growth, but those India chose failed. There is a great deal to be said for this comparison and for the policy lesson the Friedmans draw from it. I should also point out that, like most other economists of my generation, I have learned a lot from Milton Friedman's exceptionally lucid, fresh, and penetrating technical writings.[29] And I greatly respect the depth of the Friedmans' convictions.

Withal, there is an ideological—as opposed to a scientific—element in the comparison, and an instructive one at that. Of their comparison, the Friedmans write, "Economists and social scientists in general can seldom conduct controlled experiments of the kind that are so important in the physical sciences. However, experience here has produced something very close to a controlled experiment to test the importance of the difference in methods of economic organization. There is a lapse of eight decades in time. In all other respects the two countries were in very similar circumstances."[30]

An even closer approximation to the controlled experiment of the physical sciences is possible—the same one, without the "lapse of eight decades in time." It is all too often forgotten that one of the finest examples of laissez-faire policy was British rule in India. India had one of the most thoroughgoing laissez-faire policies the world has seen, and it was administered with considerable economy and efficiency in the best British civil service tradition.[31] Entrepreneurs and capitalists from all over the world were free to sell or buy in India or to set up businesses there, as were Indians themselves. No doubt there must have been favoritism to British firms, but where and when in human history was there much more laissez-faire impartiality? There was less government intervention than in Japan after the Meiji restoration. Tariffs were used only to raise revenue and part of the time there were not even revenue tariffs. Those who incorrectly ascribe most economic development to state intervention might claim that India failed to grow because it did not have an independent government that could engage in economic planning and promote development. This argument is not, however, open to the advocate of laissez-faire ideology, for that ideology does not require an active independent government, and in any case the experience of Hong Kong argues that colonies can grow with extraordinary rapidity.[32]

A half-century or more of laissez-faire did generate some growth in India, but nothing comparable to what occurred in Japan. Laissez-faire led to some change and loosening of India's caste system, and some new special-interest organizations emerged. My guess is that if India after World War II had followed the policies the British once required, it would have done better than it has. Nonetheless, the fact remains that more than a half-century of laissez-faire did not bring about the development of India or even get it off to a good start. The laissez-faire ideology in its focus on the evils of government alone clearly leaves something out. I submit that it is the distributional coalitions, which over millennia of history in India had hardened into castes.

Another great experiment in laissez-faire was conducted in Great Britain itself. Britain generally followed laissez-faire policies at home as well as abroad from about the middle of the nineteenth century until the interwar period. (The United States in the same period had highly protectionist policies and in this and some other respects, such as the subsidies to railroads, fell considerably short of laissez-faire.) In this book I have argued, as would the ideological enthusiasts for laissez-faire, that the free trade policy Britain followed has limited the extent of distributional coalitions there. Things could be worse in Britain, and would have been had Britain had the highly protectionist policies of Australia and New Zealand. Nonetheless, as the theory here argues, laissez-faire did not prove to be dynamically stable—Britain abandoned it. Neither was it sufficient to prevent cartelization in many sectors.

During the nineteenth and early twentieth centuries, precisely when and where laissez-faire policy was at its peak, Great Britain acquired a large proportion of its dense network of narrow distributional coalitions. It was in this same period, too, that the British disease emerged and British growth rates and income levels began to lag.

Stagflation, Unemployment, and Business Cycles: An Evolutionary Approach to Macroeconomics

7

Throughout this book I have emphasized the contributions of my predecessors and contemporaries, the parts of the present theory that are drawn from prior work, and the cumulative character of research in any science, be it physical or social. In part, perhaps, this emphasis rests on my observation that those writers who are most assertive about the novelty of their work and the failings of their predecessors are frequently the least original; if this observation is general, there is something to be said for the opposite strategy. I would prefer to construct a tower, an arch, or even a gargoyle on a great cathedral that will last for ages than to take credit for singlehandedly constructing a shack that will be blown away by the next change in the winds of intellectual fashion. Therefore, in this chapter I will continue to admire and to build upon prior contributions, but the strategy at this point raises two difficulties.

The first is that, because of the aspects of prior contributions that I shall need to discuss and the inherent difficulty of the subject, the account in this chapter cannot be quite so simple and sparing in its use of technical concepts as the previous chapters have been. Those who have never before studied any economics may have to read more slowly. I dearly hope that this admission will not stop anyone from pressing on. Naturally, I have saved the best till the last: this chapter contains some of the strongest evidence in support of the present theory and perhaps the most important application of it to current problems of public policy. Moreover, I would like to think that the noneconomist who has persevered through the book thus far is so intelligent that he or she will enjoy mastering this one climactic chapter. I realize that in saying this I flatter some readers, and perhaps indirectly and inappropriately the book as well. But I sincerely believe that it is important, for both intellectual and political reasons, to bring the laymen who have followed the argument thus far through the analysis of this last chapter. I have accordingly devoted many hours to making the argument as transparent to all intelligent readers as it is within my powers to make it. These matters are not, I like to think, explained more simply elsewhere.

The second difficulty is that the distinguished economists that I shall admire and exploit in this chapter have often disagreed, even vituperatively, with one another. This has not been a serious problem in earlier chapters. Although laymen think economists disagree about everything, there is a considerable degree of consensus about the microeconomic theory, or theory of individual firms and markets, that has helped to inspire what I have done so far. The great majority of serious, skilled economists, be they of the Right or of the Left, of this school or of that, accept basically the same microeconomic theory. They often have remarkably similar views on many practical microeconomic policies, such as the tariffs and trade restrictions discussed in the last two chapters. Unfortunately, many of the economists who use and respect the same microeconomic theory strenuously disagree about macroeconomic theory, or the study of inflation, unemployment, and the fluctuations of the economy as a whole.

This disagreement may suggest that my strategy of building upon prior work now must be abandoned. Who will agree with my praise and use of prior contributions when the authors of those contributions have spoken so disparagingly of each other's work? Nonetheless, I have learned a good deal from each of the factions. And the centuries of work on the great cathedral must continue. The quarreling masons have not been working on this part of the cathedral from an agreed design, but I believe that they have hewed out of the granite most of the building blocks that are needed.

II

Why is there exceptional disagreement about macroeconomic theory and policy? Some economists suppose that one side or another is logically in error. Although there are plenty of logical errors, they can be demonstrated to be errors by rules of logic accepted by all sides. This, and the high professional rewards for such demonstrations, pretty well ensure that a school of macroeconomic or monetary thought cannot thrive for long on logical mistakes. The degree of cunning exhibited in debate by some leading protagonists of each persuasion and their skill in the use of microeconomic theory also argue that logical errors would not be the basic source of disagreement. Admittedly, there is bias and even fanaticism in some partisans that might impair their reasoning, but if so, we still need to explain why the fanatic temperament leads to more error and disagreement in one area of economics than in another.

The matter is not so clear-cut when empirical inferences are at issue. Sometimes different schools of thought emerge principally because of different judgments about inconclusive empirical evidence. When so much depends on the empirical evidence, the rewards to the empirical researcher who can show which side is most likely right are very great. If an investigation possibly could settle the dispute, it will almost certainly be undertaken. However, as I have argued elsewhere,[1] macroeconomic and monetary policies are like public goods in that they have indivisible consequences for whole nations at the least. The cause-and-effect relationships or "social production functions" for collective goods of vast domain are especially difficult to estimate, because experiments with the large units are so costly and the small number of these large units means that historical experience provides few natural experiments. Thus the empirical effects of various combinations of monetary, fiscal, and wage-price policy in different conditions sometimes cannot be determined until additional evidence becomes available. This is probably partly responsible for the special disagreement about macroeconomics.

Another source of the disagreement is that each of the competing theories, though containing valid and even precious insights, is a special theory that properly can be applied only in particular circumstances. The circumstances in which each of the competing theories is valid are different. Unfortunately, even those who respect the economics profession as much as I must admit that *some* of the proponents of each of these theories tend, alas, to be doctrinaire. The doctrinaire exponents of these special theories, evidently overwhelmed by the valuable insights in their preferred theory and outraged that the familiar competing theories are erroneous in the particular conditions in which the preferred theory is valid, claim that their favored theory is essentially true, whereas the competing theories are essentially false. These doctrinaire economists are guilty of unconscious synecdoche—implicitly taking the part for the whole. Of course, special or incomplete theories can be extraordinarily valuable; indeed, no theory can be useful unless it abstracts from the unmanageable complexity of reality, so any useful theory must in some sense be incomplete.[2] Even the doctrinaire exponents of each of the theories recognize that their theory is simpler than the reality it is supposed to describe, but the matters from which the cherished theory abstracts are taken to be random, unimportant, exceptional, or outside economics.

Some theories can be *fatally* incomplete for some purposes—such as choosing macroeconomic and monetary policies for the United States and a number of other countries at the present time. A theory that abstracts from the very essence of a problem it is intended to solve is fatally incomplete. This chapter will endeavor to show that all the familiar macroeconomic theories, although full of profound and indispensable insights, are in this sense fatally incomplete—each theory has a hole at its very center.

A final source of the special disagreement in macroeconomics, then, is the inadequacy for present purposes of each of the familiar macroeconomic theories: if any one of them had the robust and compelling character of Darwin's theory of evolution or Ricardo's theory of comparative advantage, it might still be dismissed by some people. But it would not be dismissed, as is each of the familiar macroeconomic theories, by many of the leading scientists in the field. When scientific consensus is lacking, it is usually because the right path has not yet been found. There have been few times and places in the history of economics when an economist had a better warrant for trying an eccentric line of inquiry than in macroeconomics today.

III

The contending theories that will be considered here are the Keynesian, the monetarist, the "disequilibrium," and the rational-expectations "equilibrium" models. Often, monetarist and rational-expectations or equilibrium approaches are thought to be the same, or perhaps different parts of the same theory; most advocates of the one also believe in the other. Similarly, disequilibrium theory is often considered a more modern form of Keynesian economics. For some purposes, however, it is essential to make distinctions among, and untypical combinations of, these models, which will be the case here. There are various other labels or approaches to the economy as a whole that receive attention in newspapers and political debates from time to time without generating serious attention in the technical journals. We shall not consider any of these approaches here, since they are too vague and superficial to be of any help.

Much of the debate between the Keynesians and the monetarists centers on what determines the level of spending, or the demand in money or nominal (that is, not corrected for inflation) terms, for the output of the economy as a whole. Monetarists argue that changes in the quantity of money are the only systematic and important sources of changes in the level of nominal income, whereas Keynes's theory also attributes a large role to budget deficits and surpluses and fiscal policy in general in determining the level of demand in the economy as a whole.

Even though Keynes's theory, like the monetarist model, focuses mainly on what determines the level of aggregate demand, it is absolutely essential to remember that Keynes *began* his dazzling, world-changing book with (and built his theory in substantial part upon) the idea that one very large and quite crucial set of prices was influenced by *something* beyond changes in demand, and indeed beyond supply and demand.

Keynes began his argument by attacking the classical or orthodox postulate that "the utility of the wage when a given volume of labour is employed is equal to the marginal disutility of that amount of employment." Pre-Keynesian economists had argued that if groups of workers through unions agreed not to work unless they received a stipulated wage, and that wage resulted in unemployment, this unemployment was not involuntary unemployment, but rather was due to collective choices of workers themselves. Keynes then assumed just such a situation:

> A reduction in the existing level of money wages would lead, through strikes or otherwise, to a withdrawal of labour which is now employed. Does it follow from this that the existing level of real wages accurately measures the marginal disutility of labour? Not necessarily. For, although a reduction in the existing money-wage would lead to a withdrawal of labour, it does not follow that a fall in the value of the existing money-wage in terms of wage-goods would do so, if it were due to a rise in the price of the latter [i.e., a rise in the cost of living]. In other words, it may be the case that within a certain range the demand of labour is for a minimum

money-wage and not for a minimum real wage. . . . Now ordinary experience tells us, beyond doubt, that a situation where labour stipulates (within limits) for a money-wage rather than a real wage, so far from being a mere possibility, is the normal case. . . .

But in the case of changes in the general level of wages it will be found, I think, that the change in real wages associated with a change in money-wages, so far from being usually in the same direction, is almost always in the opposite direction. When money-wages are rising, that is to say, it will be found that real wages are falling; and when money-wages are falling, real wages are rising. . . .

The struggle about money-wages primarily affects the *distribution* of the aggregate real wage between different labour-groups, and not its average amount per unit of employment. . . . The effect of combinations on the part of a group of workers is to protect their *relative* real wage.[3]

The central role of "sticky" (slow to change) wages in Keynes's theory, and one of the institutions that can cause this stickiness, are also emphasized in Keynes's chapter on "Changes in Money Wages":

Since there is, as a rule, no means of securing a simultaneous and equal reduction of money-wages in all industries, it is in the interest of all workers to resist a reduction in their own particular case. . . .

If, indeed, labour were always in a position to take action (and were to do so), whenever there was less than full employment, to reduce its money demands by concerted action to whatever point was required to make money so abundant relatively to the wage-unit that the rate of interest would fall to a level compatible with full employment, we should, in effect, have monetary management by the Trade Unions, aimed at full employment, instead of by the banking system.[4]

To be sure, Keynes's explanation of underemployment equilibrium did not consist merely of the assumption of sticky wages; pre-Keynesian theory already ascribed unemployment to unrealistically high wage levels, and Keynes was anxious to differentiate his theory from the theory that preceded it. Indeed, Keynes argued that reductions of money wages need not bring full employment, and that if they did it involved, in essence, "monetary management by the Trade Unions." As we know, Keynes also had new ideas about the demand for money as an asset and other matters that played significant roles in his theory. Still, the fact remains that although Keynes's theory argued for changing aggregate effective demand, especially through budget deficits and surpluses, and claimed to explain depression and inflation solely from the demand side, it nonetheless began and in substantial part rested upon the assumption that there were forces that influenced wages and that, within limits and at least for a time, did so in ways that could not be explained in terms of increases or decreases in the demand for labor or individual decisions to trade off more or less labor for leisure.

Unfortunately, Keynes never provided any real explanation of why wages were sticky, or what determined why they stuck at one level rather than another, or for how long. This is all the more troublesome because, on first examination, this stickiness is not consistent with the optimizing or purposeful behavior that economists usually observe when they study individual behavior. This incompleteness of Keynesian theory—the reliance on an ad hoc premise that has not been reconciled with the rest of economic theory—has troubled the leading Keynesian economists (and, of course, anti-Keynesian economists) for some time.[5] It also has been, in my judgment, a source of some of the failures of macroeconomic policies in the 1970s.

A similar uneasiness about an unexplained stickiness of certain wages or prices has pervaded the writings on disequilibrium theory, or the theory of macroeconomics that is based on the observation that some markets do not clear (that is, do not reach a situation where everyone who wants to make a transaction at the going price can do so, so that shortages or surpluses persist). In the seminal book in this tradition, Robert Barro and Herschel Grossman emphasized this uneasiness with exemplary scientific candor:

> One other omission from our discussion is especially embarrassing and should be explicitly noted. Although the discussion stresses the implications of exchange at prices which are inconsistent with general market clearing, we provide no choice-theoretic analysis of the market-clearing process itself. In other words, we do not analyze the adjustment of wages and prices as part of the maximizing behavior of firms and households. Consequently, we do not really explain the failure of markets to clear, and our analyses of wage and price dynamics are based on ad hoc adjustment equations.[6]

Perhaps this admirable uneasiness about a theory built on an unexplained ad hoc premise explains why the authors, heralded as leaders of the Keynesian-disequilibrium counterrevolution, by the evidence of subsequent works have joined the flight from Keynesian economics.

IV

Monetarist models and rational-expectations equilibrium theory have the supremely important virtue of avoiding any appeal to sticky or downwardly-rigid wages that are themselves unexplained. Monetarist and equilibrium theorists assume that changes in the quantity of money tend to bring about proportional changes in nominal income because the price level readily adjusts, and that real output is determined by resource availability, technology, and other factors outside the scope of monetary and fiscal policy.

The monetarist and equilibrium theories usually are not guilty of assuming arbitrary wage or price levels, but they fail to provide any explanation of involuntary unemployment or of massive and prolonged unemployment of any sort. In more recent years, it is true, some enlightening arguments that can explain *some* variations in the level of employment have been introduced by monetarists and others. "Search" models, for example, have been developed, which explain some unemployment on the ground that occasionally it will be in a worker's interest to spend full time searching for the best available job. Then there are the "accelerationist" (or "decelerationist") monetarist arguments, which are offered as accounts of brief periods of unemployment and recession; if there is a lower rate of inflation (or a higher rate of deflation) than expected, various decisions that were made on the basis of the false expectations could, because of various lags (that are not well specified or explained), bring about temporary unemployment and reductions in real output.

The rational-expectations equilibrium theorists proceed to a conclusion that may lead newcomers to macroeconomics to think that I am describing the work of theoreticians who have lost absolutely all touch with reality. The conclusion is that involuntary unemployment and depressions due to inadequate demand simply do not occur! Although I am not in sympathy with this conclusion, I plead with readers to be patient, for the equilibrium theorists have put forth intellectually useful models of extraordinary subtlety (see, for example, the impressive work of Robert Lucas, Thomas Sargent, and Neil Wallace). Moreover, as I will demonstrate later in this chapter, it is possible to draw insights out of this quite fundamental theorizing and use them in another theory that might appeal also to those who believe that equilibrium theory as it stands is bizarre. One such insight is the equilibrium theorists' favorite concept of *rational expectations*. Not all the definitions of rational expectations are exactly the same, but for present purposes it is best interpreted as the notion that people making decisions take into account all available information that is worth taking into account; economically rational expectations in this sense has all along been the usual implicit assumption in microeconomic theorizing.

Equilibrium theorists explain obvious variations in the rate of unemployment over the business cycle primarily in terms of voluntary choices concerning when appears to be the most advantageous time to take leisure or education or to forgo gainful employment in order to spend full time seeking a better job. Their arguments are too complicated to summarize without violating the general constraints that govern the exposition in this volume. The key to the equilibrium theory is nonetheless clear: it is the supposition that different groups in the economy have different information or expectations of the future, and that individual workers, despite rational expectations, temporarily misperceive real wages or real interest rates. Suppose that workers expect a higher rate of inflation than actually occurs. They may then conclude that a given money-wage that is offered promises a lower real wage than they eventually can obtain. Since the worker values leisure as well as money income, he may choose to remain unemployed until he is offered a job at the real wage he ultimately can command. If the worker is mistaken about the course of the price level, he may, according to this theory, remain unemployed until he discovers that his estimate of the change in the price level was wrong. Another possibility is that the misjudgment of the prospective change in the price level leads the worker to underestimate the real interest rate, so that he overinvests for a time in education and other forms of human capital. These arguments require that the employers and those workers who choose to remain employed have different information or judgments about the future course of the price level than do the unemployed workers. If the arguments are to explain the high and prolonged levels of unemployment that sometimes occur, they also require enormous changes in the supply of labor from relatively modest changes in perceived real wages.

The models of the kind I have just described fail to persuade even many monetarist economists, and of course they do not convince Keynesians. Robert Solow, for example, finds "these propositions very hard to believe, and I am not sure why anyone should believe them in the absence of any evidence."[7] But they have attracted a huge amount of attention among macroeconomists; my hunch is that there is an intuitive perception that the models eventually could help economists to work out something better.

Although the search, accelerationist/decelerationist, and equilibrium theories, which in most formulations attribute any macroeconomic problems to mistaken expectations, can explain *some* variations in the level of employment and the rate of utilization of other resources, they are not nearly sufficient to explain the depth and duration of the unemployment in the interwar period. If the economy is always at a full employment level of output, except when and only for as long as the rate of inflation that was anticipated exceeds that which occurs, why did the depression that began in the United States in 1929 and ended only with World War II involve such an enormous and prolonged reduction in employment and real output? Consider also the case of Great Britain in the interwar period. Britain then as now used a system for measuring unemployment that by comparison with current U.S. practice understates the degree of unemployment; yet, from shortly after World War I until World War II, Great Britain almost never recorded less than 10 percent unemployment.

This interwar experience could be explained on an expectations hypothesis only if people, in the midst of the greatest depression ever, expected an inflation so dramatic that it made sense to refuse to accept any wage or price unless it was significantly above the current levels, or far above the level that would clear current markets. This is—to put it mildly—doubtful, and it is even more doubtful that most people would have persisted in such wildly erroneous expectations for a dozen years in the case of the United States or for twenty years in that of Great Britain. Neither is it credible that, when unemployment and welfare arrangements were so much less generous than today and when most workers were the only source of support for their families, the natural rate of unemployment could leave a tenth to a fourth of the work force unemployed.

The inability of the search, monetarist, and equilibrium theories to explain the magnitude and tenacity of unemployment in the interwar period suggests that they are seriously incomplete. Some of the leading advocates of the expectations-oriented theories concede this and also agree that they are not nearly sufficient to explain the great depression.

Perhaps there are analogies to monetarist and equilibrium theories in the histories of other sciences. The avoidance of ad hoc assumptions is commendable and the effort to explain unemployment and business cycles with complete fidelity to well-tested theory is similar to what I advocated in chapter 1 and have tried to do in this book. But the unwillingness in most monetarist and equilibrium theorizing to go beyond the conventionally defined borders of economics or to take a completely different perspective on the problem needs rethinking. So does the attachment to "equilibrium," even in the wake of the colossal unemployment and reduction in real output in the interwar period. Equilibrium is a useful concept only if there is disequilibrium too. If the disequilibrium approach is ruled out and the economy is deemed to be in or near equilibrium even in major depressions and recessions, what observation or set of observations possibly could tend to call the theory into question? Equilibrium theory may have something in common with the attachment of nineteenth-century physicists to the concept of an "ether" that was supposed to fill all space and suffuse itself even into material and living bodies. The work of Einstein and others has led to the total abandonment of the unnecessary concept of ether. With a similarly excessive attachment to established theory, the Ptolomaic astronomers constructed "epicycles" to reconcile their observations of the planets' orbits with their assumption that the earth was the center of the system. Even given these epicycles, additional observations often required new estimates of cycles or epicycles of particular planets, with the result that new anomalies would crop up in other parts of the system. The Copernican heliocentric astronomy as developed by Kepler and Newton offers a far simpler and more persuasive conception.[8] Probably the intertemporal elasticities of supply of labor required to explain the unemployment in Britain and the United States in the interwar period as the result of voluntary choices of workers who thought they were well advised to hold out for higher expected real wages would introduce new anomalies into our econometric studies of labor supply. These studies have not revealed any great sensitivity of the amount of labor offered to small changes in the real wage.

V

The shortcomings of monetarism and equilibrium theory probably persuaded some economists to remain a while longer with Keynesian theory, notwithstanding its utter dependence on the unexplained assumption of sticky wages. But the Keynesian model (like some of the other macroeconomic models) has lately been contradicted by stagflation, or simultaneous inflation and unemployment. A Keynesian model cannot explain how high inflation and high rates of unemployment can occur together, as they did in the 1970s, and this is a problem for some of the other macroeconomic models also. Some Keynesian economists have tried to explain recent macroeconomic experience in Britain, the United States, and some other countries in terms of negatively sloped Phillips curves (observed tendencies for wage and price increases to vary inversely with the level of unemployment). There is no need to invoke the monetarist criticisms of the Phillips-curve concept to show that it is inadequate, for it is only a statistical finding (or a statistical finding for a certain period) in search of a theory. An explanation of stagflation is not an explanation at all unless it includes a general explanation of *why* a Phillips curve should have this or that slope, and *why* the curve shifts if it is alleged to shift. Any Phillips-curve relationship must be derived from the interests and constraints faced by individual decision-makers. The lack of an adequate explanation in Keynes of stagflation or Phillips curves—especially the tendency for short-run Phillips curves to move upward and become steeper over long periods of inflation—must have a lot to do with the apparent growth in skepticism about Keynesian economics in recent years. (Although he certainly exaggerated, Lord Balogh did not miss the direction of change when he lamented that "anti-Keynesianism was the world's fastest-growth industry.")[9]

"Implicit contracts" have also been brought to bear in efforts to explain the recent stagflation in ways that can be reconciled with Keynes. Implicit contracts have been used to explain such phenomena as very long-term employment relationships and temporal variability in levels of effort asked of employees, combined with stable wage levels, and for purposes such as these they are a most illuminating concept. They are not sufficient to explain any significant amount of unemployment, much less simultaneous inflation and unemployment. Indeed, insofar as implicit contracts bear on stagflation and unemployment, they are more likely to *reduce* than increase the extent of it. Essentially, workers and employers will enter into implicit contracts, like explicit ones, only if they feel that will be advantageous. People are risk averse, as implicit contract theory rightly assumes,[10] so that, other things being equal, they will prefer to enter into contracts that *reduce* the probability of layoffs. They could even gain from slightly lower wages if this were combined with an implicit or explicit agreement that the employer would make every possible effort to keep them employed. The employers would not gain from contracts with individual workers stipulating rigid wages or other conditions that would increase the probability of layoffs; rigid wages constrain employers and deny them potential gains. The most profitable implicit contract between employers and employees would enable them to let the wage, in effect, fluctuate in such a way that employers and employees jointly maximized the difference between the value of leisure and alternative work to the employee and the marginal revenue product of labor for the employer. These functions shift, sometimes frequently, so only a flexible wage would be consistent with the employment of the mutually optimal amount of labor. Of course, wages most often are not very flexible, but the main reason for this, as we shall see later, is not implicit contracts.

It can be difficult to work out a long-term contract that is completely successful in maximizing the joint gain of the worker and the employer, since only the worker may know the value to him of his leisure time and only the employer may know how much a given amount of labor will add to his revenue. In practice the employers and employee may not succeed in finding exactly that wage and quantity of employment that will give them the maximum joint gain over an extended period. One of the possibilities is that they will make an arrangement that ends up with the worker working less than he would have worked had there been perfect information on all sides. But it is preposterous to attribute any substantial amount of unemployment to this possibility, since if the losses of this nature are large, the two parties would not have any incentive to make a long-term contract in any case and would rely instead on a series of "spot market" deals. Thus implicit contracts cannot explain any substantial amount of unemployment, and on balance almost certainly reduce unemployment. The common arrangement whereby firms strive to keep workers on the payroll even during slack times and workers in turn do extra work at rush periods without demanding an increased wage is probably the most common type of implicit contract, and it reduces unemployment.

There are also "cost-push" explanations of inflation and stagflation, which attribute the inflation or stagflation to price and wage increases by firms and unions with monopoly power. As others have shown before, the typical cost-push arguments are manifestly unsatisfactory. They offer no explanation of why there should be continuing inflation or why there should be more inflation in one period than in another. They do not explain why an organization with monopoly power would not choose whatever price or wage it found most advantageous as soon as it obtained the monopoly power, after which point it would have no more reason to increase prices or wages than a pure competitor. In the absence of some adequate explanation of why organizations with monopoly power do not take advantage of that power when they first acquire it, or some explanation of why monopoly power should increase over time in a way consistent with the history of inflation or stagflation, the cost-push arguments are unsatisfactory. They must also be accompanied by some account of why governments or central banks would provide increased demand after the alleged cost-push had increased wages and prices, so that the cost-push would culminate in inflation rather than in unemployed resources. (With the theory offered in this book and some other ideas, one could construct a valid theory of inflation that would have a faint resemblance to the familiar cost-push arguments, but these arguments have been the source of so much confusion that there is probably more loss than gain from doing so.)

VI

What must we demand of a macroeconomic theory before we can find it even provisionally adequate? First, the theory should be deduced entirely from reasonable and testable assumptions about the behavior of individuals: it must at no point violate any valid microeconomic theory. This means, in turn, that it must not contain ad hoc, unexplained assumptions about anything, including sticky or downwardly rigid wages or prices; such rigidities may be introduced only if they are in turn explained in terms of rational individual behavior or rational behavior of firms, organizations, governments, or other institutions (and the presence of such institutions must again be explained in terms of rational individual behavior). I think the vast majority of economists, whatever existing macroeconomic theory they might prefer, agree that a macroeconomic theory should make sense at a microeconomic level as well. This is evident from the support for the work on the microeconomic foundations of macroeconomic theory going on in all camps (consider, for example, the wide influence of Edmund Phelps's volumes on the microeconomic foundations of macroeconomics).[11]

Second, an adequate macroeconomic theory must explain *involuntary* as well as voluntary unemployment and major depressions as well as minor recessions. There are, of course, large numbers of people who voluntarily choose not to work for pay (such as the voluntarily retired, the idle rich, those who prefer handouts to working at jobs, those who stay at home full time to care for children, and so on) and, given the way unemployment statistics are gathered in the United States and other countries, no doubt some of these show up in the unemployment statistics. Yet common sense and the observations and experiences of literally hundreds of millions of people testify that there is also involuntary unemployment and that it is by no means an isolated or rare phenomenon. Depressions in the level of real output as deep as those observed in the Great Depression in the interwar period surely cannot be adequately explained without involuntary unemployment of labor and of other resources. The Great Depression was an event so conspicuous that the whole world observed it, and the political and intellectual life in most countries was revolutionized by it. Only a madman—or an economist with both "trained incapacity" and doctrinal passion—could deny the reality of involuntary unemployment. The first condition set out above entails that the involuntary unemployment is not adequately explained unless it can be shown to be possible even when every individual and firm or other organization involved is rationally acting in its own interest; the *motive* generating the involuntary unemployment, that is, the interests that are directly or indirectly served by it, must be elucidated.

Third, the theory must explain why the unemployment is more common among groups of lower skill and productivity, such as teenagers, disadvantaged racial minorities, and so on. This outcome may seem only natural to the laity, but many of the prevailing theories about variations in employment and unemployment do not predict the pattern that is observed. The search-theory approach (like the notion of "frictional unemployment") predicts the most unemployment in "thin" markets where buyers and sellers are less numerous; an individual must search longer to find a counterpart for his employment contract. Generally, professional and other highly skilled workers are the most specialized and operate in the thinnest markets, and they should by the search theory have the highest unemployment rates. The largest single labor market is that for unskilled labor, where search unemployment should be lowest.

Fourth, the theory must be able to accommodate both equilibrium and disequilibrium, among other reasons because neither concept is empirically operational without the other.

Fifth, an adequate macroeconomic theory must be consistent with booms as well as with busts—with periods of unusual prosperity and with periods of underutilized productive capacity. It must be consistent with what we loosely call the "business cycle," although the absence of strong regularities in the length and extent of periods of prosperity and recession suggests that "business fluctuations" would perhaps be a better term. In other words, as Kenneth Arrow points out,[12] the theory must be consistent with the observation that neither depressions nor full-employment levels of production appear to sustain themselves indefinitely.

Sixth, the theory should be able to explain, without ad hockery, the really dramatic differences across societies and historical periods in the nature of the macroeconomic problem. If economic history were more widely taught in economics departments, the need for this requirement would long ago have been obvious, but modern trends in economics and econometrics have meant that economic history has, alas, been crowded out and even belittled.

Seventh, since the greater the explanatory power of a theory, other things being equal, the greater the likelihood that it is true, the theory ideally should be able, at least in its full or complete form, to explain some other, extra-macroeconomic phenomena. This is not an absolute requirement, but we should be uneasy if it is not met and reassured if it is. I must repeat again that the theory need not be monocausal, so that any number of factors that are exogenous to it may be terribly important, for macroeconomic problems as well as for other matters.

Eighth, as we already know from chapter 1, the theory should be relatively simple and parsimonious.

I submit that the following theory, when combined with familiar and straightforward elements from the four macroeconomic theories set out earlier in this chapter and with what has been presented in earlier chapters of this book, meets all eight of the above conditions. Partly to underline the simplicity of the argument, especially in contrast to many of the recent contributions to macroeconomics, and partly to reach students and policy-makers, the discussion will use only the most basic and simple theoretical tools.

VII

I shall first explain, subject to the constraints entailed in the first of the above conditions, one source of the involuntary unemployment of labor. Even though it is natural to begin with the simplest and most straightforward source and type of unemployment, it is vitally important *not* to use this first explanation in isolation from the rest of the argument. There is also unemployment or underutilization of machinery and other forms of capital in a depression or a recession, and although this usually does not conjure up such painful visions as does involuntary unemployment of labor, it also involves waste of productive capacity and in addition often contributes to the losses workers suffer in such times, since the idle capital means that less capital is combined with labor, and the demand for labor and wages can then tend to be lower than they might otherwise be. The demand for labor obviously depends on what is happening in the product markets in which the firms that employ labor sell their output, so the *amount* of involuntary unemployment of labor most definitely cannot be determined without looking at conditions in product as well as labor markets.

It would be easy but unhelpful to explain involuntary unemployment in terms of some allegedly persistent tendency of those involved to choose outcomes that are inconsistent with their interests. So I shall assume rational expectations, in the sense that individuals take into account all the information that it pays them to take into account—all available information that they expect will be worth more to them than it costs.

We also must define *involuntary* unemployment *very* strictly. If we let a wide variety of situations count as involuntary unemployment, it would again be easy to explain its existence, but nothing much would be gained. In particular, we must be certain that we do not include in our definition any voluntary unemployment, which is easily explicable as a preference for leisure or home-produced output over the earnings from work. I do this by reference to figure 1. This depicts, in the *MC* (marginal cost) or supply curve, the value of the time of workers in the form of leisure, home-produced goods, and any other opportunities. The demand for labor, or *MRP* (marginal revenue product) curve, consists of *points* on the separate marginal revenue product of labor curves of firms in diverse industries that have a demand for whatever type of labor is at issue.[13] In the interest of saving a few moments of time for those intellectually versatile noneconomists who have persevered through this chapter, I point out that *MC* or the marginal cost curve for labor is assumed to rise because as more labor is taken, workers with a lesser attraction to the labor force must be persuaded to take paid employment, and because each worker must be paid more to forgo leisure

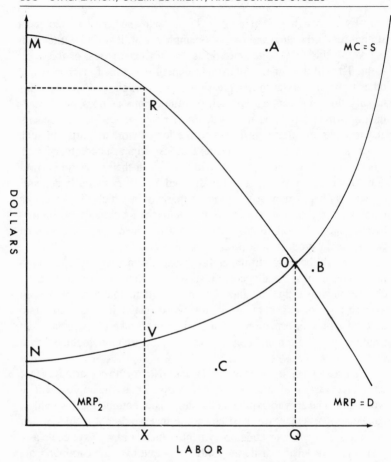

the more hours of work he has already supplied. The D curve declines because, among other reasons, the law of diminishing returns entails that additional labor of a given type will eventually add smaller increments to output.

At points to the right of the intersection of the two curves, such as point B, there can be no involuntary unemployment; the value of leisure or alternative opportunities is above point B, so no one will accept a job at that wage level, and when the amount of labor given by point B is already employed the employers would find that wage level B would cost more than the additional labor was worth to them anyway. In terms of the first quote from Keynes earlier in this chapter, we would have to move leftward to the intersection of the two curves to find the point where "the utility of the wage . . . is equal to the disutility of that amount of employment." Similarly, if anyone demanded a wage level such as that at point A there would also not be involuntary unemployment, because A is higher than the marginal revenue product of labor; the worker would be asking for a gift more than a job, for any employer will lose money from employing him at that wage. At a point such as C there is similarly no involuntary unemployment; this is below the value of time in alternative uses and the worker does not accept any job that pays only a wage of C.

We could also postulate a different type of labor with so little value to employers that the MRP curve was for all or almost all of its length *below* the MC curve, as MRP_2 is. In this depressing case, the worth of that type of labor is so low that no employer would gain from taking it, even if the wage were so low that even a normally industrious worker would not take it. A case such as this may be more tragic than involuntary unemployment, but we must not confuse it with involuntary unemployment. We know that patients in a hospital are not working, but we do not count them as or usually describe them as unemployed; the problem of people who cannot be productive, or whose productivity is so low that no one could gain from hiring them even if they put a negligible value on their time, is a problem of unproductive resources, not a problem of unemployment of resources—it does not imply any unutilized productive capacity.

There can be involuntary unemployment only in the roughly triangular area MNO. There is involuntary unemployment in our strict sense *only* if a worker's employment would add an amount to an employer's revenue that is greater than the value that the worker puts on his time, taking the value of leisure and all other opportunities for the worker into account.

Similarly, if a worker is unemployed because he believes that it is in his best interest to spend more time searching for work and therefore declines inferior employment opportunities while searching, this again is not involuntary unemployment. Personal observation may tell the reader that it is easier to get a job if one already has one, and that this type of search unemployment is rather rare. Whether this is true or not, if this type of unemployment occurs we must not call it involuntary; the worker is simply investing his time in the way that he believes will maximize lifetime income and satisfaction. If this type of unemployment were somehow prohibited, the national output and welfare would decline in the long run, since the worker in question presumably knows his interests and situation better than anyone else. On the other hand, if there is a social institution or public policy that inefficiently increases search costs or time spent in job queues, the extra searching is then required by the institution or policy, and this extra searching is no longer an investment that generates a social gain: any *extra* search unemployment due to such arrangements is defined to be involuntary.

Suppose, arbitrarily, that only *OX* workers are employed; there is then strictly involuntary unemployment of *XQ* workers, as that many have a marginal revenue product in excess of the marginal cost of their time. Note now the triangular area *RVO*, giving the area that is both above the marginal cost of the relevant labor and below the marginal revenue product of labor curve. This area represents a social loss, for the time of the workers would be worth more to employers than it is worth to themselves. Above all, *note that mutually advantageous bargains can be worked out between the unemployed workers and the employers;* they both will be better off by agreeing to an employment contract at a wage level between the two curves. *This will always be true if there is involuntary unemployment in the strict sense.*

In a Keynesian "unemployment equilibrium" these same gains would accrue to both employers and employees from making an employment contract; as time goes on, more such contracts will be made, so the "unemployment equilibrium" is not an equilibrium at all. Keynes was also talking about genuinely involuntary unemployment. The difficulty now being described is in fact a staff stuck right through the heart of Keynes's explanation of unemployment. I hasten to add that several others, such as Don Patinkin, have found this difficulty in Keynes earlier, usually by somewhat different paths, and that this is one of the reasons so many good economists have been searching for a solid microeconomic foundation for Keynesian economics, or else for an alternative to it. The fact remains that we do not have a satisfactory explanation of involuntary unemployment in Keynes, or for that matter in disequilibrium theory.

The involuntarily unemployed workers and employers in the real world do not have perfect knowledge, of course, and they may not know for a time of the gains they would acquire if they made a deal. Thus some of the workers might not become employed for a time. They would have to search, as would the employers, to obtain the mutual gains. Still, there need be no involuntary unemployment, because the workers would either continue at other jobs while they looked for better work, or else they would decide that the best way they could use their time was to invest it in searching; and as we indicated that sort of investment is not involuntary unemployment any more than investment in education is. One could appeal, as some equilibrium theorists do, to asymmetries in information that would make employers and employees estimate the *MRP* or *MC* curves differently, but this is an arbitrary and empirically implausible solution. Such misperceptions presumably could not last for twenty-year periods, such as the unemployment in Britain between the wars, or could not confuse such a large proportion of the work force as was unemployed in the United States from 1929 until World War II. We must seek some stronger and more durable influence preventing the mutually advantageous transactions between the involuntarily unemployed and present or prospective employers.

VIII

For the economist, it is natural to ask who in the government or else-where might have an interest in blocking the mutually advantageous transactions with the involuntarily unemployed. The president and governing political parties would not have any direct interest in blocking such transactions; they would risk losing the votes of both the prospective employee and the prospective employer. Everyday observation tells us that incumbents wish to run for re-election on "peace and prosperity" or "you never had it so good" platforms. The population at large would not want to block the transaction out of general human sympathy, and the business community as a whole would want the extra employment because of the extra demand it would bring to business in general.

The main group that can have an interest in preventing the mutually profitable transactions between the involuntarily unemployed and employers is the workers with the same or competitive skills. They have a substantial interest in preventing such transactions, for their own wages must be lowered as extra labor pushes the marginal revenue product of labor down. The only way that the existing workers can prevent the mutually advantageous transactions is if they are organized as a cartel or lobby or (as is very often the case) are in one way or another informally able to exert collusive pressure. The only other group that could have such an interest would be a monopsonistic (or buyers') cartel or lobby of employers; it would need to block mutually advantageous transactions between individual employers and workers to keep wages below competitive levels. No model of involuntary unemployment or theory of macroeconomics that ignores the motive that makes unemployment occur can be satisfactory.

The foregoing account has for expository reasons focused only on the labor market and *temporarily* assumed no cartelization or governmental intervention in the rest of the economy, where prices are perfectly flexible. This ensures that employers always will be able to sell their outputs. Of course, the same argument applies to the market for other factors of production and to product markets, where these applications are often much more important. The downward sloping curve in the figure could just as well have been a demand curve for a product and the upward sloping curve the supply curve or marginal cost of producing it. If something, such as a price that was too high, created underutilization of productive capacity, there would be the possibility of mutually advantageous gains in the triangle. Again, the only party that could have an interest in blocking these mutually advantageous transactions between buyers and actual or potential sellers would be the firms that profited from a noncompetitive price. They could prevent the mutually advantageous transactions only if they were organized as a lobby or cartel or could collude informally or tacitly.

As disequilibrium theorists such as Edmond Malinvaud have shown,[14] the price that does not clear the market (that is, consummate all mutually advantageous transactions) in a product market can also contribute to unemployment of labor or excess capacity in other product markets. Later in this chapter I shall consider the combined effects of distributional coalitions in both factor and product markets at the same time. Because of the findings of the disequilibrium theorists and of what I will present later, the above analyses of the labor market cannot be used in isolation and must be applied together with similar analyses of other factor markets and product markets.

The more extensive the special-interest groups and the non-market-clearing prices lobbying and cartelization bring about, the greater the variations in the rates of return for similar workers and for capital. The greater these variations, the more it pays to search for the higher returns. This extra search, however, is not a socially efficient expenditure on the gathering of information, and it is required only because of the special-interest groups, so it also generates involuntary unemployment. Some time is spent in job queues because of the non-market-clearing prices and wages, which further increases involuntary unemployment.

IX

We shall soon see that the above approach has some surprising and testable implications when placed in a general equilibrium context, but it will first be necessary to refer back to Implication 6 in chapter 3. That implication was that distributional coalitions generate slow decision-making, crowded agendas, and cluttered bargaining tables. In many cases, we found, it was also advantageous for these coalitions to be quantity-adjusters rather than price-adjusters.

The implication explains why many prices and wages in some societies are sticky. It takes a special-interest organization or collusion some time to go through the unanimous-consent bargaining or constitutional procedures by which it must make its decisions. Since all the most important decisions of the organization or collusion must be made in this way, it has a crowded agenda. Since the distributional coalition often has to lobby or bargain with others, it may face other organizations or institutions with crowded agendas, so bargaining tables may be cluttered, too. Thus it can be a slow process for a price or wage that is influenced or set by lobbies or cartels to be determined. Once the price or wage is determined, it is not likely to change quickly even if conditions change in such a way that a different price or wage would be optimal for the coalition. So special-interest groups bring about sticky wages and prices.

It is widely observed that prices and wages are less flexible downward than upward. Malinvaud, for example, speaks of the "commonly believed property according to which prices are more sticky downward than upward,"[15] and my colleague Charles Schultze's influential early work on stagflation builds partly upon that premise.[16] This observation is puzzling; any decision-makers, however much monopoly power they have, should choose the price or wage that is optimal for them and should on average lose just as much from a price that is too high as from one that is too low. It might seem, then, that if prices are sticky for any reason they should be equally sluggish going in each direction. There is observed stickiness going each way but many observations that this stickiness is more extreme or systematic on the down side. A cartel or lobby with slow decision-making will take time deciding either to raise or to lower prices and presumably its collective decision-making procedures are equally slow in each direction.

We can see from the analysis that led to Implication 6 that there is nonetheless an asymmetry. If one member of a cartel charges a lower price than the agreed-upon price, that hurts the others—they get fewer sales and lower prices. If a cartel member charges a higher price than the agreed-upon price, on the other hand, there is no harm to the others in the cartel. If there is a reduction in demand a cartel may wish that it had chosen a lower price, but because of the conditions adduced in the discussion of Implication 6 the decision to lower the cartel price will come only after some delay. If, from a position of equilibrium, there is a sufficiently small increase in demand facing the firms in the cartel, each firm can sell a little more at the old cartel price and enjoy increased profits, although not as much of an increase as if the cartel price had been adjusted promptly. Now consider an unexpected increase in demand so large that each firm can get *more* than the cartel price. No firm could have an objection if any other firm charged more than the cartel price, so for a time there will be upward flexibility in prices. The argument requires that monopolistic cartels are more common than buyers' cartels, and this appears to be the case.[17] A testable implication of the theory is that the converse phenomenon would be evident in monopsonistic cartels.

The location of price and wage stickiness across industries is also consistent with the theory. The theory implies that in sectors where there is special-interest organization there will be more stickiness, and (because of Implication 3) in industries where there is a fairly small number of firms that can collude more easily, there will on average be less price flexibility than in industries with so many firms that they cannot collude without selective incentives. Those large groups that are organized because of selective incentives may have even slower decision-making.

The sluggish movement of wages that are set by collective bargaining is well known. Wage flexibility appears to be particularly great in temporary markets where organization is pretty much ruled out, as in the markets for seasonal workers, consultants, and so on. There also appears to be less flexibility in manufacturing prices than in farm prices (except when farm prices are determined by governments under the influence of lobbies). This has been noted by observant monetarists as well as by Keynesians. Phillip Cagan, a leading monetarist, summarizes the evidence clearly and fairly:

> While manufacturing prices have at times fallen precipitously, as in the business contractions of 1920–21 and 1929–33, usually they

do not. To be sure, the available data do not record the secret discounting and shading of prices in slack markets, and actual transaction prices undoubtedly undergo larger fluctuations than the reported quotations suggest. The difference between reported and actual prices [will be] discussed further. It is not important enough, however, to invalidate the observed insensitivity of most prices to shifts in demand.[18]

F. M. Scherer and many others also present data indicating that there are greater fluctuations in farm and commodity prices than in prices in concentrated manufacturing industries.[19]

The present theory also predicts that there will be more unemployment among groups in the work force that have relatively low skills and productivity, as our list of conditions for a suitable macroeconomic theory suggested it should. As Implication 6 explained, distributional coalitions will more often than not bargain for a wage or price and permit employers or customers to make some of the decisions about who gets the resulting gains, so that the coalition will be able to minimize divisive conflict over the sharing of the gains of its collective action. When wages and salaries are set above market-clearing levels, the employer will choose and attract more qualified employees than with competitive wages, and the less productive may find that at the wage levels that have been established it is not in an employer's interest to hire them. If the less-qualified and the employers were free to negotiate any employment contracts they wished, the wages would vary with productivity, and workers with positive but relatively low productivity would find it easier to obtain jobs. The worker who is trained for a high-skill occupation but does not get a job because he or she has below-average skills for that occupation will oftentimes be able to get a job in a lower-paying occupation with lower average qualifications; but the unskilled worker is less likely to have any such inferior alternative employment to turn to. Of course, other factors are also important. For example, some of the construction and manufacturing activities that have strong unions and high wages are also sensitive to the business cycle and accordingly have unstable employment patterns.

X

Implication 6 also tells us something about how those prices and wages influenced by special-interest groups will react to unexpected inflation or deflation. A cartel or lobby will seek whatever price it believes best, but for the reasons explained in chapter 3 it will seek agreements or arrangements that last for some length of time. Collective bargaining agreements in the United States offer a clear, though perhaps extreme, example of this; they customarily last for three years.

Now suppose that there is unexpected inflation or deflation. With unexpected inflation the price the special-interest group obtained will become lower in relation to other prices than the group wanted or expected it to be, but the group will not quickly be able to change the relevant agreement or legislation. Since the cartel or lobby could only have gained from setting a supracompetitive or monopoly price, unexpected inflation will make the relative price it receives less monopolistic than intended. The price will also be closer to market-clearing levels than expected. An unexpected inflation therefore reduces the losses from monopoly due to cartelization and lobbying and the degree of involuntary unemployment. In a period of unexpected inflation an economy with a high level of special-interest organization and collusion will be more productive than it normally is.

In a period of unexpected deflation, by contrast, the price or wage set by a distributional coalition will for a time be even higher than the coalition expected or (if it had gotten its way completely) even higher than it desired. This will mean that the losses from monopoly are greater than normal and that the relative prices are even farther above market-clearing levels than normal, so involuntary unemployment will be unusually high.

We now have a better explanation than has previously been available for the familiar observation that in most economies *unexpected* inflation means reduced unemployment and a boom in real output, whereas *unexpected* deflation (or disinflation) means more unemployment and a reduction in real output. Although it has been shown in formal general-equilibrium models (in which special-interest groups were not taken into account) that ''money is neutral,'' that inflation has no effect on relative prices and no impact on real output, we now see why this conclusion does not hold for most economies in the real world.

Naturally, if inflation rises to triple-digit levels (as it has in several countries) and there is great uncertainty about the future rate of inflation, special-interest groups will then seek to lobby or to bargain for prices or wages that are indexed to the rate of inflation. I have not examined the process when inflation rates are that high, but I would hypothesize that the economic results in real terms of higher-than-expected inflation or unexpected disinflation in such circumstances would be sensitive to the imperfections of the available price indexes. And these imperfections are substantial even in the best of circumstances. Strictly speaking, each consumer needs a separate price index if he or she is going to be perfectly indexed against inflation, because each consumer tends to buy a different bundle of goods and the price of each good tends to change by a different amount. But this proof that no special-interest organization could find an ideal price index for all its members is of minor importance when compared to the great shortcomings of the existing price indexes, even in the countries with the best statistics. The very substantial mismeasurement of the rate of inflation in the United States by the Consumer Price Index is well known. Some of the defects of this index could be corrected readily were there no lobbies resisting such correction, but other difficulties cannot in practice be solved. There is no way adequately to measure the changes in the quality of products, for example, and no way to adjust appropriately for the fact that consumers will take relatively less of whatever products rise most in price, so these goods will be overweighted in the price index. These and other problems are so difficult in practice that in the United States in the 1950s and early 1960s, when measured rates of inflation were already significant, skilled economists were seriously debating whether there was in fact any inflation at all.[20] Thus the impact of unexpected inflation or unexpected deflation is usually mitigated by indexing only in those cases where inflation has proceeded for some time at high levels.

XI

It is now time to extend the argument by recognizing that there are many different industries or sectors in the economy and that what happens in each sector affects and is affected by what happens in other sectors: that is, the argument must be put in a general equilibrium context.

To understand the present theory fully in a general equilibrium context, we must draw upon an important but inadequately appreciated insight of Robert Clower's.[21] The essence of Clower's insight can be seen by returning to figure 1. As we remember, there were unexploited gains unless mutually advantageous trades had entirely eliminated the triangular area. All the gains can be captured only if the price for at least the last unit of labor sold is the one given by the intersection of *MRP* and *MC* (demand and supply curves). If that price is not achieved, or if for any reason not all of the mutually beneficial trades are completed, the incomes of both the unemployed workers and the employers will be smaller. When we shifted to cartels in product markets it was obvious that the same point held: all the mutually advantageous transactions will not be consummated unless the price is right, at least for the last unit, and if all the gains from trade are not achieved, incomes on both demand and supply sides will be lower. If we now think of a complete general equilibrium system, as Clower did, we see that if there is not exactly the right price in *every* market, there will be unexploited gains from trade. If the general equilibrium system does not come up with an ideal vector of prices, then, there will be lower incomes throughout the economy. These losses—that is, the absence of the gains from many mutually advantageous but unconsummated transactions throughout the economy—will mean that aggregate demand for the economy's output is less than it would have been had the perfect vector of prices existed, and it could be very much less. Thus Clower discerned a factor that in principle could make the output of the economy as a whole fluctuate.

For some time, Clower's fundamental insight did not receive much attention. Later it was exploited by the disequilibrium theorists, but with the demoralization of some of these theorists by the lack of any explanation of why markets did not clear and the exodus from Keynesian types of thinking, its use seems to have diminished. I have been told by a deservedly eminent macroeconomist that if a general equilibrium system does generate a mistaken vector of prices, people can immediately gain from making the trades that will correct that vector of prices, and the system therefore quickly converges on the full employment level of output, so Clower's point is insignificant. I suppose that Clower's insight has not received more attention because most economists believed that there was nothing to stop the mutually advantageous trades; they would take place, if not promptly, then after only a modest lag, so Clower's point was of only transitory significance.

If my argument is right, there are those who do have an interest in blocking the mutually advantageous trades, and in some societies they are organized to block them, sometimes indefinitely. In stable societies these interests become *better* organized over time, so the problem, far from being a mere lag, can increase with time. The inefficiencies that result from special-interest groups, which my analysis in previous chapters indicates can be very large indeed, in turn affect the level of demand. Of course, if the accumulation is gradual, as I claim it is, no large macroeconomic fluctuations need emerge from this accumulation alone.

Now suppose that there is unexpected deflation or disinflation, or a sudden rise in the price of oil, or any other major change that entails that the economy can reach its full potential, or even return to its normal level of real output, only if it has new prices throughout the economy. As we know from the preceding account of unexpected deflation and disinflation, in an economy with a dense network of distributional coalitions the terms of trade will shift in favor of the organized sector. The slow decision-making explained by Implication 6 will keep the sector with organized special-interest groups from adjusting for a time, whereas what Sir John Hicks has aptly called the "flexprice" sector will adjust immediately. Accordingly, the degree of monopoly in the society and the number who are searching, queueing, or unemployed in non-market-clearing sectors increases. With an increase in the degree of monopoly and an increase in the amount of time spent in searching, queueing, and unemployment, there is less income in the society, and demand in real terms falls off. In other words, because of slow decision-making, crowded agendas, and cluttered bargaining tables, it can take a considerable time in some societies for a vector of prices as good as the pre-deflation or pre-shock vector to emerge. The result is a reduction in the demand for goods and for labor and other productive factors throughout the economy: there is a recession or depression.

Those prices set by distributional coalitions at monopolistic and above-market-clearing levels before the unexpected deflation or unexpected shock will now tend to be even higher than before, not only because of the direct effects of the deflation or the shock, but also because of the reduction of demand in real terms due to the general equilibrium effects that Clower and the disequilibrium theorists have pointed out. This in turn makes long-term investment risky, so investment spending can also fall off fast. Each of these developments will exacerbate the others, so there can be a vicious downward spiral, although the tendency of special-interest organizations and collusions to readjust their prices to the new situation will eventually offset the forces that reduce real output.

Though Malinvaud and the other disequilibrium theorists simply assumed some non-market-clearing prices and wages, their analyses of the process now being described is quite similar. Malinvaud most usefully has pointed out that in such circumstances there is "Keynesian" involuntary unemployment as well as "classical" involuntary unemployment.[22] The former, very loosely speaking, is the additional unemployment brought about because the quantity of goods purchased in the product market has fallen off due to non-market-clearing prices in those markets, which in turn reduces firms' demands for labor and multiplies the loss in employment due to wages that are above market-clearing levels. When wages are above market-clearing levels but the prices of goods are not, the involuntary unemployment that results is defined as "classical." Malinvaud judges that Keynesian unemployment is more common than classical unemployment.

According to my argument, we would need to look at the pattern of special-interest organization by sector to determine this, and the answer would vary from place to place and time to time. But whether Malinvaud is right or not, it is absolutely certain that the extent of involuntary employment cannot be understood, even to a first approximation, by looking at the coalitions in the labor market alone. I began with involuntary unemployment due to cartelization in the labor market because that is the simplest case to understand, but it need not be the most important source of involuntary unemployment; all types of cartels and lobbies need to be taken into account together for a satisfactory analysis of the involuntary unemployment of labor or the underutilization of any other resource.

As the earlier account of unexpected inflation should make clear, the opposite process tends to occur when unexpected inflation or major favorable exogenous events (such as major technological innovations or resource discoveries) happen. An economy can enjoy a boom in which the loss from its distributional coalitions is less than normal, and this can bring about a similar spiral of favorable effects until the special-interest groups have adjusted to the new situation, the promising investment opportunities have all been exploited, and so on.

Thus we have an explanation of frequent fluctuations in the level of real output or business cycles in societies with a significant degree of institutional sclerosis. This approach—the Clower-Olson approach, if I may call it that—is at no point inconsistent with any valid microeconomic theory.

XII

Now that I have put the argument in a general equilibrium context, we must examine the fact that some prices are not determined or directly influenced by distributional coalitions, even in a relatively sclerotic economy; there is in most economies not only a sector in which disequilibria persist for long periods but also a sector where prices can never be more than momentarily out of equilibrium. If a market is not cartelized or politically controlled, workers who cannot get employment because wages or prices are too high to clear markets in the sectors under the thrall of special interests are free if they choose to move into the flexprice sector.

If they do not reflect on the matter, some economists might argue at this point that this freedom of movement will ensure that there is full employment. The hurried economist might suppose that, even in the most highly cartelized and lobby-ridden economy, so long as any sectors remain open to all entrants, there will be no involuntary unemployment.

One of the lesser problems with this argument is that it ignores the time it would take for resources to shift sectors. The sticky character of the prices and wages in the organized sector implies that the flexible prices will initially absorb the whole of any unexpected deflation or disinflation, thereby making the relative prices in the cartelized or controlled sector even higher than before. The decrease in aggregate demand and higher relative prices together imply a substantial reduction in the quantity of goods and labor demanded in the organized sector. Thus full employment could require a substantial migration to the flexprice sector. Some of the owners of unemployed resources may suppose that because of either government action or equilibrating forces any recession or depression will be temporary and then it may not pay to move to the flexprice sector. Such a move will sometimes involve considerable monetary and psychic costs; consider, for example, the uprooting of families in major cities in order that they might seek employment in the rural areas where many of the goods with flexible prices are produced. Moreover, many of the resources used in the fixed-price or disequilibrium sector will not have more than a fraction of their normal value if shifted to the other sector; factories and machines are often constructed to serve only specialized needs, and workers with considerable industry-specific or firm-specific human capital may be able to do only unskilled work for a time in other industries or firms. Some people describe themselves as unemployed if the only available work involves not only a change of occupation but a great change of status as well. And at the same time they might be too old to invest in a new skill requiring as much education, training, or service with a single firm as their prior skill. Unwillingness to invest in a second profession may be due to a deplorable conservatism in many individuals of middle age or older, but it surely often exists, and when it does, a full employment equilibrium literally could arrive only after most of those in the category at issue have retired. As Keynes wisely said, in the long run we are all dead.

Even if we take a timeless view of macroeconomic fluctuations and we unrealistically ignore the costs of the resource reallocation to the flexprice or equilibrium sector whenever aggregate demand is substantially less than expected, the fact that there are always some flexible prices need not ever insure full employment. A second problem with the hurried economist's general-equilibrium argument is that it overlooks what can best be described as the "selling apples on street corners" syndrome.

Though we are all distressed at the thought of unemployed workers who are reduced to selling apples, the economist who knows that the economy is a general equilibrium system will realize, if he does not let his emotions overcome his powers of analysis, that an increase in the number of those selling apples on street corners represents a helpful and equilibrating response to the situation. If there is a great increase in the number of people selling apples, we may reasonably infer that that sector is not organized and accordingly has flexible prices. Thus the move of unemployed resources into selling apples is a helpful shift of resources into the flexprice sector and is symbolic of the many other such shifts that take place. This "selling apples" argument is not, I insist, a parody, but rather a correct statement of *one* aspect of the matter; that this is so becomes evident when we consider the loss of welfare that would occur, for consumers as well as for workers, if streetcorner vending were prohibited during a depression.

What needs to be added is that *if distributional coalitions are ubiquitous and the unexpected deflation is considerable,* and the great obstacles to resource reallocation described above are overcome, the amount of resources that must transfer into the flexprice sector will be so great in relation to the size of the sector that prices in that sector, which already has borne the brunt of the reduction of the fall in aggregate demand, will fall *much* further. The ratio of prices in the flexprice sector to prices in the fixprice sector will be abnormal and the returns to resources employed in the flexprice sector will become very low indeed. In prosperous times, selling apples on street corners should bring the normal rate of return for industries with free entry, but with a large unexpected deflation it will become so low that this occupation is considered synonymous with abject unemployment. Herbert Hoover was accused of terrible insensitivity and political ineptness when he spoke of people who made great profits during the Great Depression selling apples on street corners; we can now see that his analysis was theoretically implausible as well.

The main point is this: what happens to the streetcorner vending of apples in a depression is what happens to *all* industries with free entry. In the United States in the 1930s, for example, the historic migration from farm to city was reversed. This reallocation of resources served a purpose, but the farm prices that were associated with this shift and the drop in aggregate demand were so abnormally low in relation to industrial prices and wages that there was widespread and effective political support for programs to raise farm prices. These prices were to some extent stabilized, and this was done *by requiring that some land and other resources by law remain unemployed* until a price ratio more nearly resembling the historic "parity" was established. It may be supposed that this action was a historical aberration. I offer the further hypothesis that it was not (similar things happened in many other countries) and that generally when a similar derangement of relative price levels occurs, government intervention to limit this abnormal fall in prices in flexible markets will occur.

When the proportion of cartelized and lobby-influenced prices becomes sufficiently great, any substantial reduction in aggregate demand will lead to underutilization of resources. This is partly because of the difficulties of resource reallocation in the short run. But it is partly because the shift of resources to the flexprice sector will eventually be so large in relation to the size of that sector that it will result in factor rewards so low that they are not distinguished from unemployment, or to additional government restriction of output or factor use to protect returns in the flexprice sector. (One result of the contribution that flexible prices make to regaining employment during a depression is that the flexprice sector diminishes further.) Although the abjectly low levels of return during a depression in the selling-apples or equilibrium sector in an economy with exceptional numbers of special-interest groups do not strictly qualify as involuntary unemployment by the very severe definition set out earlier in this chapter, it is surely not an abuse of language to describe them as "involuntary *under*employment." There is also in such times a notable increase in the incentive to search for openings in the disequilibrium or fixprice sector; queueing and search unemployment (which now is involuntary because of the institutionally determined disparities in prices and wages for resources of the same intrinsic value) rises dramatically.

XIII

The macroeconomic argument offered in this chapter has not touched on the relative significance of changes in quantity of money as compared with fiscal policy in influencing the level of spending or nominal demand. Nothing said so far precludes either the contention that the quantity of money is the only significant determinant of the level of nominal income or the contention that fiscal policy is also an important determinant. What determines the level of nominal spending is for the most part a separate matter that need not be discussed here, and this book has perhaps endeavored to cover too much territory as it is. I will accordingly leave any effort to explain the determinants of spending, or to deal with other respects in which the above argument is incomplete, to a future publication, in which I would not feel inhibitions about dealing with technical matters. In the meantime, my hope is that other economists, particularly those who (unlike myself) have specialized in monetary or macroeconomics, will find what has been said here worthy of extension and formalization; the progress will be incomparably greater if more than one person is involved. Until an analysis of the determinants of aggregate spending has been incorporated into the theory, we must be careful not to suppose that the theory here is sufficient to specify *all* of the macroeconomic characteristics of a period. It is not. One must recognize, for example, that there were extremely unstable and mainly deflationary monetary and fiscal policies in the early 1930s, and less unstable but mainly inflationary policies in the late 1960s and 1970s, in any comparison of those two periods.

What has been said above is sufficient, however, to show that this argument explains involuntary unemployment without at any point contradicting anything we know about microeconomics and the effects of the incentives facing individual decision-makers. No other macroeconomic or monetary theory succeeds in doing this. Still, it would be nice to see if the present theory has further testable implications that are different from those of other macroeconomic theories. If the further testable implications of the present theory should be confirmed, whereas those of competing macroeconomic theories should not, that would be important evidence to strengthen the macroeconomic argument here and the theory presented in the book as a whole.

Happily, there is a marvelously apt empirical test that bears on the validity of the present argument and also on that of all the alternatives that have been discussed. Keynes's *General Theory,* monetarism, disequilibrium theory, and equilibrium theory are all alike in claiming generality for all types of monetized economies, or at the least in failing to set out any conditions that tell the economist what special set of economies the theory is intended to explain. Keynes emphasized the generality of his theory even in his title and showed no hesitancy in using it to offer a new interpretation of mercantilistic economies and policies, although the underdeveloped mercantilistic economies were much different from the Western economies in Keynes's time. Similarly, many monetarists are ready to pass strong judgments on monetary and macroeconomic policies in economies of the most diverse kinds and levels of development and often make sweeping assertions; Milton Friedman's argument that inflation is "always and everywhere a monetary phenomenon" is one example of this monetarist claim to generality. If anyone should think that I have overstated the claims to generality of the established theories, he or she surely would concede that none of the existing theories spells out any ways in which macroeconomic or monetary problems will be vastly different in different types of societies or different historical periods. The generality and lack of distinctions among societies of various types no doubt reflects the depressingly unhistorical, unevolutionary, comparative-static, and institution-free character of much of modern economics.

By contrast, the present theory predicts that macroeconomic problems will be different in different societies. The above analysis makes it clear that if special-interest groups (or anything else) create only a *small* number of nonclearing markets in an economy, the problems due to these distortions will appear as sectoral, microeconomic, or local problems. An unexpected deflation or disinflation might make these problems worse, but because the problems are confined to a relatively small number of sectors, there would be no general depression or *macroeconomic* malady. An unexpected deflation or disinflation will not be terribly serious, because the harm it does will be confined mainly to a few sectors and the spillover of resources into the huge flexprice sector will be small in relation to the size of that sector, and thus fairly innocuous. Deflation or disinflation will influence the price level and nominal income but need not create much involuntary unemployment or have any substantial or sustained impact on the level of real output. In other words, the economy free of special-interest groups and the processes and legislation they bring about would behave much the way the less cautious monetarists and equilibrium theorists say that all economies do.

On the other hand, when an economy reaches the point where distributional coalitions are ubiquitous and the fixprice sector is large in relation to the flexprice sector, the theory offered here predicts that the macroeconomic situation will be different. An unexpected deflation or disinflation will then bring widespread losses and suffering from forced movement from the fixprice to the flexprice sector, from falling prices in the flexprice sector, from unemployment of those who could not or would not move, from increases in queueing and searching costs, and at the same time substantial losses of real demand that further aggravate problems because the vector of relative prices diverges far from the pre-deflation vector for that society and even farther from the ideal vector. The economy that has a dense network of narrow special-interest organizations will be susceptible during periods of deflation or disinflation to depression or stagflation. The present theory implies that some societies or periods of history will not suffer much involuntary unemployment or large losses of real output even from unexpected deflation or disinflation, whereas other societies will suffer significant involuntary unemployment and losses of real output. In addition, it predicts that any society with unchanged borders that enjoys continued stability will over time gradually shift from the former state to the latter.

XIV

Unfortunately, my knowledge of recent comparative macroeconomic experience across the world is not yet great enough to permit me to do the cross-sectional part of this empirical test as well as I would like. I

shall be forced to consider only the largest countries and one prototypical smaller country. There is also the problem that different countries
(or historical periods) may have had different monetary and fiscal policies partly or even largely because of political accidents or other causes
exogenous to my theory. The degree of fluctuation in the level of real
output and the extent of involuntary unemployment in my model depend
not only on the length of time societies have had to accumulate special-
interest groups, but also on the predictability and stability of monetary
and fiscal policies and on the extent of any exogenous shocks an economy has faced. Thus one society (or historical period) could have had
relatively minor business cycles and little involuntary unemployment,
even though it had had a high level of special-interest organization,
whereas another society with less institutional sclerosis may have had
extraordinary monetary and fiscal instability. At least partly for these
reasons, this cross-section or international comparison portion of the
empirical test that has just been set out will not be at all compelling.

Yet it appears that Japan and, to a lesser extent, Germany have
been able to keep unemployment of labor at lower levels during the
stagflation that set in during the 1970s than have the United States and,
especially, Britain. Unemployment statistics are gathered on different
bases in different countries and are not comparable, with statistics in
many other countries understating the degree of unemployment in relation to U.S. measures. However, the U.S. Bureau of Labor Statistics
has converted the unemployment rates for the major foreign countries
into figures comparable with those of the United States. These figures
show that in 1975–76 Great Britain had an unemployment rate of about
5 percent and the United States about 8 percent, whereas Germany had
an unemployment rate of about 4½ percent and Japan only 2 percent.[23]
I do not have up-to-date comparable figures, but more recently the
situation has become more striking, with U.S. unemployment rising
above 9 percent in 1982 and British unemployment rates rising well
over 12 percent even without adjustment.

Of course, any number of factors may be involved. But a glance at
the inflation rates of these countries does not seem to support either the
notion that expansive (that is, inflationary) monetary and fiscal policies
will rule out unemployment or the argument of some monetarists that
"inflation causes recession" or higher unemployment. From 1972 to
1979 the annual average rate of inflation was highest in Great Britain, at
15 percent, and fairly high in the United States, at 9.1 percent. Contrary

to Keynesian demand-management notions both countries had high unemployment. Germany's inflation record, 5.5 percent, like its unemployment record, was better. Yet success at keeping down the inflation rate apparently is not essential to full employment, either; the Japanese rate of inflation was second highest, at 10.6 percent, whereas its unemployment rate was far and away the lowest.

Moreover, as my theory would lead the reader to expect, there has been more concern and difficulty in Britain than in any other country over "social contracts" and "incomes policies." Both the aspirations for such contracts and the failure of such policies is not, by my argument, surprising in a country with strong special-interest groups of a narrow kind. Germany has had not only fewer but also more encompassing special-interest organizations, and each of these features may very well have something to do with its better record on both inflation and unemployment.

There are all sorts of special circumstances in each of the four countries that help to account for the results, such as the special role in West Germany of guest workers, who may sometimes be sent home when unemployed. But we must also remember that West Germany and Japan have faced much larger shocks from the higher price of oil, since both are utterly reliant on oil imports. The United States, although a net importer, is one of the world's largest oil producers; and Britain, during this very period, has had the colossal good fortune to become an oil exporter. Still, only polar cases and large countries have been considered, so no conclusions are yet in order.

It is not possible to examine the experience of all countries, but there is one small country so prototypical that it is worth special attention. As I pointed out in chapter 6, Taiwan (like Korea, Hong Kong, and Singapore) has enjoyed fantastically high postwar growth rates. The Japanese occupation, we recall, had repressed special-interest organization in Taiwan, so the rapid growth is in accord with the theory offered in this book. If the argument in this chapter is right, countries with Taiwan's nearly complete absence of special-interest organization should be able to maintain something approximating full employment and full-capacity production even during an unexpected deflation or disinflation. By my reading of the statistics, Taiwan has in fact experienced dramatic disinflations with only relatively minor losses of real output. Those who have given the matter specialized attention also seem to have observed this. Erik Lundberg writes:

The postwar period began with the consumer price index rising about tenfold a year during 1946–49 and about 500 percent in 1949–50. By 1950–51 the rate of inflation was still out of control (80 to 100 percent a year). It is of great interest to determine how this very rapid inflation was dampened so quickly and brought down to manageable proportions by 1952 without a depression or a severe break in economic growth. . . .

Another central issue is Taiwan's success in bringing down the relatively high rate of inflation during 1952–60 (7 to 8 percent a year) to a remarkable stable value of money—the GNP deflator rising by 2 to 3 percent annually—and with a minimum of fluctuation. This achievement cannot be explained solely by monetary and fiscal policies.[24]

XV

Clearly the preceding examples do not provide any definitive empirical test.* But let us now look at changes in the United States over the relatively brief period since World War II. Since monetarists have in general been more resistant than Keynesians to suggestions that structural and institutional changes were among the causal factors in postwar inflationary experience, it may be expedient to take some of our facts once again from that careful monetarist writer, Phillip Cagan.

Cagan examined data on the changes in prices and in output for the United States since 1890. He found that the tendency for prices to fall during recessions has declined over time. He observes that

the change in rates of change [of prices] from each expansion to the ensuing recession became less negative and, in the last two cycles, the change became positive—that is, the rate of price increase in the recession exceeded that in the expansion, perverse cyclical behavior not exhibited before. The distinctive feature of the postwar inflations has not been that prices rose faster in periods of

---

*Another cross-sectional test was suggested when this book was in press: unemployment rates according to my theory ought to be higher in those states of the U.S. in which a larger proportion of the labor force is unionized. They are. Regressions on unemployment rates by state from 1957 to 1979 show that this relationship is statistically significant, and far stronger than the relationship between the percentage of the labor force in manufacturing and unemployment. The regressions neglect the important indirect effects of distributional coalitions other than labor unions, but these indirect effects are usually not confined to the state in which the coalition exists.

cyclical expansion—many previous expansions had much higher rates—but that they declined hardly at all, or even rose, in recessions. . . . The startling failure of the 1970 recession to curb the inflation was not a new phenomenon . . . but simply a further step in a *progressive* post-war development. . . . The phenomenon of rising prices in slack markets is quite common. . . .

Part of the smaller amplitude of cyclical fluctuations in prices reflects the reduced severity of business recessions since World War II, for which some credit goes to the contribution of economic research to improved stabilization techniques. Nonetheless, in addition to the smaller cyclical contractions in aggregate expenditures, the response of prices to a given amplitude of contraction has declined, so that now proportionately more of the contraction in expenditure falls on output.[25]

Jeffrey Sachs has also in a recent article corroborated Cagan's finding with somewhat different methods.[26]

Although the finding that what is loosely called *stagflation* has emerged recently is commonplace, there are two features of Cagan's observations that deserve to be emphasized. The first is his insistence that there has been a *progressive* or *gradual* emergence of this problem. This is certainly correct—the puzzling experience of the 1970s was foreshadowed, for example, in the 1950s, when the cost-push arguments first appeared. Yet nothing like this was evident early in the century or in previous centuries.

A second important feature of Cagan's observations is the point that, because of the changing behavior of prices, over time *an increasing proportion of the effect of any reduction in aggregate demand shows up as a reduction in real output.* Cagan does not discuss this, but straightforward observation suggests there has been a similar development in several other countries. This is exactly what the theory here would lead us to expect, but it is not implied by any of the nonevolutionary and institution-free macroeconomic theories.

XVI

The same tendency for unexpected deflation or disinflation to lead to more unemployment and larger losses of real output as time goes on appears in more dramatic form when we take a long-range historical perspective. Even though the reliable data needed to make definitive judgments about macroeconomic and monetary history in earlier centuries are lacking, the qualitative evidence and the scattered data that do exist are sufficient to have generated almost a consensus among economic historians about certain broad outlines of historical experience. These broad outlines, well-known as they are to economic historians, somehow have not been taken into account in either the Keynesian or the monetarist theories.

Perhaps the most prominent trend in all macroeconomic history has been the tendency in countries such as Britain and the United States for reductions in aggregate demand, whatever their causes, to have more and more impact on the level of real output as time progressed. This pattern is evident since at least the eighteenth century. There were great (and unpredicted) fluctuations in the price level, but these fluctuations did not, at the time of the Industrial Revolution and during most of the nineteenth century, bring about large-scale unemployment or substantial reductions in real output. In still earlier eras of history, economies were relatively parochial, with trade barriers of the kind described in chapter 5 around small communities, so it is difficult to speak of uniform national macroeconomic developments. But in the mercantilistic period Britain, particularly, had become a centralized state with few internal barriers to trade. This meant it could, and did, easily experience nationwide inflations and deflations. After this jurisdictional integration and the civil war and political instability of the seventeenth century, the inflations and deflations appear to have had only minor and transitory effects, if any, on the level of employment or real output. Similarly, the United States from the onset of its national history was a national economy that could, and did, experience inflations and deflations, but again these appear to have had only a small impact on the level of employment and real output.

While situations began to change somewhat in the latter part of the nineteenth century, the years from the peak of inflation of the Napoleonic Wars in 1812 to the low point in 1896 nonetheless will serve to illustrate the point. Over that period in Great Britain the price level fell by more than one-half. The price level in the United States fell even more. Yet during that period the Industrial Revolution continued in Britain and the United States also enjoyed remarkable growth and prosperity. Broadly speaking, the longest period of peaceful growth in per capita income that the world has ever seen took place in a period in which the price level was, more often than not, falling. As the nineteenth century wore on, the bottom years of the cycle probably brought increasing unemployment, but by comparison with twentieth-century experience the downswings in the cycle brought relatively small reductions in real output.

There were, of course, many "panics" and "crises" even in the early nineteenth century. It was naturally when the price level fell that those who had borrowed money tended to have the hardest time paying it back; they were paying a higher real interest rate than they would have paid had the price level not fallen. As the Populist movement in the nineteenth-century United States indicates, those who had borrowed money when prices were higher certainly did not like the deflation. When prices fell and some firms could not pay their debts, there could be a panic, especially in view of the unstable banking system (particularly in the United States), which often led to bank failures. These panics and crises depressed expectations and led to some reductions in employment and real output, but in terms of the experience of the 1930s, or our sense of what would result from comparable falls in the price level today, the effects were relatively minor and brief.

This can best be illustrated by comparing the depression of the interwar years with what was perhaps the greatest previous U.S. monetary contraction. Milton Friedman and Anna Schwartz say that "to find anything in our history remotely comparable to the monetary collapse from 1929 to 1933, one must go back nearly a century to the contraction of 1839 to 1843."[27] Indeed, as some detailed estimates by economic historian Peter Temin show, the contraction in the money supply was even greater in 1839–43 than in 1929–33. *The fall in the price level was substantially greater: −31 percent in 1929–33 and −42 percent in 1839–43.* But consumption in real terms, which decreased by 19 percent from 1929 to 1933, increased 21 percent from 1839 to 1843. More dramatically still, *the real gross national product, which decreased by no less than 30 percent from 1929 to 1933, increased by 16 percent from 1839 to 1843.* (See table 7.1 below, reproduced from Temin's *Jacksonian Democracy*.)[28] As Temin aptly points out in another book,[29] the unemployment of resources in the United States in the depression that started in 1929 had no precedent in any prior contraction:

> The economic contraction that started in 1929 was the worst in history. Historians have compared it with the downturns of the 1840's and the 1930's, but the comparison serves only to show the severity of the later movement. In the nineteenth-century depressions, there were banking panics, deflation, and bankruptcy, in various proportions. But there is no parallel to the underutilization

Table 7.1. Comparison of 1839–1843 with 1929–1933 (in percent)

	1839–43	1929–33
Change in money stock	−34	−27
Change in prices	−42	−32
Change in number of banks	−23	−42
Change in real gross investment	−23	−91
Change in real consumption	+21	−19
Change in real gross national product	+15	−30

NOTE: The 1839–43 data are taken from peak to trough of the respective series, and dates differ somewhat. Data on money and banks are from late 1838 to late 1842; data on prices, from calendar-year 1839 to calendar-year 1843; data on GNP, etc., from census-year 1839 (year ending May 31, 1839) to census-year 1843.

SOURCE: 1839–43—Tables 3.2, 3.3, 5.2 [in Peter Temin, *The Jacksonian Economy* (New York: W. W. Norton, 1969, 1975)]; Gallman, private correspondence; U.S. Historical Statistics, p. 624; 1929–33—Ibid., pp. 116, 143, 624, 646.

of economic resources—to the unemployment of labor and other resources—in the 1930's.

The value of goods and services in America fell by almost half in the early 1930's. Correcting for the fall in prices, the quantity of production fell by approximately one-third. Unemployment rose to include one-quarter of the labor force. And investment stopped almost completely. It was the most extensive breakdown of the economy in history.

The difference in the character of the macroeconomic experience between the nineteenth and twentieth centuries is evident even in the language of daily life. Although some writers have exaggerated the newness of the term, the fact remains that unemployment is a term that came into common use only late in the nineteenth century. The *Oxford English Dictionary* states that the word *unemployment* has been in common use since about 1895, but E. P. Thompson points out that the word can occasionally be found in Owenite and Radical writings as early as the 1820s and 1830s.[30] Early observers of unemployment tended to use such circumlocutions as "want of employment" or "involuntary idleness." The usual German word for unemployment, *arbeitslosigkeit,* was also rarely used before the 1890s. The usage of the French word *chomage* goes back to the Middle Ages, but this word also has connotations of leisure, as in the expression *un jour de chome* for a day or holiday on which no work is normally done.[31] If the falling price level in the early nineteenth century had led to widespread and continuing unemployment of labor or other resources, some word to describe such an important, if not tragic, state of affairs would surely have come quickly into common usage in the languages of all the relevant countries.

The extent to which a reduction in aggregate demand is reflected in unemployment of resources and reductions in real output must be distinguished from the magnitude of fluctuations in aggregate demand. The years since World War II, as Cagan pointed out, have by historical standards been relatively stable, in part because of what economists and governments have learned about stabilization policy. But the evidence cited shows that because of increasing inflexibility of prices, as time goes on, a stable society suffers more unemployment and a greater loss of output for any given reduction in aggregate demand.

This historical evidence, like the international comparisons cited earlier, is not explained by any of the conventional macroeconomic theories. They say nothing at all about what historical periods or societies would suffer the most unemployment and loss of real output when there is unexpected deflation or disinflation. Their emphasis on generality leaves the impression that the consequences of bad fiscal or monetary policies would be much the same in all monetized economies. The theory offered here, by contrast, does predict the international differences and the gradual changes over time in stable societies that we have observed.

XVII

The time and the place where Keynes developed his brilliant theory, the parts of the world where it became the orthodoxy, and the character of the Great Depression also fit with the argument. Keynes was, of course, working out his dazzling ideas in Great Britain in the 1920s and 1930s. The society in which he wrote had accumulated far more special-interest organizations and collusions than any other society at that time. The pattern of demand for exports and other goods that the British economy faced was far different from that before the war, and the industries in which Britain had comparative advantage had changed, too. Britain thus needed a new structure of relative wages and prices and a considerable reallocation of resources. In the absence of price and wage flexibility and in the presence of entry barriers, the reallocation of resources proceeded slowly; there was a great deal of unemployment of resources. For a time this problem was exacerbated by Churchill's overvaluation of the pound in the mid-1920s. Still, if the relevant wages and prices had fallen enough, British resources would nonetheless have been fully employed. But the British institutional structure had been developing for a long time, and the relevant wages and prices did not fall in the short run, and some not even in the medium. In a sufficiently long run, these wages and prices would have adjusted, but by then, as Keynes well knew, a good proportion of the population at issue would be dead. Thus Keynes's *General Theory* is, in fact, an ingenious and enlightening but by no means truly "general" theory. Had Britain emerged from World War I with the clean institutional slate that Germany had after World War II, Keynes would probably not have written the book.

The problems that Britain faced and the diverse difficulties of other countries at the time Keynes worked out the ideas in the *General Theory* (and the *Treatise on Money*) were made very much more serious by the reverse jurisdictional integration and rampant economic nationalism in the world economy after World War I. The Austro-Hungarian empire was divided at Versailles into many smaller states. In general these new nations were economically nationalistic and protectionist. The Soviet Union had relatively little trade with the outside world. Protection increased dramatically elsewhere as well; even Britain and the British Empire abandoned free trade policies. On top of this, the world economy was further deranged by extravagant demands by the European allies for reparations from the defeated nations, unrealistic demands by the United States for repayment of the debts its allies had contracted during the war, and beggar-thy-neighbor and other foolish exchange-rate policies in many countries. The loss of potential gains and even past gains from trade in the world economy must have been very large indeed. By the logic described earlier this loss would have reduced the real demand for output everywhere, especially the demand for exports.

The huge and prosperous United States might have survived these international difficulties without calamity had it chosen the right policies. In addition to making other mistakes, the United States joined in the restrictionist and protectionist binge; it slapped unprecedented quotas on immigration and passed the Fordney-Macomber and then the still higher Smoot-Hawley tariffs. Although labor unions favored and were implicated in the immigration restriction legislation, for example, it is important to emphasize that by modern American standards only a very modest proportion of the labor force was unionized. The efforts of employers to keep out unions by following union wage scales and the concentration of unions in conspicuous and important labor markets gave them an influence far beyond their membership, but this membership in the 1920s was decreasing.

As Implication 3 predicts, small groups organize first, and small groups of business firms appear to have been far and away the largest source of the problem. There was, as Lester V. Chandler aptly described it, "the trade association movement of the 1920s. Strongly approved by Herbert Hoover as Secretary of Commerce, trade associations were established in virtually every major industry and in many minor ones. . . . Many, probably most, of the trade associations restrained competition."[32] The success they met in initiating an orgy of tariff-raising in a country and a period with a relatively strong support of free-market ideology suggests how strong they must have been; this suggestion is confirmed in several studies by leading political scientists.[33] The tariff is the mother of all manner of combinations and collusions, and further business cartelization and oligopolistic collusion were greatly facilitated. This in turn must have encouraged slow consensual and constitutional decision-making about prices, especially in the industrial sector.

The extremely unstable American banking system of the time, the satiation of the opportunities for investment in certain sectors, the limitation on the demand for American exports due to foreign tariffs, the adverse impact on investor confidence of the stock-market crash, and perhaps still other factors brought about a reduction in spending. When this happened, many prices, especially in the manufacturing sector, naturally did not fall promptly or in proportion to the reduction in demand. And indeed the statistics that have already been discussed show that, whereas agricultural prices and other flexible prices fell dramatically, a host of other prices, particularly in concentrated and organized industrial sectors, fell slowly and by relatively little. With these inefficient prices the gains from trade were much less than before and real incomes and demands for output lower, and this, in combination with the deflation and the volatility of investment spending that Keynes emphasized, meant that the demand for labor and other factors of production fell dramatically, and by so much that rigidities in the labor market that would not have been nearly so serious by themselves had substantial quantitative effects.

Even then, the unemployment problem would not have been so serious or so prolonged but for what followed. There were intense complaints in the apple-selling or flexprice markets about the disproportionate drops in prices and low returns. In addition, the laissez-faire doctrine that all would be well if the government left the economy alone (except, in some versions, for providing protection against foreign competition) was largely discredited in the minds of most Americans by the manifest failure of capitalism and the conservative administrations of Coolidge and Hoover to prevent the depression. There followed an avalanche of measures designed to intervene in markets by fixing prices and wages at "fair," "reasonable," or "full cost" levels—that is, at levels that would be profitable for the firms and workers who were already securely established in the market, but that would make it unprofitable to hire the additional workers or sell the extra goods that would have brought the economy back to prosperity. These efforts began in the Hoover administration. The Davis-Bacon Act of 1931, for example, made it illegal for contractors or subcontractors on federal construction projects to pay less than what the secretary of labor deemed to be the prevailing wage rate in that locality, which was typically the union wage rate in the fairly heavily unionized construction industry. The Norris-LaGuardia Act of 1932 ended the use of the powers of courts to limit combination in the labor market.

Then came the National Recovery Administration (NRA) created in 1933. It not only allowed but enthusiastically encouraged each industry to set up a "code of fair competition" and a "code authority." The codes of fair competition typically required "fair" behavior with respect to output, prices, and various trade prices, and also "fair" wages, hours of work, collective bargaining, and so forth. It is estimated that 95 percent of industrial employees came to be covered by these codes.[34] Although the NRA also stipulated minimum wages and rules against wage-cutting, the interests of the trade associations of business firms seemed more significant. As Franklin Roosevelt later described it, the "codes were developed, as a matter of Administration policy, from proposals initiated from within the industries themselves. All but a few of them were sponsored and initially proposed by at least one trade association. [The NRA gave] industry the opportunity for self-government, many trade associations which had been inactive for years came to life again and many industries which did not have trade associations hastened to organize them."[35] In 1935 the Supreme Court declared the NRA unconstitutional. Some of its activities were transferred to other agencies and diverse acts (such as the National Labor Relations Act of 1935 and the Wagner Act of 1937) were passed to maintain wages and promote unionization. Unionization meanwhile had increased significantly and no doubt greatly influenced the wage policies of many firms who feared independent or "outside" unionization; by the spring of 1934, one-fourth of all industrial workers were employed in plants with company unions, which were usually organized after strikes or organizing efforts by independent unions.[36] Membership in independent unions rose from somewhat more than three million in 1932 to eight million in 1938.

In short, the onset of the depression led to the official promotion of business and labor combinations and to legislation and regulation that prohibited ever more unemployed labor and other resources from making mutually advantageous contracts: more and more workers, consumers, and firms were prohibited from making the deals that would have filled up the triangular areas like those depicted in figure 1. In addition, the Agricultural Adjustment Act and other legislation fixed some farm prices and mandated the nonuse or unemployment of acres of land and of other agricultural resources because farm prices were fantastically low, among other reasons because of a migration of unemployed resources into agriculture.

In these circumstances policies to increase aggregate demand, such as those advocated by Keynes, made a lot of sense. To the extent that deflation could be stopped and prices increased, the prices set in nominal terms by the slow-moving combinations and regulatory processes were made lower in relative terms and thus less harmful. Since interest rates were already low and some people apparently were hoarding money, it is also not astonishing that Keynes would feel that increasing the money supply might not be sufficient and would advocate deficit spending by government. I do not know just what contribution each policy or development made to the increasing aggregate demand during the New Deal years. There was an inflow of gold and some monetary expansion, but most famously there was Franklin Roosevelt's controversial budget deficits. The combined effect of Roosevelt's expansionary demand policies, confidence in the banking system due to federal deposit insurance, some monetary expansion, and slow downward adjustment of some cartelistic prices and wages was evidently greater than all the increases in unemployment of resources brought about by the new cartelization and governmentally set minimum prices and wages. Unemployment was somewhat lower and real output somewhat higher in 1940 than it had been when Roosevelt took office in 1933.

Thus it is hardly surprising that Keynes had a profound impact upon the United States, and indeed upon the whole English-speaking world, most of which has enjoyed unusual political stability and accumulated dense networks of special-interest groups. From this perspective it is no accident that postwar German opinion, for example, has not been nearly as susceptible to Keynes. As always, many factors were involved; the number of technically trained economists has been many times larger in the English-speaking world than elsewhere, and thus there were more who were enthralled with the subtlety and sophistication of Keynes's book.

We are now in a position to see that, although an expansion of aggregate demand such as Keynes advocated in a depression can sometimes offset the effects of special-interest groups and unwise macroeconomic policies, the level of aggregate demand is at best a secondary and temporary influence on the level of involuntary unemployment. Involuntary unemployment can only be explained in terms of the interests and policies that rule out mutually advantageous bargains between those who have their own labor or other goods to sell and those who would gain from buying what is offered. A low level of or even a drop in aggregate demand is neither a sufficient nor a necessary condition for involuntary unemployment. That a declining or low level of aggregate demand need not cause a depression or involuntary unemployment is evident not only on theoretical grounds but also from the historical experience cited earlier in this chapter.

That involuntary unemployment can result with a high and increasing level of aggregate demand is evident from the fact that, whatever level of inflation is anticipated, a distributional coalition still has an incentive to set real prices or wages at levels that will block mutually advantageous trades outside the coalition and thus keep the market from clearing; if unemployed resources eventually could get employment in the flexprice sector, there would still be some involuntary unemployment due to the excessive queueing and searching brought about by the gratuitous disparity in returns to homogeneous resources. That involuntary unemployment can occur with a high and increasing level of aggregate demand is also demonstrated by the recent stagflation; in some years in which GNP in money terms has increased, there has also been high unemployment. There must have been an increase in aggregate spending or the higher nominal GNP could not have been purchased, yet unemployment remained and sometimes increased.

Since inadequate aggregate demand is not the main or ultimate source of involuntary unemployment, continuous, fast-changing demand management with fine tuning does not make sense. This is not only because, as others have pointed out, our knowledge is not good enough for fine adjustments, but also because demand management is not the main dial in any case. It was a great idea in the depths of the U.S. depression in 1933—when no one had a reason to fear any harmful inflation and when many special-interest organizations were in the process of trying to lower their prices from 1929 levels and did not expect price increases—to try to offset the mischievously high prices in the fixprice sector by using every method to augment aggregate demand. The extra spending could offset the drop in demand caused by the unemployment and the monopolistic pricing and might also help by raising the price level and thus changing the relative prices in the fixprice sector. But such an expansion may do little but bring about more inflation if the organizations are accustomed to demand management and will offset any expected expansionary fiscal or monetary policy by setting still higher prices. Sometimes, as I have shown elsewhere,[37] monetary and possibly fiscal policy can be changed faster than the distributional coalitions can alter their prices, and this opens up the possibility that demand management can achieve some gains in real output by changing policies after most of the distributional coalitions have chosen their prices. But changeable and unpredictable policies can have costs of their own, so this does not appear to be a permanent solution.

The ultimate source of the problem is that Keynes did not explain the inflexibility of many wages and prices or point out that such an explanation should be the very *core* of *any* macroeconomic theory, so some of his followers assumed they were more or less arbitrarily determined. Keynesians talked a lot about the "core" rate of inflation—that is, the rate of increase of those prices and wages that change relatively slowly—but what determined which prices and wages were the core ones, and what made them change, was not in their theory. If these core prices and wages were arbitrarily determined or the resultant of exhortatory "incomes policies," there was no reason to suppose they would be greatly affected by increases in aggregate demand, so some Keynesians in the 1970s recommended even more expansive policies to cure the unemployment, thereby generating pointless inflation.

There are similar holes, just where the core ought to be, in the monetarist and equilibrium theories. These theories contain little or no theory of what makes some prices change only rarely and slowly; this is one of the reasons they offer no explanation of involuntary unemployment. Many economists in both Keynesian and monetarist camps have often referred to minimum-wage laws, labor unions, and the like as sources of sticky wages and unemployment, but passing references are not nearly enough. They do not explain what interests these sticky prices serve or how they emerged. If the most important phenomena in macroeconomics—the ones that give rise to unemployment and fluctuations in the level of real output—are not integrated into a macroeconomic theory, then that theory is like Hamlet without the Prince of Denmark.

XVIII

To say that Keynes's theory is crucially incomplete, and incomplete in a way that has been profoundly misleading, does not deny the magnitude of his contribution to macroeconomic theory. In a sense, he created the field. Keynes's emphasis on the demand for money as an asset, on the special volatility of investment as compared to consumption expenditure, and on expectations have enormously enriched our understanding of macroeconomic and monetary problems. Most of the monetary and business cycle theory that appeared before his *General Theory* now seems terribly primitive. Keynes, with the help of Hicks, also provided the intellectual framework needed to consider the supply and demand for money simultaneously with the intentions to save and invest. Having done all this and more, Keynes hardly can be blamed for failing to provide a theory of supply-price, such as has been offered here. But he should have pointed out the risks and limitations inherent in this omission and should not have claimed a specious generality. His reputation in the very long run might have been greater had he been more attentive to the cumulative nature of any science and less emphatic about the extent to which he differed from his predecessors.

One of the reasons I think it is important to emphasize Keynes's contribution to macroeconomic analysis and debate is that some of the monetarist and equilibrium-theory writing, for all its value to me and to the profession, has almost seemed to be inspired by a desire to demonstrate that the exact opposite of what Keynes concluded or recommended was right. Sometimes polemical victory has seemed to be more important than creativity. My impression may be wrong and unfair and, if so, I apologize. But why, then, have so many brilliant and valuable criticisms of Keynesian economics said little or nothing about involuntary unemployment, or about the manifest failure of the American economy and some others automatically to sustain full-employment levels of output? Above all, when millions of people are alive and ready to testify to the massive suffering and terrifying unemployment of the interwar period, why build a macroeconomic theory on the assumption that the economy is at or near an ether-like equilibrium and that neither involuntary unemployment nor deep and prolonged depressions can occur? And why complain vociferously about the rapidly increasing and harmful influence of government and the perniciousness of labor unions, but then build macro models on the assumption that the economy is essentially free of governmentally or cartelistically set prices, or is even perfectly competitive?

My hope is that the debate over Keynes soon can be left to the historians of economic thought, freeing the colossal talents in all the schools to focus on macro models that follow the monetarists and equilibrium theorists in their insistence that the macro theory must rest on valid microeconomic theory, and that follow Keynes in recognizing that involuntary unemployment is possible and that a laissez-faire economy in a stable society will not permanently and automatically sustain a full-employment level of output. It may be that I emphasize these conditions simply because they are conditions satisfied by my own theory, but I would be interested to see what arguments any skilled economist would propose for why a macroeconomic theory should not meet both of these conditions (or, for that matter, all the conditions for an adequate macro theory in the list set out earlier in this chapter).

XIX

For the most part, I am leaving the policy implications of the theory offered in this book aside for now. It would require another book to explore all the implications of the present theory in combination with familiar microeconomic theory and other considerations. Besides, it is best to focus first on getting the theory right, leaving the policy implications until later (among other reasons, because it is less likely that preconceptions about the "right" policy will distort the theory). It may be useful, nonetheless, to say a few tentative words.

The most important macroeconomic policy implication is that the best macroeconomic policy is a good microeconomic policy. There is no substitute for a more open and competitive environment. If combinations dominate markets throughout the economy and the government is always intervening on behalf of special interests, there is no macroeconomic policy that can put things right. In the invaluable but perhaps misleading language of Milton Friedman and Edmund Phelps, the "natural rate of unemployment"—essentially, the rate of unemployment when the price level or inflation rate generally expected is the one that actually occurs—will be very high. The need for better microeconomic policies and institutions has been most eloquently stated by the British economist James Meade, who said that "the natural rate of unemployment is unnaturally high." This statement is true not only for his own country, but to an extent for many others as well, not least the United States.

A second policy implication, also unoriginal, is that the disinflationary policies needed in so many countries at the present time should, in most cases, be steady and gradual policies, as well as resolute and believable ones. It has sometimes been suggested by economists who place almost exclusive emphasis on "expectations" that if the public actually could be made to believe that the government or central bank would institute a truly anti-inflationary policy and adhere to that policy for a long period, then a short and sharp contraction would solve the problem. Such a policy can work in a society with few distributional coalitions but not in one with many. The slow decision-making of such coalitions entails that they will not be able to adjust quickly, however certain they may be about the government resolve and however deep the short slump will be. Although it is an extreme case, consider again the Danish cartel referred to in chapter 3, which took ten years to adjust its policy despite disappearing profits. There is at the same time considerable evidence that special-interest groups do eventually adjust to the reality in which they find themselves. One example is the wage cuts sometimes accepted by unions when the firms that employ them are about to go broke.

The third and last macroeconomic policy implication to be considered at the moment is that tax and subsidy schemes designed to lower the natural rate of unemployment can in some societies make an important, if probably only temporary, contribution, when—and only when—they are combined with good monetary and fiscal policies. When the natural rate of unemployment is unnaturally high, it can be lowered somewhat by special taxes on firms that raise wages by a greater percentage than, say, the expected increase in productivity in the economy at large. Alternatively, if it is politically more feasible, firms can be given a subsidy that diminishes when they grant such an increase. This will give the firm an incentive to bargain for a lower wage increase and, on getting it, the firm will have an incentive to hire more workers than otherwise, thereby reducing unemployment. A disadvantage of such a policy is that it will discourage firms for which it is optimal to upgrade the skill mix from doing so, with some loss of economic efficiency. That is one reason policies of this kind presumably should be temporary and should not be offered (as they sometimes are) as panaceas or ideal solutions. I have been advocating such policies for a decade,[38] and Henry Wallich and Sidney Weintraub (the first to propose such schemes) have been advocating them far longer. A great many eminent economists have in recent years joined the chorus, but still without the least political success. I nonetheless maintain that such policies are politically achievable. They could be palatable when combined with policies favorable to the groups that would lose something from them (for example, senior workers with good job security). Such a tax usefully could be applied as well to price increases of large firms, although it would raise difficulties of administration and enforcement. Another policy in the same spirit advocates wage subsidies to firms that enlarge their work force by taking on workers from categories in which there is high unemployment. It cannot be stressed too strongly, though, that all such policies are definitely not cure-alls and are no substitutes for good monetary and fiscal policies and sound microeconomic policies and institutions.

XX

As I mentioned at the beginning of this chapter, a macroeconomist should be slightly uneasy if a theory explains nothing besides macroeconomic phenomena and should be somewhat reassured if a theory not only meets the specified macroeconomic conditions but explains other phenomena as well. Of course, this condition echoes the argument in chapter 1 about the need for theories with broad explanatory power, consilience to explain phenomena of very different kinds, and parsimonious simplicity as well. We are back to "the standards a satisfactory answer should meet."

I hope those who remain advocates of alternative macroeconomic conceptions, and advocates of alternative explanations of the growth rate or social structure of this or that country, will ask themselves how wide a variety of phenomena their theory can explain while retaining its simplicity. The theory offered here is certainly a simple one, at least by the standards of my discipline.

The theory here is consistent with the rapid postwar growth of West Germany and Japan, with the slow growth and ungovernability of Britain in recent times, and at the same time with Britain's record as the most rapidly growing country in an earlier time. It is consistent with the slower growth of the northeastern and older midwestern regions of the United States and with the faster growth of the South and the West—and offers a statistically significant explanation of the growth of the forty-eight states as a whole.

The theory also is consistent with the rapid growth of the six nations that founded the Common Market, the rapid growth of the United States throughout the nineteenth century, and the rapid growth of Germany and Japan in the later part of the nineteenth and early twentieth centuries. The theory fits the growth of Britain and of Holland and (less clearly) of France in the early modern period and their roles in the rise of the once-backward civilization of Western Christendom. It explains the decline of old cities in the midst of these expanding countries and the scattered, transactions-intensive putting-out system. The theory is consistent with the phenomenal postwar growth of Korea, Taiwan, Hong Kong, and Singapore and with the guild-ridden stagnation of the China that was first exposed to European pressure, not to mention the similar stagnation in India. Finally, the theory fits the pattern of inequalities and the trade policies of many of the unstable developing countries, and a number of other facts as well.

The evidence is perhaps not sufficient for us to say to what extent the theory succeeds in explaining the British class structure, the Indian caste system, and the timing and character of the stronger forms of racial discrimination in South Africa. It is best to be cautious when there is not enough sound quantitative or historical information. Yet the theory certainly explains each of these phenomena far better than any other theories do.

The *same* theory that parsimoniously explained the foregoing was the one that I used with very little addition to explain involuntary unemployment, depressions and stagflation, and other macroeconomic phenomena as well, without at any point making ad hoc or unreasonable assumptions about individual behavior. And it is powerful evidence for the present theory that, unlike any other theory, it explains the pattern of the development of the macroeconomic problem over time. When we take all these explanations together, we see that the theory is powerful and consilient as well as parsimonious. It is hard to see how it could explain so many diverse phenomena so simply if it were wholly or mainly false.

But even if the theory here should to my surprise be *entirely* correct, it still considers only one among the many factors affecting the phenomena I have endeavored to explain. The overwhelming significance that other factors will sometimes have can perhaps best be illustrated by considering what would happen if the findings of future research should resonate with what I have said here, and all the pertinent specialists should in time be persuaded by my argument. Suppose further that the message of this book was then passed on to the public through the educational system and the mass media, and that most people came to believe that the argument in this book was true. There would then be irresistible political support for policies to solve the problem that this book explains.

A society with the consensus that has just been described might choose the most obvious and far-reaching remedy: it might simply repeal all special-interest legislation or regulation and at the same time apply rigorous anti-trust laws to every type of cartel or collusion that used its power to obtain prices or wages above competitive levels. A society could in this way keep distributional coalitions from doing any substantial damage. This remedy does not require any major expenditure of resources: intelligent and resolute public policies would by themselves bring great increases in prosperity and social performance. So sweeping a change in ideas and policies is extraordinarily unlikely. But this scenario is nonetheless sufficient to show that if the argument in this book or other arguments of similar import should be unexpectedly influential, then the predictions derived from this book will be falsified.

Obviously, distributional coalitions will oppose the repeal of special-interest legislation and the imposition of anti-trust policies that deny them the monopoly gains that their capacity for collective action could otherwise obtain. The limited impact of economic education in the past, even on matters on which there has been professional consensus, suggests that the coalitions will often be successful. Keynes went much too far when he wrote that the world is ruled by ideas and little else. Yet the great influence of his writings on public policy, and the more recent impact of his critics, shows that ideas certainly do make a difference.

May we not then reasonably expect, if special interests are (as I have claimed) harmful to economic growth, full employment, coherent government, equal opportunity, and social mobility, that students of the matter will become increasingly aware of this as time goes on? And that the awareness eventually will spread to larger and larger proportions of the population? And that this wider awareness will greatly limit the losses from the special interests? That is what I expect, at least when I am searching for a happy ending.

Acknowledgments

My strategy in research is to attempt to say or write something au-
dacious enough to elicit intelligent criticism, to reflect at length on that
criticism, and then to maintain the self-confidence needed unreservedly
to make every amendment, abandonment, or extension that could be
appropriate. Even if I believe a criticism is mistaken, I strive (sometimes unsuccessfully) to take that as evidence that I need to improve my
exposition. While working on this book I have accordingly obtained
criticisms from hundreds of people—experts in almost every pertinent
specialization, in most parts of the world, and from almost every ideological shading. As a result, a large part of any merit this book may
have is due to my critics.

I am indebted to each and every critic, but the number is so very
great that it is not feasible to list them all. This is not only because of the
excessive number of pages such a listing would require. I was using the
criticism-seeking strategy even before I knew I would be writing a book
along these lines, and I have been using it for so many years on this
book alone that I have undoubtedly forgotten some of those who helped.
In some cases the critics were questioners in large audiences, whose
names I never knew. In selecting for special mention some critics whose
help is recent or for other reasons especially memorable, I am no doubt
doing an unjustice to others, and even to some whose help was quite
valuable. I am deeply sorry for this and hope that those I have acciden-
tally slighted will forgive me.

Those who provided crucial help and encouragement in the earlier
and more primitive stages of this effort needed special patience, and I
am especially thankful for that. John Flemming, coeditor of the *Eco-*

nomic Journal, was an extraordinarily generous and penetrating early critic, and I am sorry that I have never sent him the ready-to-publish article that I led him to expect. Robert Solow was another invaluable source of early encouragement and help, as were Moses Abramovitz, Samuel Brittan, Sir Alec Cairncross, Walter Eltis, Daniel Patrick Moynihan, Daniel Newlon, and Thomas Wilson. Those who have done or are doing complementary or collaborative work have also been particularly helpful, most notably Kwang Choi, Jean-François Hennart, Gudmund Hernes, Dennis Mueller, and Peter Murrell.

In 1978 Robin Marris proposed and chaired a conference to assess and criticize a paper I had written òn the matters discussed particularly in chapter 4 of this book. He invited experts from various countries and specialties to this conference, some of whom wrote extended comments that are published in Dennis Mueller's *Political Economy of Growth.* I am deeply thankful to Robin Marris for promoting this conference, to Dennis Mueller for editing and contributing to the book that grew out of it, to the National Science Foundation for providing the principal funding for it, and to the Deutsche Forschungsgemeinschaft, the Centre National de la Recherche Scientifique, and the Ministry of Education of Japan for financing some of the travel to it. Finally, each of those who attended the conference or contributed papers has helped me more than he or she probably realizes. The mere listing of names and affiliations that follows does not do them justice:

Moses Abramovitz (Stanford U.), J. C. Asselain (U. de Bordeaux I), Ragnar Bentzel (Uppsala U.), James Blackman (National Science Foundation), Samuel Bowles (U. of Massachusetts), Myles G. Boylan (National Science Foundation), Camilo Dagum (Ottawa U.), James Dean (Simon Fraser U. and Columbia U.), Stephen J. DeCanio (U. of California, Santa Barbara), Edward Denison (U.S. Dept. of Commerce), Raymond Courbis (U. of Paris), John Eatwell (Trinity, Cambridge), Walter Eltis (Exeter, Oxford), Francesco Forte (U. of Torino), Raymond Goldsmith (Yale U.), Jean-François Hennart (Florida International U.), Gudmund Hernes (U. of Bergen), Sir John Hicks (All Souls, Oxford), Ursula (Lady) Hicks (Linacre, Oxford), Helen Hughes (World Bank), Charles Hulton (Urban Institute), Serge-Christophe Kolm (CEPREMAP, Paris), Hans-Juergen Krupp (U. of Frankfurt), Franz Lehner (Ruhr U. Bochum), Harvey Leibenstein (Harvard U.), Edward J. Lincoln (Johns Hopkins U.), Edmond Malinvaud (Inst. National de la Statistique, Paris), R. C. O. Matthews (Clare,

Cambridge), Christian Morrisson (Ecole Normale Superieure), Daniel H. Newlon (National Science Foundation), Yusuke Onitsuka (Osaka U.), Sam Peltzman (U. of Chicago), Richard Portes (Birkbeck, London), Frederic L. Pryor (Swarthmore College), Walter Salant (Brookings Institution), Hans Soderstrom (U. of Stockholm), Ingemar Stahl (U. of Lund), Carl Christian von Weizsacker (U. of Bonn), Hans Willgerodt (U. of Cologne), Wolfgang Zapf (U. of Mannheim).

I am similarly indebted to Roger Benjamin for bringing early drafts of part of this work to the attention of critics in political science, to Marian Ash, Myles Boylan, Jan de Vries, Stanley Engerman, I. M. D. Little, R. C. O. Matthews, and Edmund Phelps for exceptionally generous help, to Nuffield College, Oxford, and especially to Brian Barry for hospitality and comment when I had some of my early thoughts on this, to the staff of Resources for the Future and especially Emery Castle and Joy Dunkerley for patient encouragement, and to the participants in the pleasant seminars organized by the Lehrman Institute around early drafts of this book, including particularly Donald Dewey and Kelvin Lancaster. My wife, Alison G. Olson, has as a professional historian a special appreciation of the importance of prose that is whenever humanly possible free of specialized technical language, and I am indebted to her for invaluable instruction in the art of writing clearly, as well as for many other things. My brothers, Allan and Gaylord, have also helped in many ways.

My colleagues at the Department of Economics at the University of Maryland have been exceptionally generous and stimulating. I must emphasize Martin J. Bailey's patience with the delays in our collaborative work occasioned by my preoccupation with this book, Christopher Clague's years of helpful and penetrating comments on this and my other writing, and Charles Brown's and Paul Meyer's criticisms of many early drafts. Adele Krokes's help also deserves special emphasis, not only because of her incredibly patient typing and word processing, but even more because of the efficient way she helps to organize my hectic professional life. I am also thankful to those who have provided research assistance over the years I have worked on this book, especially Terence Alexander, Kwang Choi, Brian Cushing, Cyril Kearl, Douglas Kinney, Natalie McPherson, James Stafford, Fran Sussman, and Howell Zee.

Finally, there are the many kind people who have read and criticized the last two drafts. I am grateful not only to many of those named earlier, but also to Alan Blinder, Roger Boner, Barry Bosworth, Shannon Brown, Bruce Bueno de Mesquita, Martha Derthick, Dudley Dillard, Bruce Dunson, James Galbraith, John Goldethorpe, Donald Gordon, Daniel Hausman, Russell Hardin, Michael Hechter, Gail Huh, Peter Katzenstein, Donald Keesing, Robert Knight, Robert Mackay, Cynthia Taft Morris, Douglas North, Joe Oppenheimer, Clarence Stone, Maura Shaw Tantillo, Charles Taquey, Neil Wallace, Oliver Williamson, and Horst Zimmermann.

Unfortunately, there has not been time enough to do justice to many of the more recent comments. I fear I have perhaps also failed to comprehend fully some of the criticisms, and despite my general strategy I have stubbornly resisted a few, including one or two that were most severe. Thus the faults that remain in this study—and I fear, partly because of its scope, that there may be a great many—are entirely my responsibility.

Notes

CHAPTER 1

1. From "The First Book, Entitled Clio," *The History of Herodotus,* trans. George Hawlinson (New York: D. Appleton and Company, 1882), 1:121, 122.

2. Irving B. Kravis et al., *A System of International Comparisons of Gross Product and Purchasing Power* (Baltimore and London: Johns Hopkins University Press for the World Bank, 1975), especially p. 8.

3. New York: Collier, 1962, p. 476 (6th ed., London: J. Murray, 1872). For an analysis of the power of theories, see Anatol Rapoport, "Explanatory Power and Explanatory Appeal of Theories," *Synthese* 24 (1972):321–42. I am thankful to Russell Hardin for advice on the power of theories.

4. *The Philosophy of Inductive Sciences* (New York: Johnson Reprint, 1967), 2:65 (3rd ed., London: Parker, 1858); see also Paul R. Thagard, "The Best Explanation: Criteria for Theory Choice," *Journal of Philosophy* 75 (February 1978):76–92. I am thankful to Daniel Hausman for calling the concept of consilience to my attention and for his penetrating criticisms of an earlier draft of this book, and to Stephen Brush for providing helpful references on this subject.

CHAPTER 2

1. Cambridge: Harvard University Press, 1965, 1971. The 1971 version differs from the first 1965 printing only in the addition of an appendix. Some readers may have access to the first paperback edition published by Schocken Books (New York: 1968), which is identical to the 1965 Harvard version. Readers whose first language is not English may prefer *Die Logik des Kollektiven Handelns* (Tübingen: J. C. B. Mohr [Paul Siebeck], 1968), or *Logique de*

l'Action Collective (Paris: Presses Universitaires de France, 1978). Translations in Japanese (from Minerva Shobo) and in Italian (from Feltrinelli) are forthcoming.

2. There is a logically possible exception to this assertion, although not of wide practical importance, that is explained in footnote 68 of chapter 1 of *The Logic*, pp. 48–49.

3. David J. McDonald, *Union Man* (New York: Dutton, 1969), p. 121, quoted in William A. Gamson, *The Strategy of Social Protest* (Homewood, Ill.: Dorsey Press, 1975), p. 68.

4. *The Logic*, p. 85.

5. This means in turn that sometimes individual corporations of substantial size can be political combinations with significant lobbying power. On less than voluntary corporate contributions, see J. Patrick Wright, *On a Clear Day You Can See General Motors* (Grosse Pointe, Mich.: Wright Enterprises, 1979), pp. 69–70.

6. *The Logic*, pp. 132–67.

7. Erik Lindahl, "Just Taxation—A Positive Solution," in Richard Musgrave and Alan T. Peacock, eds., *Classics in the Theory of Public Finance* (London: Macmillan, 1958), pp. 168–77 and 214–33. In a Lindahl equilibrium, the parties at issue are each charged a tax-price for marginal units of the public good that is equal to the value each places on a marginal unit of the good. When this condition holds, even parties that have vastly different evaluations of the collective good will want the same amount. It would take us far afield to discuss the huge literature on this matter now, but it may be helpful to nonspecialists to point out that in most circumstances in which the parties at issue expect Lindahl-type taxation, they would have an incentive to understate their true valuations of the collective good, since they would get whatever amount was provided however low their tax-price. There is an interesting literature on relatively subtle schemes that could give individuals an incentive to reveal their true valuations for public goods, thereby making Lindahl-equilibria attainable, but most of these schemes are a very long way indeed from practical application.

8. See my primitive, early article, "The Principle of 'Fiscal Equivalence,'" *American Economic Review, Papers and Proceedings* 59 (May 1969):479–87.

9. See, for a leading example, Martin C. McGuire, "Group Segregation and Optimal Jurisdictions," *Journal of Political Economy* 82 (1974):112–32.

10. See most notably Wallace Oates, *Fiscal Federalism* (New York: Harcourt Brace Jovanovich, Inc., 1972).

11. For very early work on the limited information voters may be expected to have, see Anthony Downs's classic *Economic Theory of Democracy* (New York: Harper, 1957).

12. I am indebted to Russell Hardin for calling this point to my attention.

For a superb and rigorous analysis of the whole issue of collective action, see Hardin's *Collective Action* (Baltimore: The Johns Hopkins University Press for Resources for the Future, forthcoming).

13. There is another consideration that works in the same direction. Consider individuals who get pleasure from participating in efforts to obtain a collective good just as they would from ordinary consumption, and so are participation altruists (described in the first footnote in this chapter). If the costs of collective action to the individual are slight, the costs of consuming the participation pleasure or satisfying the moral impulse to be a participant are unlikely to prevent collective action. With the diminishing marginal rates of substitution that are described in the footnote, however, the extent of collective action out of these motives will decrease as its price rises.

14. *The Logic*, pp. 5–65.

15. The assumption that there are two firms that place an equal value on the collective good is expositionally useful but will not often be descriptively realistic. In the much more common case, where the parties place different valuations on the public good, the party that places the larger absolute valuation on the public good is at an immense disadvantage. When it provides the amount of the collective good that would be optimal for it alone, then the others have an incentive to enjoy this amount and provide none at all. But the reverse is not true. So the larger party bears the whole burden of the collective good. (The party that places the larger value on the collective good has the option of trying to force the others to share the cost by withholding provision, but it is also at a disadvantage in the bargaining because it will lose more from this action than those with whom it is bargaining.) Thus a complete analysis of the likelihood of collective action must consider the relative sizes or valuations of the collective good of the parties involved as well as the size of the group; see the references in the next note on "the exploitation of the great by the small" and other consequences of intragroup variations in valuations of collective goods.

If the corner solution with the larger party bearing all the burden does not occur, and both firms provide some amount of the collective good under Cournot assumptions, then the two firms will tend to be of exactly the same size, as in the example chosen for expositional convenience in the text. Assume that each firm has to pay the same price for each unit of the collective good and that they have identical production functions for whatever private good they produce. Since they must, by the definition of a pure collective good, both receive the same amount of it, they can both be in equilibrium under Cournot assumptions only if their isoquants have the same slope at the relevant point. That is, the isoquants describing the output that results from each combination of the private good and public good inputs for each of the firms must have the same slope if the two firms enjoying the same amount of the collective good are each purchasing some of it at the same time. Under my identical production function and factor price assumptions, the two firms must then have exactly the same output or size.

Similarly remarkable results hold for consumers who share a collective good. Either the consumer that places the higher absolute valuation on the public good will bear the entire cost or else they will end up with equal incomes! When both consumers get the same amount of a collective good, they both can be continuing to purchase some under Cournot behavior only if they both have the same marginal rate of substitution between the public good and the private good, and thus (with identical utility functions and prices) identical incomes. Unless the two consumers have identical incomes *in the beginning,* there is inevitably exploitation of the great by the small. One possibility is that the richer consumer will bear the whole cost of the collective good. The only other possibility with independent adjustment is that the public good is so valuable that the richer consumer's initial purchases of it have such a large income effect on the poorer consumer that this poorer consumer ends up just as well off as the initially richer consumer, so both buy some amount of the collective good in equilibrium. I have profited from discussions of this point with my colleague Martin C. McGuire. For a stimulating and valuable, if partially incorrect, argument along related lines, see Ronald Jeremias and Asghar Zardkoohi, "Distributional Implications of Independent Adjustment in an Economy with Public Goods," *Economic Inquiry* 14 (June 1976):305–08.

16. *The Logic,* pp. 29–31, and Mancur Olson and Richard Zeckhauser, "An Economic Theory of Alliances," *Review of Economics and Statistics* 47 (August 1966):266–79, and my introduction to Todd Sandler, ed., *The Theory and Structure of International Political Economy* (Boulder, Colo.: Westview Press, 1980), pp. 3–16.

17. No strategic interaction is observed among firms in perfectly competitive industries or among buyers of automobiles, for example. In such situations no one finds that his own interests or choices depend on the choices of any other individual in the group or industry, so they have no incentive to bargain with one another. A sufficiently large subset, if it could obtain the collective good of a bargaining organization for the subset, would have an incentive to bargain with others in the group. But when genuinely large groups are at issue, the size of the subset that is large enough to have an incentive to bargain is itself so large that the collective good of the bargaining organization for the subset cannot be obtained without selective incentives. Another way of stating the point is to say that the bargaining costs of getting the bargaining organization for the subset are themselves prohibitive, so that any further bargaining costs are irrelevant when group size increases still further, i.e., to the point that a still bigger subset would be needed. This indicates that approaches to genuinely large or "latent" groups that focus on bargaining costs and strategic interaction are not getting at the essence of the matter.

NOTES TO PAGES 38–45

CHAPTER 3

1. Niccolò Machiavelli, *The Prince,* trans. George Bull (Baltimore: Penguin Books, 1961), p. 51.

2. Edward Shorter and Charles Tilly, *Strikes in France, 1830–1968* (London and New York: Cambridge University Press, 1974), pp. 154–55.

3. Max Weber, *Theory of Social and Economic Organization,* trans. Talcott Parsons and A. M. Henderson, ed. Talcott Parsons (New York: Oxford University Press, 1947), p. 318.

4. I am thankful to Peter Murrell for help on this point.

5. Gordon Tullock and Anne Krueger are to the best of my knowledge the pioneers in this literature. For reprints of their initial articles and especially pertinent articles by Keith Cowling and Dennis Mueller, Richard Posner, and Barry Baysinger, Robert B. Ekelund, Jr., and Robert D. Tollison, plus other useful papers, see James M. Buchanan, Robert D. Tollison, and Gordon Tullock, eds., *Toward a Theory of the Rent-Seeking Society* (College Station, Tex.: Texas A. & M. University Press, 1980).

6. A measure that would reduce economic efficiency if introduced in a Pareto-efficient society could conceivably increase efficiency in a society with prior distortions. See R. G. Lipsey and R. K. Lancaster, "The General Theory of the Second Best," *Review of Economic Studies* 24, no. 63:11–32.

7. One of the questions left aside was raised by the concept of "mass movements" fashionable among sociologists in the 1950s and 1960s. This concept emphasizes that membership in organizations that are smaller than the state (and presumably small or subdivided enough so that there is social interaction among members) can reduce alienation and increase social stability. In my judgment there is an important element of truth in this concept, and I have found it useful in some of my own writings, particularly those cited in note 21 below. But this element of truth is more than offset in many societies by the contribution these organizations make to divisiveness and ungovernability, as is explained in the remainder of the discussion leading to Implication 4. The prospective publications that will relate the point from the literature on mass movements to the argument in this book, and the reasons that integration is omitted from this book, are set out in note 21.

8. Again, this qualification is introduced because of the possibility of "second-best" problems. It is, for example, possible that the monopolization of a previously competitive but highly polluting industry could increase economic efficiency if there were no effluent fee on the pollution. In this example, the logic is quite simple: the industry when competitive had an output that was inefficiently large because the social cost of its pollution is neglected by the competitive firms. Since monopolists have an incentive to restrict output, the loss from pollution would be reduced by monopolization, and if the pollution

were serious enough this could be of greater value than the market output forgone.

9. Arnold Harberger, "Monopoly and Resource Allocation," *American Economic Review* 44 (May 1954):77–87. See also Harvey Leibenstein on X-efficiency, *Inflation, Income Distribution and X-Efficiency Theory* (London: Croom Helm; New York: Harper and Row, Barnes and Noble, 1980).

10. To the best of my recollection, in a guest lecture at Princeton University in the 1960s.

11. See Dennis C. Mueller's concluding essay in the book he edited on *The Political Economy of Growth* (New Haven: Yale University Press, 1983).

12. Kenneth Arrow, *Social Choice and Individual Values,* 2d ed. (New Haven: Yale University Press, 1963). For a more accessible proof of Arrow's theorem and a survey of related issues, see Dennis Mueller, *Public Choice* (Cambridge: At the University Press, 1979).

13. See, for example, Morris Fiorina, "The Decline of Collective Responsibility in American Politics," *Daedalus* 109 (Summer 1980):25–46; this issue has the title *The End of Consensus.* See also the writings of E. E. Schattschneider, *Party Government* (New York: Farrar and Rinehart, 1942), *Politics, Pressures, and the Tariff: A Study of Free Private Enterprise in Pressure Politics, As Shown in the 1929–1930 Revision of the Tariff* (Hamden, Conn.: Archon Books, 1963), *The Semisovereign People: A Realistic's View of Democracy in America* (New York: Holt, Rinehart, and Winston, 1960), and *The Struggle for Party Government* (College Park, Md.: University of Maryland, 1948).

14. See note 12 above.

15. "How Are Cartel Prices Determined?" *Journal of Industrial Economics* 5 (November 1956):16–23.

16. *Industrial Market Structure and Economic Performance* (Chicago: Rand McNally, 1970), p. 161. I am thankful to Jean-François Hennart for calling this and the previous reference to my attention.

17. M. A. Adelman of M.I.T. made this type of argument in a seminar a few years ago at Resources for the Future in Washington. Of course, Adelman recognized that some nations with their own nationalized oil companies were not covered by the argument.

18. William Baumol, John C. Panzar, and Robert Willig, *Contestable Markets and the Theory of Industry Structure* (San Diego: Harcourt Brace Jovanovich, 1982); see also Baumol's "Contestable Markets: An Uprising in the Theory of Industry Structure," *American Economic Review* 72 (March 1982):1–15.

19. See Avinash Dixit, "A Model of Duopoly Suggesting a Theory of Entry Barriers," *Bell Journal of Economics* 10 (Spring 1979):20–32, and "The Role of Investment in Entry-Deterrence," *Economic Journal* 90 (March 1980):95–106.

20. See Richard Schmalensee, "Economies of Scale and Barriers to Entry," *Journal of Political Economy* 89 (December 1981):1228–38.

21. "Rapid Growth as a Destabilizing Force," *Journal of Economic History* 23 (December 1963):529–52; "Agriculture and the Depressed Areas," *Journal of Farm Economics* 46 (December 1964):984–88; "Economics, Sociology, and the Best of All Possible Worlds," *The Public Interest* 12 (Summer 1968):96–118; and the introduction and epilogue (coauthored) to *The No Growth Society,* edited with Hans Landsberg (New York: W. W. Norton, 1974).

One reason that I have not in this book gone into the social costs that unprecedented rapid growth can sometimes have is that it would make the present theory much more difficult to refute. The theory here makes predictions about economic growth as it is conventionally defined and (for recent periods) measured in the national income statistics issued by the governments of most developed countries. I argue in "The Treatment of Externalities in National Income Statistics" (in Lowdon Wingo and Alan Evans, eds., *Public Economics and the Quality of Life* [Johns Hopkins University Press for Resources for the Future and Centre for Environmental Studies, 1977], pp. 219–49) that the national income statistics often do not properly take account of various environmental and social side effects. These statistics nonetheless offer an objective and generally unbiased test of the present theory and in addition provide far better insight into the progress of societies and the well-being of people in them than many people realize.

Another reason why I have omitted the social disruptions that rapid economic growth can occasionally cause, and the contributions (discussed in note 7 above) that some special-interest groups can sometimes make to social stability, is that the accumulation of these groups in the long-stable societies that are a principal focus here creates the ungovernability discussed in connection with Implication 4 and also decidedly destabilizing frustrations, as more and more people come to realize that their societies are very far from being as productive (or as fair) as they could be. Thus the inclusion of the matters I have omitted does not lead to any major change in any of the conclusions here.

A final reason for excluding these matters is that I have discussed most of them elsewhere, in the publications so tediously cited above, and I will relate these and other issues to the present argument in forthcoming books. The sometimes disruptive effects of rapid growth and the relation of the economy and economic theory generally to social, political, and environmental issues will be discussed in "Beyond the Measuring Rod of Money"; this is a book that I very nearly decided to publish in the 1970s, but I decided this subject was so vast that it needed years of additional thought—I hope to finish revising it soon after this book is published. The relationship between the development of special-interest groups and other institutions and the development of stability in less developed countries will, if all goes well, be the subject of still another book. This last will be an expansion of an unpublished paper I wrote and circulated in the early 1960s under the title "Economic Growth and Structural Change" (and more recently in a revised form under the title "Diseconomies of Scale in Development"). It will emphasize the special problems of instability and inefficiency of large-scale organizations in poor societies, both now and before the Industrial Revolution.

I apologize for leaving out certain considerations that some readers may feel would affect their assessment of the importance of the theory in the present book, but surely this book is sweeping enough as it is.

22. Even if the innovation in this firm is a labor-saving innovation, a sufficiently powerful union could in principle take advantage of it to make all workers better off; it could appropriate a portion of the savings from the innovation for the workers and offer as much of this portion as was needed as an inducement to the number of workers who were no longer needed to seek employment elsewhere. The workers might do still better if the innovation in the firm were a capital-saving innovation, like the less expensive but superior computers that have been developed recently. Workers as a whole could lose from an economy-wide labor-saving innovation. The fact remains that a sufficiently powerful union could, if bargaining costs and delays are ignored, serve its members' interests by encouraging the firm with which it bargains to adopt any innovations that increased the total surplus available for profits and wages in the aggregate.

23. This special case occurs when there is such an underutilization of labor in relation to the amount of other factors that the average product of labor would increase if another laborer were added. But the profit-maximizing firm could never be in this range.

24. Sir John Hicks, "Structural Unemployment and Economic Growth: A 'Labor Theory of Value' Model," in Mueller, *The Political Economy of Growth*.

25. Strictly speaking, Hicks's proof applies only to a two-sector economy with labor as the only factor of production. The essence of this argument is, however, applicable to economies with any number of industries and factors of production.

26. To avoid complications with income effects that are of no importance here, I assume that we are speaking of an income-compensated demand curve.

27. They would not, however, necessarily want the number of workers or other sellers to fall below the point where the average product of the factor was at a maximum.

28. I am thankful to Christopher Clague for emphasizing the magnitude of the other factors involved here. These are illustrated by the endogamous rules of some groups that have average or below-average levels of wealth, power, and prestige.

29. Charles Schultze, *The Public Use of Private Interest* (Washington, D.C.: The Brookings Institution, 1977).

30. Morris Fiorina and Roger Noll, "Voters, Legislators and Bureaucracy—Institutional Design in the Public Sector," *American Economic Review, Papers and Proceedings* 68 (May 1978):256–60.

CHAPTER 4

1. Gustav Stolper et al., *The German Economy, 1870 to the Present* (New York: Harcourt Brace and World, 1967), pp. 258–61.

2. Richard E. Caves and Masu Uekusa, *Industrial Organization in Japan* (Washington, D.C.: The Brookings Institution, 1976).

3. I am grateful to Gudmund Hernes for educating me on the substantial significance of the encompassing special-interest organizations in postwar Germany.

4. For a good description and analysis of French growth from a more orthodox perspective, see J.-J. Carré, P. Dubois, and E. Malinvaud, *La Croissance Française*, which is also available in English translation as *French Economic Growth*, trans. John P. Hatfield (Stanford: Stanford University Press, 1975). I am grateful to Edmond Malinvaud for taking an early, primitive version of the present argument quite seriously and offering a severe criticism of it. I do not think Malinvaud's criticisms apply to the present book.

5. The need to draw also upon another part of the present theory to explain French experience is evident from the useful criticism of an early version of the present argument written by J.-C. Asselain and C. Morrisson, "Economic Growth and Interest Groups: The French Experience," in Dennis C. Mueller, ed., *The Political Economy of Growth* (New Haven: Yale University Press, 1983). Asselain and Morrisson show that instability and invasion by themselves are not nearly sufficient to explain the whole story of the evolution of special-interest groups and growth rates in France. Valuable as Asselain's and Morrisson's criticism is, I do not think it does full justice to the extent to which instability, invasion, and ideological division have slowed the development of French labor unions, and since the largest part of the national income is paid in wages to labor, this is quantitatively very important. There is much to be said for Asselain's and Morrisson's emphasis on how economic adversity can facilitate special-interest organization; but recessions also can weaken special-interest organizations, as the recent experience of American and British labor unions shows, and boom conditions are often periods of exceptional growth of such organizations (e.g., the growth of American labor unions in both world wars). In view of the generally ambivalent relationship between economic progress or retrogression and special-interest organization, I would continue to attribute a significant role to instability and invasion—and the wide ideological

divisions that go with them—in retarding the development of special-interest organizations. It is difficult to see how any French economic organization with a massive clientele would not have been cowed by, say, the Nazi hegemony and occupation, or that any such organization would not have been handicapped at times by the intense ideological divisions in French society.

6. See, for example, M. W. Kirby, *The Decline of British Economic Power Since 1870* (London: George Allen and Unwin, 1981).

7. Relative rates of growth must be used in this argument because the rates of growth of the slowest growing and the fastest growing countries alike were faster in the 1950s and 1960s than in any previous period, and far higher than during the Industrial Revolution. One explanation of this is the apparently increasing pace of scientific progress in the modern world. This progress is essentially exogenous to a single national economy like the British economy; it depends on the advance of science over the world as a whole rather than in any single country. Many advances in basic science in any case may often be largely independent of current economic developments and of the institutions on which the present theory focuses. In view of the importance of developments like the world's rate of basic scientific advance that are exogenous to my theory, it does not predict absolute rates of growth. Since all countries have access to essentially the same basic scientific knowledge, the relative rates of growth of different countries in any one period can depend to a great degree on the institutions and policies of that country, so the present theory can therefore generate predictions about relative rates of growth.

8. Verlag Dokumentation (Pullach bei Munchen, 1973).

9. Peter Murrell, ''The Comparative Structure of the Growth of West German and British Manufacturing Industry,'' in Mueller, *The Political Economy of Growth.*

10. Some observers are taken by the idea that Germany and Japan have grown so rapidly since World War II because, it is supposed, they were fortunate to have their existing factories and machines destroyed by bombing and other combat, and therefore had no choice but to invest in the most modern plant and equipment. Britain, by contrast, is supposed to have been cursed with a large inheritance of capital that was not up-to-date. A moment's reflection will, however, make it clear that a profit-maximizing firm that owns plant and equipment that is not up-to-date will be either better off for owning the old capital or alternatively no worse off than if it had no capital left at all. If the use of the old capital will generate receipts in excess of average variable costs, the firm will profit from using the old capital and be better off than if it did not own this capital. Should the use of the capital not generate a return above average variable costs, the profit-maximizing firm will not use it, and will be in essentially the same position as it would have been had this old capital been destroyed. The most that bombing of old capital could do is to save a country some

wrecking costs of capital goods it needed to tear down, and this hardly could be quantitatively important. Everyday observation also confirms that it is not an advantage to be forced to start from scratch. The poorest developing countries certainly do not have a lot of old machinery and factories, yet most of them are not growing very rapidly. Germany and Japan invested so heavily in the 1950s and 1960s as compared with Britain that they must have more outdated capital goods than the British do, but yet they continue to grow faster than the British. Thus nations are not being irrational when they regard the bombing of their industry as a hostile act and try to defend themselves against such bombing.

11. If we assume that the percentage of income saved rises with income, and that there are no inflows or outflows of capital, a country with a hard-working population will save and invest more than a country that is identical to it in everything except industriousness. It will accordingly grow faster. I am thankful to Tatsuo Hatta and I. M. D. Little for calling this and other possible connections between industriousness and growth to my attention.

12. Samuel Brittan, "How British Is the British Sickness?" *Journal of Law and Economics* 21 (October 1978):245–68.

13. Ibid., table 9, p. 254.

14. David Smith, "Public Consumption and Economic Performance," *National Westminster Bank Quarterly Review,* November 1975, pp. 17–30.

15. David S. Landes, *The Unbound Prometheus* (Cambridge: At the University Press, 1969), pp. 39–122. These quotations are taken from widely scattered sections of chapters 2 and 3.

16. I am grateful to Daniel Patrick Moynihan for reminding me of the purpose Smith had when using this expression: "To found a great empire for the sole purpose of raising up a people of customers, may at first sight appear a project only for a nation of shopkeepers; but extremely fit for a nation whose government is influenced by shopkeepers" (*Wealth of Nations* [New York: Modern Library, 1937], p. 579).

17. Christopher Hill, *The Century of Revolution, 1603–1709* (New York: W. W. Norton, 1961), and J. H. Plumb, *The Growth of Political Stability in England, 1675–1725* (London: Macmillan, 1967).

18. See chapter 4, "Orthodox Theories of State and Class," in *The Logic,* pp. 98–110.

19. See, for example, Mancur Olson, "The Principle of Fiscal Equivalence," *American Economic Review, Papers and Proceedings* 59 (May 1969):479–87 and Martin C. McGuire, "Group Segregation and Optimal Jurisdictions," *Journal of Political Economy* 82 (January/February 1974):112–32.

20. Cambridge: At the University Press, 1981.

21. One need not agree with George Bernard Shaw "that all professions are conspiracies against the laity" (*The Doctor's Dilemma,* 1906), for one to believe that the honored place held by the professions in modern society, and

the fact that most intellectuals are in the professions, lead many to neglect their cartelistic aspects.

22. The ruptures of medieval class patterns and barriers that apparently have been due to the sweeping changes in technology and modes of life since the onset of the Industrial Revolution suggest an intriguing extension of the present theory. If there are sufficiently drastic and rapid changes in an economy, so that utterly new industries, occupations, and modes of living rapidly arise, the existing distributional coalitions (which make decisions in the relatively slow fashion described in Implication 6) may find the new activities beyond their scope and control. Peter Murrell's finding that new industries are less likely to be controlled by distributional coalitions than old ones also calls attention to this possibility. Thus when economic growth is not only rapid but also characterized by large discontinuities, it could tend to bypass existing special-interest groups and leave them relatively less important in the society than previously. This could in the extreme even offset the accumulation of the distributional societies described in Implication 2; drastic economic instability as well as political instability can at times weaken special-interest organizations. Although extremely rapid and discontinuous growth introduces some of the social costs discussed in notes 7 and 21 in chapter 3, it is nonetheless worth looking into the possibility that public policies occasionally could be designed to promote exceptionally discontinuous and rapid growth partly because this would reduce the significance of distributional coalitions and the social rigidities they help to engender. Such policies would most often be feasible for poor developing societies that can transform their technologies by borrowing those already developed in more prosperous societies. Eventually, if time permits, I hope to examine this possible extension of the theory in a detailed way, or alternatively to provoke others to do so. The importance of this extension is due partly to the possibility that it could illuminate a way of introducing an economic and possibly quite desirable form of instability that could delay or prevent the development of institutional rheumatism.

23. The evidence that there is greater sensitivity to certain class or group distinctions and barriers in Britain than in various comparable societies is unfortunately mainly informal and anecdotal rather than quantitative. But there are mountains of casual evidence on this point, and the evidence and perceptions of British observers appear to be in close accord with those of foreign visitors to Britain. One interesting example of this is the distinctive response of British commentators on the earliest versions of the present argument, written before the implications of the theory for class and group barriers were apparent to me. Most British commentators, however generous they might be, were quick to point out that my argument did not take account of the special characteristics of one or another of the British social classes, such as the alleged bloody-mindedness of the British working class or the allegedly aloof and anticommercial

attitudes of the British upper classes, or of the British class system as a whole. At first I resisted these criticisms as only ad hoc arguments; I foolishly overlooked the fact that not a single commentator from anywhere made any similar comments about any other country, and even somehow neglected memories from my own time as an American undergraduate at Oxford—which memories strongly supported my British critics' contentions that the British class system was distinctive and harmful to British economic growth. Finally I realized that, if my argument was right, the British critics who pointed out that one had to take account of the class system also had to be right, and I then generalized my theory. Once the theory was generalized to cover social rigidities, it was almost inevitable that the additional application of it that is set out in chapter 6 would come to mind. If my theory as generalized has any value, much of the credit is due to my many British friends and critics.

Massive and consistent as the casual evidence that there is a distinctive class system in Britain seems to me to be, it is nonetheless useful to seek quantitative and systematic evidence as well. A consensus among observers obviously has meaning, but the perceptions of casual observers do not have the precision and ready comparability that is desirable. On the other hand, quantitative evidence of an incomplete or inadequate kind should not necessarily be given more weight than a vast amount of casual evidence.

Unfortunately, the types of quantitative studies that are now available do not provide appropriate tests of the hypothesis about social exclusion that my theory generates. One reason is that this hypothesis relates to social exclusion or discrimination but does not claim to explain any correlation between the status of parents and children that is due to different-sized legacies of human and other capital. As the application of the theory in chapter 6 should make clear, my theory, if correct, explains any systematic tendency to exclude, or to discriminate against the actual capabilities of any group or class of adults in a society; it does not, however, explain any differences in capabilities that are due to differences in upbringing and educational opportunities, except to the extent that these differences in turn are explained by the impact of the distributional coalitions in the parents' generation on the distribution of income. The quantitative studies of social mobility that exist now relate the social prestige of the occupations of fathers to the social prestige of the occupations of their sons. To the extent that the social prestige of the occupations that sons practice is due to the amount and kind of human capital they acquired, it is generally not explained by my theory.

A second reason why the existing quantitative studies do not provide a good test of my argument about social involution is that these studies consider social mobility from one generation to another, and the majority of the distributional coalitions in Britain and other Western countries are not strictly multigenerational. That is, most of them do not restrict membership in the coalition to their own offspring. The Indian and South African distributional coalitions considered in chapter 6 do this; so do some European coalitions such as the nobility and certain labor unions, but so far they appear to be less common in the West than single-generation coalitions. To the extent that membership in distributional coalitions is not passed from one generation to another, the exclusion and discrimination inherent in these coalitions will not be captured by studies of the degree of association between the occupational prestige of fathers and sons.

A third reason why the studies of the association between the occupational prestige of fathers and sons do not offer a sufficient test of the present theory is that they leave out so much: differences in accent, dress, or style across different social groups; the role of inherited fortunes and titled aristocracies; the degree of resentment faced by uninvited entrants to established occupations or industries; the extent to which people are conscious of or sensitive about their social or class position; attitudes toward business; and attitudes toward entrepreneurship (which probably leads to the most dramatic changes in socioeconomic position). One measure of the significance of some of these variables that the existing quantitative studies leave out is the degree to which class and social position are correlated with allegiance to political party. Here it is significant that the association between socioeconomic status and adherence to the Labour and Conservative parties in Great Britain has been very much stronger than the corresponding association between socioeconomic position and affiliation with the Democratic and Republican parties in the United States (see Reeve D. Vanneman, "U.S. and British Perceptions of Class," *American Journal of Sociology* 85:769–90). It might be objected that this British-American difference is due to the different nature of the political parties in the two countries rather than to any differences in the social structure, but since the political parties are in turn partly a reflection of the socioeconomic situation, and have the policies they do partly because of their desire to attract support, this objection is not convincing.

Although the existing types of quantitative studies of social mobility are by no means sufficient to test the present theory, they are nonetheless extremely useful for a variety of purposes. They also seem to show faint traces of the involutional process that my theory describes. Donald J. Treiman and Kermit Terrill, in "The Process of Status Attainment in the United States and Great Britain" (*American Journal of Sociology* 81 [November 1975]:563–83), find the rate of social mobility marginally lower in Britain than in the United States. Similarly, the data in papers by Robert Erikson, John Goldethorpe, and Luciene Portocarero ("International Class Mobility in Three Western European Societies," *British Journal of Sociology* 30 [December 1979]:415–41; "Social Fluidity in Industrial Nations: England, France, and Sweden" [mimeo]) suggest that Sweden (whose more encompassing coalitions have a smaller incentive to exclude than their narrower counterparts in Britain) has somewhat more social mobility than England.

I am grateful to Otis Dudley Duncan, John Goldethorpe, Robert Hauser, Keith Hope, Donald Treiman, and Reeve Vanneman for helpful conversations or correspondence about social mobility, but it should not be assumed that they are in agreement with what I have said.

24. In Mueller, *The Political Economy of Growth.*

25. On Swedish economic history and policy, see Assar Lindbeck, *Swedish Economic Policy* (Berkeley and Los Angeles: University of California Press, 1974); for a discussion of the advocacy or adoption of policies consistent with growth, see especially pp. 24, 229–30, and 246.

26. I am thankful to Sten Nilson of the University of Oslo for this suggestion, and for letting me see his draft on "Organizations in Norway after 1955"; see also Lindbeck, *Swedish Economic Policy,* especially p. 6.

27. This paper on the Scandinavian experience is being prepared in collaboration with Gudmund Hernes of the University of Bergen.

28. *The Logic,* chapter 3.

29. On emulation and the desire for large scale in relatively undeveloped countries, see Alexander Gerschenkron, *Economic Backwardness in Historical Perspective* (Cambridge: Harvard University Press, 1962), pp. 5–30.

30. See Jeffrey G. Williamson and Peter H. Lindert, *American Inequality* (New York: Academic Press, 1980) and Allen Kulikoff, "The Progress of Inequality in Revolutionary Boston," *William and Mary Quarterly* 28 (July 1971):375–412.

31. Williamson and Lindert, *American Inequality.*

32. See Richard Nisbett and Lee Ross, *Human Inference: Strategies and Shortcomings of Social Judgment* (Englewood Cliffs, N.J.: Prentice-Hall, 1980), especially chapter 3.

33. Kwang Choi, "A Study of Comparative Rates of Economic Growth" (forthcoming, Iowa State University Press) and Kwang Choi, "A Statistical Test of the Political Economy of Comparative Growth Rates Model," in Mueller, *The Political Economy of Growth.*

34. Spearman rank correlation coefficients between years since statehood and *LPI, PN,* and per capita *LPI, PN* were respectively $-.52$, $-.67$, $-.52$, and $-.52$, and the correlation coefficients were in every case significant.

35. Farm organization membership need not be correlated with union membership, but farm groups focus almost exclusively on the farm policies of the federal government, and any losses in output due to them must fall mainly on consumers throughout the United States, rather than in the state in which the farmers are organized, so farm organization membership probably should not be included in tests on the forty-eight contiguous states. By contrast, the victims of any barriers to entry or restrictive practices by unions or professional organiza-

tions are likely to be disproportionately from the area in which the special-interest organization operates.

36. Choi, "A Study of Comparative Rates of Economic Growth."

37. C. Vann Woodward, *The Strange Career of Jim Crow*, 3rd rev. ed. (New York: Oxford University Press, 1974).

38. If all goes well (it rarely does), I shall devote my presidential address to the Southern Economic Association to this question; it will be published in the *Southern Economic Journal* in early 1983.

39. I am thankful to Ed Kearl for help on this point.

40. I am grateful to Moses Abramovitz, Geoffrey Brennan, and Simon Kuznets for giving me a fuller appreciation of the salience of this distinction.

41. "Thoughts on Catch-Up," October 1978, manuscript distributed to the conference on "The Political Economy of Comparative Growth Rates," University of Maryland, December 1978.

42. See Moses Abramovitz, "Notes on International Differences in Productivity Rates" in Mueller, *The Political Economy of Growth*.

43. As I argued earlier, differences in per capita income induce migration that tends to eliminate the differentials. Thus within any country with freedom of movement the model here should be tested on changes in total rather than per capita income. The significance of migration is shown by the fact that the catch-up hypothesis performs much better with per capita than with total income as the dependent variable; indeed, it then decisively outperforms the independent variables suggested by our model.

44. *America's Third Century* (New York: Harcourt Brace, 1976), pp. 72–74.

45. Choi, "A Study of Comparative Rates of Economic Growth," and "A Study of Comparative Rates of Economic Growth among Large Standard Metropolitan Statistical Areas" (unpublished manuscript, 1979).

46. Peter Murrell, "Comparative Growth and Comparative Advantage: Tests of the Effects of Interest Group Behavior on Foreign Trade Patterns," *Public Choice* 38 (1982):35–53, and "The Comparative Structure of Growth in the Major Developed Capitalist Nations," *Southern Economic Journal* 48 (April 1982):985–95.

CHAPTER 5

1. Edwin M. Truman, "The European Economic Community: Trade Creation and Trade Diversion," *Yale Economic Essays* 9 (Spring 1969):201–51; Mordechai Kreinen, *Trade Relations of the EEC: An Empirical Investigation* (New York: Praeger, 1974), pp. 25–55. See also John Williamson and Anthony Battrill, "The Impact of Customs Unions on Trade in Manufactures," in Melvyn G. Krauss, ed., *The Economics of Integration* (London: George Allen & Unwin, 1973).

2. Bela Balassa, "Trade Creation and Trade Diversion in the European Common Market," *Economic Journal* 77 (March 1967):17.

3. Fernand Braudel, *Capitalism and Material Life,* trans. Miriam Kohan (New York: Harper and Row; London: George Weidenfeld and Nicolson, 1973), pp. 439–40.

4. M. J. Daunton, "Towns and Economic Growth in Eighteenth-Century England," in Philip Abrams and F. A. Wrigley, eds., *Towns in Societies* (Cambridge and New York: Cambridge University Press, 1978), p. 247.

5. Charles Pythian-Adams, "Urban Decay in Late Medieval England," in Abrams and Wrigley, *Towns in Societies,* pp. 159–85.

6. Domenico Sella, *Crisis and Continuity, The Economy of Spanish Lombardy in the Seventeenth Century* (Cambridge: Harvard University Press, 1979), p. 136. On these matters see, for example, Jan De Vries, *The Economy of Europe in an Age of Crises* (Cambridge: At the University Press, 1976); Dudley Dillard, *Economic Development of the North Atlantic Community* (Englewood Cliffs, N.J.: Prentice Hall, 1967); Henri Pirenne, *Economic and Social History of Medieval Europe* (London: Routledge and Kegan Paul, 1936); and Douglass C. North, *Structure and Change in Economic History* (New York and London: W. W. Norton, 1981).

7. Braudel, *Capitalism and Material Life,* pp. 404–05.

8. Herbert Kisch, "Growth Deterrents of a Medieval Heritage: The Aachen Area Woolen Trades before 1790," *Journal of Economic History* 24 (December 1964):517–37.

9. Adam Smith, *An Inquiry Into the Nature and Causes of the Wealth of Nations,* ed. R. H. Campbell, A. S. Skinner, and W. B. Todd (Oxford: Clarendon Press, 1976), p. 146.

10. See, for example, Christopher Hill, *The Century of Revolution, 1603–1709* (New York: W. W. Norton, 1961), and J. H. Plumb, *The Origins of Political Stability in England, 1675–1725* (Boston: Houghton Mifflin, 1967).

11. I am grateful to Jan De Vries for helpful conversations about the Dutch Republic as well as other matters. See, for example, William Doyle, *The Old European Order, 1660–1800* (Oxford: Oxford University Press, 1978), p. 31; Richard W. Unger, *Dutch Shipbuilding before 1800* (Amsterdam: Van Gorcom, 1978); and Robert DuPlessis and Martha C. Howell, "Reconsidering the Early Modern Urban Economy: The Cases of Leiden and Lille," *Past and Present* 94 (February 1982), pp. 49–84.

12. See, for example, Charles Cole, *Colbert and a Century of French Mercantilism* (New York: Columbia University Press, 1939), especially volume 1, chapter 7, and volume 2, chapter 12; Doyle, *The Old European Order,* map 7, p. 401; Pierre Goubert, *Cent Mille Provinciaux Au XVIIᵉ Siecle: Beauvais et le Beauvaises de 1600 à 1730* (Paris: Flammarion, 1968).

13. I am grateful to Wolfgang F. Stolper for calling this expression to my attention.

14. In Dennis C. Mueller, ed., *The Political Economy of Growth* (New Haven: Yale University Press, 1983).

15. White Plains, N.Y.: International Arts and Sciences Press, 1973. On similar findings on growth and protection in developing countries see Ian Little, Tibor Scitovsky, and Maurice Scott, *Industry and Trade in Developing Countries, A Comparative Study* published for the Organization for Economic Cooperation and Development by Oxford University Press, 1970.

16. See Dumas Malone, ed., *Jefferson and His Times,* 2:166; see also Thomas Jefferson's letter to James Madison in which he says, "I hold it that a little rebellion now and then is a good thing, and as necessary in the political world as storms in the physical," quoted in Merrill Peterson, ed., *The Portable Thomas Jefferson* (New York: Viking, 1975), p. 417. I am thankful to Connie Schulz for help at this point.

17. Charles P. Kindleberger, *Europe's Postwar Growth* (Cambridge: Harvard University Press, 1967).

18. For a related argument about "contradictions," see Samuel Brittan, "The Economic Contradictions of Democracy," *British Journal of Political Science* 5:129–59, reprinted as chapter 23 of Brittan's *Economic Consequences of Democracy* (London: Temple Smith, 1977).

CHAPTER 6

1. Max Weber, *The City,* trans. and ed. Don Martindale and Gertrud Neuwirth (New York: Collier Books, 1962), pp. 95–96.

2. David B. Weisberg, *Guild Structure and Political Allegiance in Early Achaemenid Mesopotamia* (New Haven: Yale University Press, 1967); Isaac Mendelsohn, "Guilds in Babylonia and Assyria," *Journal of the American Oriental Society* 60 (1940):68–72, and "Guilds in Ancient Palestine," *Bulletin of the American Schools of Oriental Research* 85 (1942):14–17.

3. See, for example, Theodore W. Schultz, *Transforming Traditional Agriculture* (New Haven: Yale University Press, 1964).

4. London: Longmans, Green, 1909; reprint ed., Taipei: Ch'eng-wen, 1966, p. 24. See also John Stewart Burgess, *The Guilds of Peking* (New York: Columbia University Press, 1928; reprint ed., Taipei: Ch'eng-wen, 1966); Peter J. Goles, "Early Ching Guilds," and Sybille Van Der Sprenkel, "Urban Social Control," in G. William Skinner, ed., *The City in Late Imperial China* (Stanford: Stanford University Press, 1977), pp. 555–80 and 609–32, respectively.

5. Morse, *The Guilds of China,* p. 21.

6. Ibid., pp. 21, 27, and 11.

7. "Chinese Guilds or Chambers of Commerce and Trades Unions," *Journal of the [North] China Branch of the Royal Asiatic Society* 21 (1886):141.

8. Ibid., pp. 182–83.

9. Shannon R. Brown, "The Partially Opened Door: Limitations on Economic Change in China in the 1860's," *Modern Asian Studies* 12 (1978):187.

10. Ibid., and Shannon Brown, "The Ewo Filature: A Study in the Transfer of Technology to China in the 19th Century," *Technology and Culture* 20 (July 1979):550–68; "Modernization and the Chinese Soybean Trade, 1860–1895," *Comparative Studies in Society and History* 23 (July 1981):426–42; "The Transfer of Technology to China in the Nineteenth Century: The Role of Direct Foreign Investment," *Journal of Economic History* 39 (March 1979):181–97; and Shannon R. Brown and Tim Wright, "Technology, Economics, and Politics in the Modernization of China's Coal Mining Industry, 1850–1895," *Explorations in Economic History* 18 (January 1981):60–83.

11. "More than any other mature non-Western state, China has seemed inadaptable to the conditions of modern life," in John K. Fairbank, *Trade and Diplomacy on the China Coast* (2 vols., Cambridge: Harvard University Press, 1953; reprint ed. in one vol., Stanford: Stanford University Press, 1969), p. 4.

12. Alvin Rabushka, *Hong Kong: A Study in Economic Freedom* (Chicago: University of Chicago Press, 1979).

13. See, for example, Susan B. Hanley and Kozo Yamamura, *Economic and Demographic Change in Preindustrial Japan, 1600–1868* (Princeton: Princeton University Press, 1977).

14. Milton Friedman and Rose Friedman, *Free to Choose* (New York: Avon Books, 1981).

15. In this account of Japan, I have drawn particularly on conversations with my friend Yasukichi Yasuba of Osaka University, who may not, however, necessarily agree with my argument. I have also been particularly helped by William Lockwood's *The Economic Development of Japan* (Princeton: Princeton University Press, 1968); Johannes Hirschmeier, *The Origins of Entrepreneurship in Meiji Japan* (Cambridge: Harvard University Press, 1964); W. G. Beasley, *The Meiji Restoration* (Stanford: Stanford University Press, 1972); and John W. Hall and Marius B. Jansen, eds., *Studies in the Institutional History of Early Modern Japan* (Princeton: Princeton University Press, 1968).

16. Angus Maddison, *Class Structure and Economic Growth* (New York: W. W. Norton, 1971), p. 43.

17. Ibid., pp. 22–23.

18. Jewaharlal Nehru, *The Discovery of India*, ed. Robert I. Crane (New York: Anchor Books, Doubleday and Company 1946, 1960). The quotes are from widely scattered sections of the book, and presented in a different order here than they are in the book. I believe that they nonetheless fairly represent Nehru's views on these matters.

19. W. H. Hutt, *The Economics of the Colour Bar* (London: Merritt and

Hatcher Ltd. for The Institute of Economic Affairs Ltd. by Andre Deutsch Ltd., 1964).

20. Ibid., p. 62.

21. Ibid., p. 69.

22. There is the possibility, mentioned in the last chapter, that exporters would want a tariff in order to engage in price discrimination. On the politics of the discrimination against rural export industries in many developing countries, see the works of Robert H. Bates, especially *Markets and States in Tropical Africa* (Berkeley: University of California Press, 1981). I am grateful to Barry Weingast for calling Bates's work to my attention.

23. Washington, D.C.: The Brookings Institution, 1975.

24. Introduction, Mancur Olson, ed., *A New Approach to the Economics of Health Care* (Washington, D.C.: American Enterprise Institute, 1982).

25. Actually, as the "Cambridge controversy" shows, there is the possibility of paradoxical results when dealing with capital in the aggregate. Strictly speaking, I should have said, "the price of each type of machine or other capital good will tend to fall as more of each is accumulated."

26. Mancur Olson and Richard Zeckhauser, "The Efficient Production of External Economics," *American Economic Review* 60 (June 1970):512–17; Mancur Olson, "The Priority of Public Problems," in Robin Marris, ed., *The Corporate Society* (London: Macmillan, 1974), pp. 294–336; "The Principle of Fiscal Equivalence," *American Economic Review: Papers and Proceedings* 59 (May 1969):479–87; "The Treatment of Externalities in National Income Statistics," in Lowdon Wingo and Alan Evans, eds., *Public Economics and the Quality of Life* (Baltimore: Johns Hopkins University Press for Resources for the Future and the Centre for Environmental Studies, 1977), pp. 219–49; and U.S. Department of Health, Education and Welfare, *Toward A Social Report* (Washington, D.C.: U.S. Government Printing Office, 1969), written with others.

27. I have been working off and on since the early 1960s on "Diseconomies of Scale and Development"—that is, on the special problems the less developed countries have in creating stable and effective large-scale institutions, and on similar problems that the European societies also faced in preindustrial times. My hope is that eventually that argument, in combination with the present theory, would help us understand this problem.

28. Friedman, *Free to Choose,* pp. 49–55.

29. See, for example, the next chapter of this book, and also my article with Martin J. Bailey and Paul Wonnacott, "The Marginal Utility of Income Does Not Increase: Borrowing, Lending, and Friedman-Savage Gambles," *American Economic Review* 70 (June 1980):372–79. See also Mancur Olson and Martin J. Bailey, "Positive Time Preference," *Journal of Political Economy* 89 (February 1981):1–25.

30. Friedman, *Free to Choose,* p. 49.

31. See, for example, Vera Anstey, *The Economic Development of India,* 4th ed. (London: Longmans, Green, 1952), pp. 107–14 and 345–63. The extreme laissez-faire character of British policy in India is evident even in articles concerned with the exceptions and inconsistencies in it; Sabyasachi Bhattacharya quotes British officials ruling out progressive taxation for India on the noninterventionist principle that it was "no part of the functions of fiscal arrangements to equalize the affairs of men." (See his "Laissez Faire in India," *Indian Economic and Social History Review* 2 [January 1965]:1–22.)

32. Alvin Rabushka, *Hong Kong: A Study in Economic Freedom* (Chicago: University of Chicago Press, 1979).

CHAPTER 7

1. In "Beyond the Measuring Rod of Money," (book, forthcoming), and in "Environmental Indivisibilities and Information Costs: Fanaticism, Agnosticism, and Intellectual Progress," *American Economic Review, Papers and Proceedings* 72 (May 1982):262–66, and (quite unsatisfactorily) in "Evaluating Performance in the Public Sector," in Milton Moss, ed., *The Measurement of Economic and Social Performance: Studies in Income and Wealth,* vol. 38, National Bureau of Economic Research (New York: Columbia University Press, 1973), pp. 355–84.

2. That is one reason why I believe there can be no satisfactory monocausal theory.

3. *The General Theory* (London: Macmillan and Co., 1945), scattered quotations from pp. 5–15.

4. Ibid., pp. 262–67.

5. See, for example, Edmund S. Phelps, ed., *Microeconomic Foundations of Employment and Inflation Theory* (New York: W. W. Norton, 1969).

6. *Money, Employment, and Inflation* (Cambridge: At the University Press, 1976), p. 6.

7. In "Alternative Approaches to Macroeconomic Theory: A Partial View," *Canadian Journal of Economics* 12, no. 3 (August 1979):342.

8. See Owen Gingerich, "Crisis versus Aesthetic in the Copernican Revolution," in Arthur Beer and K. A. Strand, eds., *Vistas in Astronomy,* vol. 17 (Oxford: Pergamon Press, 1975), pp. 85–95; Thomas S. Kuhn, *The Copernican Revolution* (Cambridge: Harvard University Press, 1957); Kenneth F. Schaffner, *Nineteenth-Century Aether Theories* (Oxford: Pergamon Press, 1972); Lloyd S. Swenson, Jr., *The Ethereal Aether* (Austin: University of Texas Press, 1972).

9. *Challenge Magazine* 22 (1979):67.

10. Martin J. Bailey, Mancur Olson, and Paul Wonnacott, "The Marginal Utility of Income Does Not Increase: Borrowing, Lending, and Friedman-Savage Gambles," *American Economic Review* 70 (June 1980):372–79.

11. See the anthology cited in note 5 above and Edmund S. Phelps, *Inflation Policy and Unemployment Theory* (New York: W. W. Norton, 1972).

12. In "What Macroeconomic Theory Is Best," a paper read at a session I organized at the Southern Economic Association meetings in New Orleans, November 1981.

13. Note that the argument speaks of "points on the marginal revenue curves" rather than of such curves or aggregations of such curves. The *MRP* curve of a firm is not the demand curve for a factor when there is more than one variable factor. A change in the price of a factor affects the demand for it not only through substitution and output effects, but in other ways as well. For an analysis of some of the complexities of this relationship, see Charles Ferguson, "Production, Price, and the Theory of Jointly Derived Input Demand Functions," *Economica* 33 (November 1966); "'Inferior Factors' and the Theories of Production and Input Demand," *Economica* 35 (May 1968); and *The Neoclassical Theory of Production and Distribution* (London: Cambridge University Press, 1969), chapters 6 and 9.

14. Edmond Malinvaud, *The Theory of Unemployment Reconsidered* (Oxford: Basil Blackwell, 1977).

15. Ibid., p. 102.

16. *Recent Inflation in the United States,* Study Paper no. 1, Joint Economic Committee of the U.S. Congress (Washington, D.C., 1959).

17. I am thankful to Peter Murrell for calling this point to my attention.

18. Phillip Cagan, *The Hydra-Headed Monster: The Problem of Inflation in the United States* (Washington, D.C.: American Enterprise Institute, 1974). Also in Cagan's *Persistent Inflation* (New York: Columbia University Press, 1979).

19. F. M. Scherer, *Industrial Market Structure and Economic Performance* (Chicago: Rand McNally, 1970), p. 291.

20. I am thankful to Michael Parkin and Robert Barro for impressing me with the importance of the point that coalitions would in many circumstances have an incentive to index agreements, and to Stanley Engerman for reminding me of the debate about whether there was really inflation in the 1950s and early 1960s.

21. Robert W. Clower, "The Keynesian Counterrevolution: A Theoretical Appraisal," in F. H. Hahn and F. P. R. Brechling, eds., *The Theory of Interest Rates* (London: Macmillan; New York: St. Martin's, 1965).

22. Malinvaud, *The Theory of Unemployment Reconsidered*, p. 31.

23. *Monthly Labor Review,* April 1977. The inflation rates cited in the next paragraph are from Arnold Harberger and Sebastian Edwards, "International Evidence on the Sources of Inflation," unpublished manuscript.

24. See, for example, Erik Lundberg, "Fiscal and Monetary Policies," in Walter Galenson, ed., *Economic Growth and Structural Change in Taiwan*

(Ithaca: Cornell University Press, 1979), pp. 263–307. I am especially thankful to Howell Zee for help on this issue.

25. Cagan, *Persistent Inflation*. The quotation is from scattered sections of Cagan's essay.

26. Jeffrey Sachs, "The Changing Cyclical Behavior of Wages and Prices: 1890–1976," *American Economic Review* 70:78–90.

27. *A Monetary History of the United States, 1867–1960* (Princeton: Princeton University Press, 1963), p. 299.

28. Peter Temin, *The Jacksonian Economy* (New York: W. W. Norton, 1969), table 5.1, p. 157.

29. *Did Monetary Forces Cause the Great Depression?* (New York: W. W. Norton, 1976), p. xi.

30. E. P. Thompson, *The Making of the English Working Class* (New York: Pantheon, 1964), p. 776, n. 2. I am grateful to Peter Murrell for this reference. The word *unemployed* goes much further back, and was used, for example, to describe fallow land; note this passage from *Paradise Lost:* "Other creatures all day long rove idle unimploid, and need less rest" (iv, 617).

31. See John A. Garraty, *Unemployment in History* (New York: Harper and Row, 1979), p. 4.

32. *America's Greatest Depression, 1929–1941* (New York: Harper and Row, 1970), p. 226.

33. See E. E. Schattschneider, *Politics, Pressures, and the Tariff* (New York: Prentice-Hall, 1935) and E. Pendleton Herring, *Group Representation Before Congress* (Washington, D.C.: Brookings Institution, 1929), especially p. 78.

34. Chandler, *America's Greatest Depression*, p. 230. I have also been greatly helped on the NRA and the history of the Great Depression by reading an unpublished paper by Martin N. Baily and chapter 9 of Friedman and Schwartz, *A Monetary History of the United States, 1867–1960*.

35. As quoted in Chandler, *America's Greatest Depression*, p. 231.

36. Ibid., p. 232.

37. "An Evolutionary Approach to Inflation and Stagflation," in James H. Gapinski and Charles E. Rockwood, eds., *Essays in Post-Keynesian Inflation* (Cambridge, Mass.: Ballinger Publishing Company, 1979), pp. 137–59.

38. "On Getting Really Full Employment without Inflation," in David C. Colander, ed., *Solutions to Inflation* (New York: Harcourt Brace Jovanovich, 1979), pp. 183–87; and "'Incentives-Based' Stabilization Policies and the Evolution of the Macroeconomic Problem" in Michael P. Claudon and Richard R. Cornwall, eds., *An Incomes Policy for the United States: New Approaches* (Boston, The Hague, and London: Martinus Nijhoff, 1981), pp. 37–77. The latter paper is in large part the same as the one cited in n. 37.

Index